A16A
100 -

Outstanding Studies in

Early American History

EDITED BY

John Murrin
Princeton University

A Garland Series

Servants into Planters

The Origin of an American Image: Land Acquisition and Status Mobility in Seventeenth-Century South Carolina

Aaron M. Shatzman

Garland Publishing, Inc.
NEW YORK & LONDON 1989

Library of Congress Cataloging-in-Publication Data

Shatzman, Aaron M.
Servants into planters: the origin of an American image: land acquisition and status mobility in 17th-century South Carolina/ Aaron M. Shatzman.
p. cm.—(Outstanding studies in early American history)
Includes bibliographical references.
ISBN 0–8240–6197–7 (alk. paper)
1. South Carolina—History—Colonial period, ca. 1600–1775. 2. South Carolina—Social conditions. 3. Land tenure—South Carolina—History—17th century. 4. Social mobility—South Carolina—History—17th century. 5. Indentured servants—South Carolina—History—17th century. I. Title. II. Series.
F272.S48 1990
975.7'02—dc20 89–48048

Printed on acid-free, 250-year-life paper
MANUFACTURED IN THE UNITED STATES OF AMERICA

For Karen

Contents

Preface

Among the greatest pleasures of publication is the opportunity it provides to express gratitude. Few students can have been more fortunate than I in the friends, colleagues, and universities that encouraged their scholarly endeavours.

At Washington University in St. Louis, I learned that History was worth my time and efforts, and that scholarship was to be cherished. The four years I spent on the campus of Stanford University were equally rewarding, for there I learned the craft of the professional historian. A James Birdsall Weter fellowship from Stanford University supported a full year's research in South Carolina.

Virtually all my research was conducted in the Search Room of the South Carolina Archives in Columbia, where I encountered men and women whose courtesy and professional behavior made my work far easier and more pleasant than it might have been. I wish especially to mention Wylma Wates and R. Nicholas Olsberg who provided me with solid advice, and Alexia Helsley, Ruth Trice, Robert Mackintosh, Jamie Lee Bedford, Pat Durlach, and Harold DeLorme whose attention, assistance, and friendship has meant much to me.

Peter Wood offered advice and encouragement at an early stage of this work. Agnes Leland Baldwin has been a steady source of help to me. Both have generously shared the results of their own research with me. Carl N. Degler and John M. Murrin read the manuscript, and improved it.

I have had the privilege of working with a group of scholars who have provided me with examples not only of outstanding research and writing, but also of kindness, generosity, decency, and humanity. I wish to acknowledge, in this context, William Danforth, Burton Wheeler, Peter Riesenberg, and Kevin Herbert at Washington University; Barton J. Bernstein, Don E. Fehrenbacher, Linda Kerber, and George H. Knoles at Stanford University; and Alice Drum at Franklin and Marshall College.

Three teachers have shaped my life and my work more than any others. John M. Murrin, by his example, showed me that I wanted to be a historian, and that early America was too fascinating to be ignored. The late David M. Potter gave me encouragement and provided me with a model of behavior that only those who knew him can comprehend. And Carl N. Degler, by his honesty, fairness, good judgment, and tolerance, has taught me what it means to be a scholar. These men gave me more than their time. They have given me standards I can only attempt to meet.

Doris Suits and Chuck Bartelt prepared the manuscript for publication with great care. Grateful acknowledgment goes also to Mary Ross and Brian Cook of Garland for their editorial guidance and encouragement.

My parents, Ben and Miriam Shatzman, have supported me in countless ways. My wife, Karen, who was a historian *before* she was a physician-epidemiologist, understands what it means to be a scholar, and knows how much she means to me.

AMS

Introduction

By the time Charles II assumed the monarchy of Britain in 1660, Europeans had firmly established themselves in the Americas. For more than a century and a half the New World had provided a focus for European activities, ranging from voyages of discovery, to expeditions of exploration, to actual efforts at colonization. The Spanish, Portuguese, French, and Dutch, as well as the English, had engaged in such activities. The settlements they created dotted the American landscape from Canada to South America. These outposts of Europe occupied territories so varied that such different economic enterprises as gold mining, fur trapping, sugar cultivation, and cattle grazing were able to be attempted. And the Americas were so vast that all sorts of social and political experimenters were able to find open space in which to erect ideal societies without interference from established communities with vested interests.

By the second half of the seventeenth century Europeans had learned that while the huge amount of free space in America allowed them to attempt to live according to designs for which the Old World had neither the room nor the patience, the wilderness might also act as a destructive force which corrupted individual behavior and shattered communities created to realize the dreams of European social philosophers. If the English Puritan efforts to build a city on a hill in Massachusetts Bay, or the Spanish missionary Vasco de Quiroga's creation of Indian communities in New Spain modeled on Thomas More's Utopia represent using the open space of America to experiment socially, and to succeed if only for a brief period, then surely the French attempt to establish an ideal Catholic absolutist state in Canada illustrates the negative impact of the frontier on such use of the New World.[1]

---

[1] The best statement of the argument that the New World served primarily as open space in which ideas and plans imported from the Old World were able to be tried out, and in which they both flourished and shaped the future, is contained in Louis B. Hartz, *The Founding of New Societies: Studies in the History of the United States, Latin*

But even when communities created according to an imported scheme failed to develop in conformity with the master plan, Europeans did not respond by leaving the Americas. Those Frenchmen who refused to accept low status and limited freedom as "habitants" in an ideal feudal society in Canada, and instead ran off into the woods to hunt and to trap, nevertheless remained in the colony. Indeed, they flourished in the New World, even if they became less French and more Indian in the process. If Englishmen in Virginia failed to find gold or precious stones or large groups of docile Indians willing to serve as a labor force, they nevertheless learned that both they and tobacco could thrive in the colony. In other words, even when Europeans discovered that America was not exactly what they thought it would be before they came, and even if they acted or lived differently from the ways they thought they would live or act, they almost always stayed in the New World. Thus they came to realize that frequently land was valuable even if it contained no gold, silver, or precious stones. They came to understand that in some places they or their countrymen would have to perform hard work in order to succeed. At the same time, some leaders recognized that there were many men and women living in the Old World to whom working on the land in an alien environment seemed attractive, and represented an opportunity to improve immediately their standard of living, if not their social status. Some, in fact, were so attracted by the prospects of life in America that they would voluntarily give up a degree of freedom and their labor for a specified period in order to reach the New World.

European experience in the New World taught those who ruled in the Old World that they as well as their nations might derive substantial rewards from having their countrymen seize and inhabit portions of the Americas. As a place to occupy their idle, to enrich their poor, to reward their retainers, to display their power, to provide needed supplies of food or raw materials, to locate new wealth, to discover new trade routes to the Far East, to protect routes already in use, to supply ships engaged in trade, or to create new markets for their own production, America seemed compellingly attractive. Thus, by the middle of the seventeenth century, Europeans had a fairly good idea of just what America was. And they knew they wanted to live in it or to rule it. Some wanted both.

America, South Africa, Canada, and Australia (New York, 1964). The opposite view, commonly associated with Frederick Jackson Turner, that America was a place which transformed European ideas and immigrants into American ideas and Americans, has influenced many scholars. Perhaps the most useful example in this context is Sigmund Diamond's essay on the French experience in Canada, "An Experiment in 'Feudalism': French Canada in the Seventeenth Century," *William and Mary Quarterly*, 3rd Series, XVIII (January, 1961).

Servants into Planters

The Origin of an American Image: Land Acquisition and Status Mobility in Seventeenth-Century South Carolina

CHAPTER ONE

The Establishment of the Carolina Colony

If the Americas were a magnet that attracted the attention of many Europeans, the area itself which the English named Carolina and colonized during the last quarter of the seventeenth century had drawn the interest of Britain's rivals in America. In fact, the international conflicts played out on a large scale during the colonial era throughout the New World were waged in microcosm in Carolina. More than a century before any Englishman settled there, agents of both the Spanish and the French crowns had explored the area, erected communities, and fought for permanent possession of it.

During the second decade of the sixteenth century three Spanish expeditions reached Carolina, culminating in the establishment of an actual, though short-lived, settlement.[1] In 1561 Spaniards returned to Carolina, both to reaffirm their claim to it and to deter visits from representatives of other powers who might wish to use the area as a base from which they might trade with or attack Spanish settlements in the New World. However, no effort was then made to create a permanent settlement.[2] The French clearly were undeterred by Spanish claims of

---

[1] These expeditions were led by Francisco Gordillo in 1520-21, Pedro de Quexos in 1525, and Lucas Vasquez de Ayllon in 1526. Ayllon's force included more than 500 people from Hispaniola, but the settlement he erected collapsed after his death, with most of the colonists departing for Santo Domingo. See Peter H. Wood, *Black Majority: Negroes in Colonial South Carolina from 1670 through the Stono Rebellion* (New York, 1975), pp. 3-4; Joseph I. Waring, M.D., *The First Voyage and Settlement at Charles Town 1670-1680* (Columbia, 1970), pp. 1-4.

[2] Wood, *Black Majority*, p. 5. Philip II determined in 1561 to end Spanish colonization efforts in the area. Waring, *First Voyage*, pp. 4-5.

sovereignty over or visits to the area, for in 1562 two ships and about 150 settlers left France to establish a colony in Carolina. The expedition built a fort, armed it with eight guns, and garrisoned it with 28 men. Like the earlier Spanish effort, this French attempt to create a lasting settlement failed under the impact of inadequate supplies and mutiny.[3] In 1564 both Spanish and French expeditions appeared in the area, and the French erected a fort near the mouth of St. John's River in what is now Florida. This was attacked by Spaniards who chose to tolerate neither Frenchmen nor the attacks they launched on Spanish trading vessels from an American base.[4] The Spanish promptly replaced the French fort with one of their own. The French responded by attacking and destroying it in 1567. A year earlier, in 1566, the Spanish had created a fortified settlement on Parris Island. It was abandoned in 1577, when a second effort was made to establish a permanent Spanish presence there. This endured for a decade before being abandoned. Meanwhile, the French had enjoyed no greater success in their colonization efforts. Their final serious attempt at settlement, which probably was located near the mouth of the South Edisto River, was ruined by the Indians.[5]

The legacy of European efforts to colonize Carolina during the sixteenth century, then, was wholly negative. No enduring colony had been founded. No profitable crops had been planted, much less harvested. No precious metals had been discovered or mined. Mutiny, murder, death, destruction, conflict, and desertion marked the Old World's initial seven decades of actual experiences in the area. The Spanish were firmly and profitably situated in the Caribbean, Mexico, and South America. It seemed reasonably clear that, given the valuable inter-American trade among Spanish colonies and especially between the colonies and Spain itself, even if they were unwilling or unable to settle Carolina themselves, Spaniards were not about to tolerate any other nation's occupation of an area from which attacks on that trade, or even competitive trading ventures might be launched. Anyone contemplating a colonization effort in Carolina had to consider that Spanish power in the Americas had been sufficient to deter French interlopers. More telling, the Spanish themselves, even with

---

[3] *Ibid.*, p. 6.

[4] This successful attack came by land. An earlier effort by sea had been driven back by the French. However, the French fleet was destroyed by a storm, and the Spanish executed the survivors. *Ibid.*, pp. 7-8.

[5] *Ibid.*, pp. 8-11.

all of their experience in American colonization, had not been able to erect an enduring colony in Carolina. At the start of the seventeenth century Carolina seemed to offer little to those who might organize and support attempts to settle in the New World, and virtually nothing to individuals who sought a place in America to begin a new life, to take up land in peace, to work, to thrive, and perhaps to prosper.

The failure of early European colonization efforts in Carolina worked to deter further attempts at settlement there. Both the French and the Spanish were sufficiently disenchanted with the area that they neglected it, and for some time no other European power sought to send settlers there. But while the early experiences of Europeans in Carolina must have been discouraging to anyone contemplating colonization ventures there, the history of French and Spanish failures did not prove paralyzing. For there were Englishmen intrigued by the prospects in America of adventure, wealth, or freedom from the close scrutiny of religious and political leaders at home. And since the Spanish had, by reaching the New World earliest, secured for themselves those areas which seemed to offer the best physical qualities, virtually the only open places available to English adventurers were those which appeared to be the least attractive. Carolina certainly fit into that category, and it was the English who finally succeeded in establishing a permanent European presence there.

It is possible to argue that in some measure Englishmen succeeded where Frenchmen and Spaniards had failed precisely because of the earlier efforts of their rivals. For well before any Englishman set foot on Carolina soil, prior French and Spanish experiences there dictated patterns of thought and behavior which would help the newcomers to succeed. First, since the Spanish were firmly established to the South, and since they had consistently acted to thwart settlement efforts by the French, it was only prudent to assume that any English colony in Carolina would be similarly threatened. Thus the defense of any expedition and the protection of any community had to be paramount concerns from the outset. This meant, of course, that males would dramatically outnumber females even though leaders wanted to create permanent settlements intended to sustain themselves and to grow through reproduction. Second, anyone contemplating a colonization venture in Carolina knew from the beginning that it was not a place full of gold, silver, diamonds, or rubies. Nor were the natives likely to be transformed into a docile and willing labor force to enrich a few English overlords. Rather, it seemed likely that in order to survive in Carolina, Englishmen would have to work. But while such foreknowledge would prove a boon to prospective settlers, it would not ensure success. For even if they were able to defend themselves from Spaniards and Indians, and even if they worked diligently, it was still not clear that Carolina would provide a suitable location for a prosperous colony. Nevertheless, in the seventeenth century the land was available, and some Englishmen were interested in acquiring it.

It is not certain that the first Englishman granted the territory either wanted it or, having received it from the crown, was interested in using it. Although Spain claimed the area in America lying between the 31st and 36th parallels of north latitude by virtue of Ponce de Leon's expeditions of 1513, DeSoto's exploration of 1539, and attempts at settlement undertaken in the 1520's, 1566, and 1577, Charles I of England chose in 1629 to grant that part of the New World to his Attorney General, Sir Robert Heath. Yet, as one scholar has noted, for the succeeding 32 years, "neither Sir Robert nor his heirs did anything toward developing Carolina, and we seldom find it referred to in any written or printed documents of that day by the name that Charles I had given it with the intention of perpetuating his own name therein."[6]

Thus, for about 30 years after the initial grant of the territory by an English monarch, Englishmen neglected the area. But the Restoration that brought Charles II to the throne in 1660 provided circumstances in which Englishmen more determined than Heath to use open space in America, were able to secure from the crown the right to try. Land in America provided Charles with a means by which he could reward or repay those who had given him assistance. And among those who had provided support to the crown both during the Civil Wars as well as after the execution of Charles I, was Sir John Colleton, a Barbadian planter. Colleton had found it expedient to leave England for Barbados after serving as a colonel in the royalist army, "and immediately after the Restoration . . . like so many other royalists, he set out for London to claim his reward."[7] Charles II responded by knighting Colleton and appointing him to the Council for

---

[6] A. S. Salley, Jr., *The Origin of Carolina* (Columbia, 1926), p. 3. In the 1630's an attempt was made to settle a colony of Huguenots in Carolina. At about the same time an agent was sent to Virginia to lead settlers into Carolina. Both these efforts yielded no results and Carolina "remained as before a land unoccupied by Englishmen." Charles M. Andrews, *The Colonial Period of American History*, Vol. III (New Haven, 1964), pp. 189-90.

[7] M. Eugene Sirmans, *Colonial South Carolina: A Political History, 1663-1763* (Chapel Hill, 1966), p. 4; Robert M. Weir, *Colonial South Carolina: A History* (Millwood, NY, 1983), pp. 48-49; Andrews, *Colonial Period*, III, p. 184.

Foreign Plantations, whose membership included Sir William Berkeley, Governor of Virginia;[8] Sir Anthony Ashley Cooper; Edward Hyde, Earl of Clarendon, the king's first minister; and Sir George Carteret, treasurer of the Navy and vice-chamberlain of the royal household.[9]

Sir Anthony Ashley Cooper had, like Colleton, owned property in Barbados. His plantation, like those of numerous Barbadian investors, had failed as wealthy sugar planters with vast estates and ample capital engrossed smaller properties whose owners simply could not bear the competition.[10] While many Barbadians were able to survive by farming small properties, large numbers of settlers lost their land.[11] As the process by which a few large property owners came to control most of the land continued, many residents perceived that their prospects in Barbados were dim. Needless to say, the "crop failures, epidemics, fires, and hurricanes" which "damaged the colony's precarious economic and social well-being . . . combined with land scarcity" to encourage thoughts of departure among "all elements of the population." In 1669 alone, about four percent of the population, or 2,000 individuals, quit the island.[12] Thus both Cooper and Colleton were personally familiar both with American colonization and a situation in Barbados which might work to provide experienced colonists for some new American colonial venture.

Scholars generally agree that Colleton initially formulated the notion of planting a new English colony in Carolina. He gathered with

---

[8] Appointed in 1661. Sirmans, *Colonial*, p. 4.

[9] *Ibid.*, p. 4; Andrews, *Colonial Period*, pp. 183-87; John W. Brinsfield, *Religion and Politics in Colonial South Carolina* (Easley, SC, 1983), p. 2.

[10] Andrews, *Colonial Period*, III, p. 185.

[11] Vincent T. Harlow, A *History of Barbados, 1625-1685* (Oxford, 1926), and Richard S. Dunn, *Sugar and Slaves: The Rise of the Planter Class in the English West Indies, 1624-1713* (Chapel Hill, 1972), cover this story in detail. See Harlow, pp. 306, 309, 338-40. Richard Waterhouse, in "England, the Caribbean, and the Settlement of Carolina," *American Studies* 9 (December, 1975), suggests that aside from those driven off their land by an inability to compete with big sugar planters, others, some of whom had quite substantial assets, sought to leave Barbados because of increasing labor costs caused by a shortage of slaves, competition from other colonies which were producing sugar (such as Jamaica), and because Barbadian soil was becoming exhausted. All these factors led to reduced profits and may have impelled planters in Barbados to quit that island. See pp. 267-70.

[12] Wood, *Black Majority*, pp. 8-9.

seven other prominent gentlemen as co-petitioners, and asked Charles to grant them the territory. In addition to Cooper, Sir William Berkeley, Edward Hyde, and Sir George Carteret, all from the Council for Foreign Plantations, the petitioners included the Duke of Albemarle, Lord Berkeley (Sir William's brother), and William Craven, Earl of Craven. Of these eight men, six involved themselves in both the Royal African and Hudson's Bay Companies. Five were members of the Council of Trade.[13] Thus, not only were these exceedingly prominent men, they were also deeply interested in colonial affairs, and had helped to shape colonial policy. In March, 1663, they received from the crown a charter naming them proprietors of Carolina.[14]

Having secured title to a vast territory, the proprietors set out to fill it with people. Since these men were hardly novices in dealing with colonization, they knew that success depended on attracting settlers who would pay rents and produce profitable crops. The proprietors defined success in economic terms—they did not seek to erect in the Carolina wilderness an ideal social or religious or political community. In the words of one scholar, their "motives were frankly commercial."[15] Thus the very first meeting of the proprietors concluded with a decision to advertise the colony and to invite settlers from New England, Barbados, and later, from Bermuda. While a group from New England did attempt to settle in the province almost at once, the first serious, large-scale, and well-planned effort by Englishmen to migrate to the new colony was organized, as might have been anticipated, in Barbados.[16] There, Sir Thomas Modyford and Peter Colleton (Sir John's son) gathered together two hundred Barbadians, identified as the Barbadian Adventurers, who each agreed to contribute 1000 pounds of sugar in order to finance their planned settlement. In return, each was to receive 500 acres of Carolina land. In the summer of 1663 they engaged Captain William Hilton to explore the Carolina coast. He returned with a favorable report, and promptly was ordered back to confirm his initial opinions. From August

---

[13] Sirmans, *Colonial*, pp. 4-5.

[14] *Ibid.*, p. 5. Andrews, *Colonial Period*, III, pp. 186-87, 191-93. The charter was modified in June 1665, to extend the boundaries to north latitude 290. *Ibid.*, p. 197.

[15] Wood, *Black Majority*, p. 13.

[16] The New Englanders actually did settle briefly in the Cape Fear region. Their community did not survive. Andrews, *Colonial Period*, III, pp. 192-93; Wood, *Black Majority*, p. 14.

10, 1663, until January 6, 1664, he was at sea, exploring Carolina itself from August 26 until December 6.[17]

If a colonizing venture in Carolina were to attract settlers, and especially if those given the opportunity to participate were asked to contribute funds to the enterprise—to risk their own, as opposed to the proprietors' capital—then the place had to seem appealing. This was most critical in the case of Carolina, whose early history involved nothing but a series of failed attempts by Europeans to establish enduring and profitable settlements there. Therefore, Hilton's report must have been eagerly awaited. To those promoting colonization in Carolina, it proved gratifying.

Captain Hilton's report did not ignore or gloss over the dark side of Carolina. He told of encounters with Indians who acknowledged his presence by shooting arrows at him and his men. He told how his men had been compelled to fire their guns to protect an exploration party from an Indian "creeping on the Bank as they thought to shoot at them." But he also narrated pleasant encounters with natives who provided food. Such frankness extended to Hilton's report of the country itself. One area he "judged . . . to be [of] little worth . . . the Land sandy and barren . . . a place fitter to starve Cattel in our judgement, then to keep them alive." About a different location he said, "we took some view of the Land on both sides of the River there, finding some good Land, but more bad." Nevertheless, on balance it was clear that Hilton found Carolina appealing and attractive. His negative comments must have served to make more credible his overall view that the place was overwhelmingly good. For he had found "good Soyl, covered with black Mold, in some places a foot, in some places half a foot." He reported that "the Country abounds with Grapes, large Figs, and Peaches; the Woods with Deer, Conies, Turkeys, Quails, Curlues . . . Herons; and as the Indians say, in Winter, with Swans, Geese, Cranes, Duck and Mallard . . . and on the Sands: Oysters in abundance, with great store of Muscles. . . . The Rivers [are] stored plentifully with Fish that we saw play and leap." Another area displayed "woods stor'd with abundance of Deer and Turkies everywhere. . . . Also we saw great store of Ducks . . . Also . . . innumerable of Pines, tall and good for boards or masts. . . . We saw several Mulberry-trees, multitudes of Grape-vines, and some Grapes which we did eat of." Just prior to his departure Hilton received "very good Salt" from Indians who

[17] Alexander S. Salley, Jr., *Narratives of Early Carolina, 1650-1708* (New York, 1967), pp. 33-34; Weir, *Colonial*, pp. 51-52.

"made signes pointing to both sides of the Rivers mouth, that there was great store thereabouts." Carolina, it was clear, was bountifully endowed with a variety of assets. There was reason to believe that any number of commercial enterprises might succeed there. If Frenchmen and Spaniards had failed, the cause could not have been that the area lacked resources. Determined, hard-working, adequately-supplied English settlers surely would prosper in the environment Hilton encountered.[18]

But a group of English colonists had already been to Carolina. They had come from New England, so they were not unfamiliar with life in the New World. And they had brought with them both hogs and cattle—they had, in other words, intended to stay. Yet they had not prospered. Rather, they had been miserable in Carolina, and had soon departed. Moreover, before quitting the colony, these settlers posted a "writing" at the entrance to a river, "the contents whereof," said Hilton, "tended not only to the disparagement of the Land about the said River, but also to the great discouragement of all those that should hereafter come into those parts to settle." All Hilton could do in response was "affirm" that the area embraced "as good Land, and as well Timbered, as any we have seen in any other part of the world, sufficient to accomodate thousands of our English Nation. . . ."[19] Yet no matter how positive an impression Carolina had made on Hilton and his crew, and in spite of his open, honest, and thus seemingly reliable report, Carolina must have remained a place about which prospective settlers or investors were uncertain. It had a good and a bad side. It had potential, to be sure. No one could doubt its resources. But in spite of its bounty, no Europeans had been able to prosper there over a long span of years.

The Barbadians were sufficiently encouraged by Hilton's narrative of his voyage that their agents, Colleton and Modyford, wrote the proprietors suggesting conditions that would lead them to undertake a settlement effort in Carolina. But even before they received the Barbadian proposals, the proprietors had published their own "Declaration and Proposals to all that will Plant in Carolina," in which they outlined their own intentions. These included granting land on the basis of the number of persons a given planter brought to the colony. Such a headright system dovetailed nicely with the situation in Barbados, where people were

---

[18] "A Relation of a Discovery, by William Hilton, 1664," *Salley*, Jr., *Narratives*, pp. 44-53.

[19] *Ibid.*, p. 53.

plentiful while land was becoming increasingly scarce. Almost at once after Hilton's return, a group of Barbadians had left for Carolina under the command of John Yeamans, a planter, to establish a community at Cape Fear. A year and a half later, Yeamans led another group of Barbadians to the same area, and a group of Virginians had formed a community a little to the north, in Albemarle Sound. Given these bursts of activity, the initial prospects for the Carolina venture seemed bright.[20]

However, any optimism generated by such early attempts to use Carolina soon passed. While the settlement at Albemarle Sound survived and served as the basis for the colony of North Carolina, the first "Charles Town," erected about twenty miles up the Cape Fear River, like all the earlier settlements built by Europeans in Carolina, failed. Although an agreement made with the proprietors by Yeamans' son, Major William Yeamans, clarified the terms by which land would be conveyed, and in spite of the definition of authority in the settlement through the appointment of the elder Yeamans (now a knight) as governor, the settlement did not flourish. As one historian has noted, "trouble followed trouble and from the beginning misfortune dogged their path." Supply vessels were delayed or destroyed by storms. The master of one vessel, Captain Stanyarne, "went mad and leapt overboard." Colonists felt abused by the quitrents collected on behalf of the proprietors and were dissatisfied by the way lands were being allocated.[21] Although favorable reports from the colony were publicized in Britain[22] (which may have

---

[20] Andrews, *Colonial Period*, III, pp. 194-97; Wood, *Black Majority*, pp. 14-11.

[21] Andrews, *Colonial Period*, III, pp. 197-99; Wood, *Black Majority*, pp. 16-17; Salley, Jr., *Narratives*, pp. 78-79.

[22] See "A Brief Description of the Province of Carolina," by Robert Horne, 1666, in *ibid.*, pp. 66-73; and "A Relation of a Voyage on the Coast of the Province of Carolina, 1966," by Robert Sandford, in *ibid.*, pp. 82-108. Horne described the province as "fertile," and claimed the population numbered "800 persons." He recited the customary list of trees which grew there, but added that there were "mulbury-trees, and the Silkworm breeding naturally on them, with many other Trees for Fruit and for Building, for Perfume and for Medicine, for which the English have no name. . . . The Woods are stored with Deer and Wild Turkeys . . . of a more pleasant tast than in England." In addition to these natural endowments, Horne testified that the settlers "have brought with them most sorts of seeds and roots of the Barbadoes which thrive very well. . . . They have Indico, Tobacco very good, and Cotton-wool; Lime-trees, Orange, Lemon, and other Fruit-Trees they brought, thrive exceedingly: They have two crops of Indian-Corn in one year. . . . Here are as brave Rivers as any in the World, Stored with great abundance of Sturgeon, Salmon, Basse, Plaice, Trout, and Spanish

"materially aided the proprietors in securing settlers for the lower part of the province as well as for the upper part"),[23] by the autumn of 1677 the settlement at Cape Fear had failed, and the site was abandoned.

Just as their infant settlement on the Cape Fear River in Carolina collapsed, so too did the original body of proprietors decline. Colleton died, and his proprietorship passed to his son Peter. Albemarle's failed health caused him to retire from public affairs. By 1670 he too was dead, and was replaced by his 17-year old son Christopher. Clarendon had fled into exile after falling from power. Age may have led others to become disenchanted, if not with colonization, then at least with the prospect of undertaking major (and perhaps expensive) new efforts to restructure or reinvigorate their colonial holdings. Carteret was past 70 and the Berkeleys and Craven were over 60.[24] The proprietors had attempted to found a colony and make a profit with minimal inconvenience and virtually no expenditure of their own funds. Their first efforts, launched under the charter of 1663, had required each to contribute only £75. Between 1663 and 1666 their total expenses had run to only £600 8 s. 3 d., much of which had paid not for supplies to be sent to Carolina, but rather for the charters (£106 for the first, £71 for the second), and for "a great seal."[25] They had relied on the lure of free land and generous terms to attract colonists to Carolina who would pay their own way. They had counted on men and women already in America and experienced in colonization largely to support themselves in the wilderness. They had believed that a situation in Barbados which made land scarce and people plentiful would work to their advantage. To a degree, they were correct on all counts. But in order to succeed, a new colony in Carolina would require both the careful attention as well as the steady financial support of the proprietors. This was the clear lesson of the very first years of English settlement in Carolina.

Mackrill. . . ." Horne went on to declare that in spite of hard work and inadequate housing at the outset of life in Charles Town, "yet not one of them was ill, but continued well all the time." *Ibid.*, pp. 68-70.

[23] *Ibid.*, p. 65.

[24] Andrews, *Colonial Period*, III, p. 199; Sirmans, *Colonial*, p. 6.

[25] Wesley Frank Craven, *The Southern Colonies in the Seventeenth Century 1607-1689* (Baton Rouge, 1970), p. 333; *Collections of the South Carolina Historical Society, Vol. 5* (Charleston, 1897), pp. 56-67. Hereafter this volume will be cited simply as *Shaftsbury Papers*.

If other proprietors were uninterested in the Carolina colony or too old to act vigorously to revitalize it, Anthony Ashley Cooper (who would become the Earl of Shaftsbury in 1672) was neither.[26] Ashley had managed to hold office "under Charles I, Parliament, Cromwell, and Charles II"—a rare feat, and ample testimony to his political acumen.[27] In the summer of 1666 Ashley had been ill, and while traveling to the waters at Astrop, he stopped at Oxford. There he met the former Oxford don and now practitioner of medicine, John Locke. Locke impressed Ashley, who reacted by retaining him as his personal physician, secretary, and children's tutor. With Ashley's support, Locke came to hold the positions of secretary to the Council for Trade and Plantations and secretary to the proprietors.[28] Together Ashley and Locke assumed direction of the colonization of Carolina.

Originally the Carolina proprietors had aimed at using America to make a profit. They had ignored the opportunity to attempt to erect an ideal community in the open space they possessed. Now Ashley and Locke determined that these two goals were not mutually exclusive—that an ideal community could also be a profitable community—and that if a new effort were to be undertaken to settle Carolina, it might be good to create a society built in accordance with what they deemed to be an ideal pattern. They recognized that while economic profit was a worthwhile goal, they might simultaneously strive to make a social and political statement—to demonstrate that a society organized along lines they considered ideal would produce happy colonists who prospered as they lived in peace and enjoyed social harmony. All this would, of course, enrich the proprietors, as new immigrants surely would flock to such a place, take up land, pay rents, and buy as well as produce goods.

In April of 1669 Ashley "asserted his leadership" as he convinced the proprietors that a new effort at colonization was worthwhile, and that they, not prospective settlers, would be required to assume the responsibility for its success. Thus, each proprietor agreed to contribute £500 to finance the attempt, and pledged to provide up to £200 a year for the next four years in additional funds, if necessary. The money would purchase "Shipps Armes, Ammunition, Tooles, provisions" and other

---

[26] I shall refer to him as Lord Ashley. In 1667 he was 46 years old, the youngest of the original proprietors.

[27] Sirmans, *Colonial*, p. 7.

[28] *Ibid.*, pp. 7-8; Andrews, *Colonial Period*, III, pp. 199-200.

required supplies, and pay for the "shipping" of them, along with colonists, to "the Settlement of Port Royall within the Province of Carolina."[29] Thus, this was to be an entirely new venture, one which broke dramatically with earlier efforts to settle Carolina with Englishmen. First, the proprietors were now committed to absorbing the initial costs themselves. Second, they abandoned the Cape Fear region and determined to situate their settlement further south. And third, Ashley now proceeded to recruit colonists from England itself to accompany the three ships he purchased soon after the decision was taken to make a new effort. While no one doubted that Englishmen, and especially Barbadians, already residing in America would provide a substantial segment of the new community's population, it now seemed appropriate to send out men and women directly from Britain. Within three months over 100 such persons committed themselves to the enterprise.[30]

The three vessels, the *Carolina*, the *Port Royal*, and the *Albemarle*, left the Downs for Carolina in August 1669, under the command of Captain Joseph West. In addition to supplies, colonists, and instructions to the expedition's leaders, the ships carried a copy of a fascinating document, the Fundamental Constitutions of Carolina, which Locke and Ashley had drafted during the summer. In it they outlined their image of the ideal society they hoped to see erected in Carolina. Through adoption of the Constitutions, Ashley and Locke sought to bring to realization ideas formulated by James Harrington which suggested that political order might best be attained, and social harmony ensured, by carefully maintaining a balance between the influence of the aristocracy and that of the common people. And since influence, or power, was associated with the control of real property, the Constitutions discussed real property in great detail. On the one hand, the Constitutions guaranteed that the nobility would be composed only of men who held vast amounts of land—Carolina would be the home for no persons whose titles bore no relation to their wealth, influence, or power. At the same time, the Constitutions provided for widespread ownership of land by freeholders. Indeed, the total share of Carolina land owned by commoners would always exceed

---

[29] *Shaftsbury Papers*, pp. 91-92; Sirmans, *Colonial*, p. 7; Craven, *Southern Colonies*, pp. 334-35. Only five of the proprietors, the Duke of Albemarle, the Earl of Craven, Sir Peter Colleton, Sir George Carteret, and Lord Ashley seem to have paid their shares in time to provide funds for the expedition. *Shaftsbury Papers*, p. 151.

[30] Craven, *Southern Colonies*, pp. 334-35; Sirmans, *Colonial*, p. 7; Andrews, *Colonial Period*, III, p. 200.

that controlled by the aristocracy. The Fundamental Constitutions thus included a planned pattern of land holding, to be established at the outset of settlement and perpetuated over time, in which precisely two-fifths of all real property in the colony was held by either the proprietors or their own hereditary nobility. The remaining three-fifths was to be owned by ordinary free persons.

Land in Carolina was, as stated in the Constitutions, to be divided into squares, each to consist of 12,000 acres. Counties would be composed of 40 of these tracts. Of the 40 squares in each county, eight would become seigniories—one for each of the proprietors. An additional eight squares in every county, identified as baronies, were to be allocated to the nobility.[31] The other squares were to be distributed among the county's freeholders according to the headright system, by which land would be granted according to both the time of arrival in Carolina (those reaching the colony earliest got larger parcels than those coming later), and to the type of person whose passage to the province the claimant had financed (free adults and male servants merited more land than did female servants or children).[32] The hereditary nobility would consist of landgraves, caciques, and manor lords, invested with traditional prerogatives and entrusted with traditional responsibilities (every barony and seigniory was to have its own manorial court). At the apex of the nobility were the proprietors themselves, whose members constituted the palatine court. The eldest proprietor would serve as the lord palatine of Carolina.[33] Freeholders were to be represented in the Assembly, with every owner of at least 50 acres enfranchised to vote for those who held at

[31] *Shaftsbury Papers*, p. 94. The entire document fills pages 93-117 and contains 111 articles. It is identified as "Shaftsbury Papers:—First Set of the Constitutions for the Government of Carolina; by John Locke," p. 93; Weir, *Colonial*, pp. 53-58.

[32] The headright system employed in the earlier settlement at Cape Fear was not specifically discussed in the Fundamental Constitutions. It was fully detailed in instructions annexed to the commission for the colony's first governor, which accompanied the first fleet from England, and which were dated July 27, 1669. *Shaftsbury Papers*, p. 121. One hundred fifty acres were to be granted for every free person and male servant over sixteen years of age arriving prior to March 25, 1671, and 100 acres for each woman servant and male servant under 16. The land allocations declined in size to 100 acres for free persons arriving after March 25, 1672, and to 70 acres for free persons reaching Carolina after March 25, 1673.

[33] *Ibid.*, p. 101. Article 32.

least 500 acres.[34] Thus, the people's representatives would, by definition, be men of some substance. While they would always be more prevalent in the Assembly than the local nobility (each county would be represented by its landgrave and its two caciques, plus four elected freemen), the fact that the parliament would sit as one unified body with each member having a single vote did not mean that Ashley and Locke were handing power to the common people, for the Assembly could not initiate legislation. It could only react to laws proposed by the Grand Council, composed exclusively of noblemen. Additionally, since the proprietors or their appointed deputies would also sit in the parliament, if they chose to unite with the local nobles the combined voting strength thus created would overwhelm that of the freeholders until Carolina grew so large that nine counties existed.[35] The Constitutions further stipulated that the proprietors might veto laws passed by the Assembly. The document guaranteed religious freedom, requiring only that settlers participate in some organized religious group,[36] and it both recognized and validated Negro slavery.[37]

Thus did Ashley and Locke contemplate the future in Carolina. Needless to say, neither they nor the larger group of proprietors expected the Fundamental Constitutions to be implemented at the outset of settlement in Port Royal. This was made clear in the text of documents which Captain West carried to Carolina in addition to the Constitutions.[38] First, they sent a blank commission to Sir John Yeamans in Barbados, authorizing him to serve as Governor. However, they left Yeamans the option of inserting the name of anyone he chose in the event he wished to

---

[34] *Ibid.*, p. 110. Article 66. Ashley feared that, as Harrington argued, "A nobility . . . overbalancing a popular Government is the utter bane and destruction of it." At the same time, "A Nobility . . . in a popular Government not overbalancing it, is the very life and soul of it." Ashley once wrote, "It is as bad as a State of Warr for men that are in want to have the makeing Laws over Men that have Estates." See Sirmans, *Colonial*, p. 10; *Shaftsbury Papers*, p. 468, for quote from Ashley.

[35] Sirmans, *Colonial*, pp. 9-13.

[36] *Shaftsbury Papers*, pp. 114-15. Articles 87-95.

[37] *Ibid.*, p. 115 Article 101.

[38] West received a variety of documents which included his own commission and one for a surveyor general, as well as instructions for himself and others. *Ibid.*, pp. 117-32.

decline the post. Second, they provided a set of instructions for the new governor and his officials to follow in establishing the settlement. These demonstrate that the proprietors were not about to try to impose an ideal medieval social and political order on a wilderness colony. Rather, they instructed the new officials to "summon all ye freeman . . . And . . . elect five persons who being joyned to ye five deputed by ye respective Propriet^{rs}, are to be ye Counsell. . . . Yo^{u} are to sumon ye Freehoulders . . . to elect twenty persons, wch together wth o^{r} Deputys for ye present are to be y^{r} Parliament. . . ." The proprietors then proceeded to specify the precise terms under which land could be conveyed to the colonists. The only attempt to comply with the plan outlined in the Fundamental Constitutions was an instruction to lay out land "in Squares containeing each, 12000 Acres. . . ." Any of these taken up by a proprietor would be identified as a "Signiory;" any taken up by a landgrave or a cacique would become a "Barrony." Each square settled by "the people shall be a Collony." The officials were told to preserve "the proporcon of twenty-fower Collonyes to eight Signiorys & eight Barronyes."[39] But aside from these provisions, it is clear that the proprietors considered the implementation of the Fundamental Constitutions to be a goal to be achieved some time in the future, once a settled community had been established. Ashley, Locke, and the proprietors "were not," as one scholar has aptly observed, "impractical utopians bent on establishing feudalism in a virgin land. . . ."[40]

Captain West's own instructions were eminently practical, focusing on the acquisition of additional settlers in Ireland, and of seeds, plants, and provisions in Barbados. In fact, West was told "to carry" the seeds and roots "in a tubb of earth, y^{t} they may not dye before yor arrivall att Port Royall," and instructed as to the specific type of soil in which they were to be planted (ginger and cane, the proprietors said, "love a rich soyle & light mould"), as well as the exact season in which the planting

---

[39] *Ibid.*, pp. 120-211

[40] Sirmans, *Colonial*, p. 9. A somewhat different view has been offered by Wesley Frank Craven, who wrote: "The effort to transplant into America the feudal usages of England's rural society may seem foolish in the light of previous and subsequent experience. Yet it should be recognized that the proprietors naturally saw a worthy model in a familiar social and political order which offered substantial testimony to the advantages . . . of some sort of balance between an aristocracy and the more popular forces of 'democracy'." *Southern Colonies*, p. 341. A harsher judgment of the plan has been offered by Charles M. Andrews, who refers to it as an "archaic and cumbersome form of colonial management." *Colonial Period*, III, p. 222.

was to be done.[41] The proprietors were not, then, dreamers. They were experienced in colonization. They had tried in the past to settle Carolina and had failed. This time they intended to succeed.

The proprietors' three vessels left England after August 17. Their first destination was Kinsale, Ireland, where West was to recruit additional colonists. Instead of enlisting new recruits there, the expedition suffered a number of desertions. The ships then headed for Barbados, where in November the *Albemarle* was wrecked in a storm. Sir John Yeamans, who had accepted command of the enterprise, replaced the *Albemarle* with a rented sloop, *The Three Brothers*, and proceeded to lead his fleet to the Carolina coast. Bad weather in the Caribbean persisted, and the ships were driven apart by storms, with *The Three Brothers* ending up in Virginia, the *Carolina* in Bermuda, and the *Port Royal* wrecked in the Bahamas. In Bermuda Yeamans chose to give up his command and to return to Barbados. He filled in the blank governor's commission with the name of "an old Puritan now approaching the age of eighty," William Sayle, whom Yeamans himself described as "a man of no great sufficiency."[42] When the colonists finally departed from Bermuda in February 1670, they encountered continuing foul weather. The *Carolina* was not able to reach Port Royal until the end of March. *The Three Brothers*, which had been blown from Virginia far to the south of its goal, to what is now Georgia (where a number of passengers and the ship's master were captured by Spaniards), finally appeared on the Carolina coast at the end of May.[43]

Although the expedition's goal had been Port Royal, the first community (named Charles Town) erected in the new colony was situated well to the north, several miles up the Ashley River, on a site the settlers named Albemarle Point. Apparently, friendly Indians were waiting to greet the colonists when they landed on the Carolina coast. The natives urged the immigrants to consider settling to the north of Port Royal, in their own territory known as Kiawah. Perhaps these Kiawahs were seeking allies to protect them from the Westoes, who dominated the territory to

---

[41] *Shaftsbury Papers*, pp. 125-26.

[42] Craven, *Southern Colonies*, p. 343; Sirmans, *Colonial*, p. 16.

[43] *Ibid.*, p. 16; Craven, *Southern Colonies*, pp. 343-44.

the south, in the direction of the Savannah River.[44] The natives were persuasive, so the settlers decided to examine both prospective sites for their colony. The *Carolina* proceeded to explore the area around Port Royal, while the sloop headed for the land suggested by the Kiawahs. After these explorations the colonists decided they preferred to live near the Kiawahs. Governor Sayle, therefore, led his vessels through what is now Charleston harbor and up the Ashley River as far as the first major stream. On a bluff they believed to be well situated for defense, the colonists began to build a settlement.[45]

The settlers at the new Charles Town confronted two central problems at the outset. First, given the proximity of Spanish settlements and warlike natives, the colonists had to concern themselves with the defense of their community.[46] Thus, the first major construction undertaken at Charles Town was a palisade which, when completed by autumn, surrounded the town. The proprietors had furnished plenty of arms, and the colonists were quick to train in their use. Second, in spite of continued support from the proprietors, the settlers lacked sufficient food. Soon after depositing its passengers on Albemarle Point, the *Carolina* headed to Virginia to secure enough corn, peas, and meal to last the settlement eight months. The colonists did carry out some planting to bolster their food supply, but the weather failed to support these efforts. Rainfall proved inadequate and crops consistently failed. At one point during the winter of 1671-1672, food was in such short supply that the Council, "Upon consideracon . . . of the scarcity of provisions now growing in this Collony which will require a more frugall disposition of the provisions now remaining . . . ," commanded "that noe person . . . shall have or receive . . .

---

[44] This has been suggested by Craven, *Southern Colonies*, p. 344. The Westoes "enjoyed the unsavory reputation of being not only skillful warriors but maneaters as well." Waring, *First Voyage*, p. 26. Thus, the colonists may well have chosen to settle in Kiawah as opposed to Port Royal in order to maintain their distance from the Westoes.

[45] The stream is now known as Old Town Creek. See Waring, *First Voyage*, pp. 24-25; Craven, *Southern Colonies*, p. 344. The site of Charles Town was moved to a place called Oyster Point at the junction of the Ashley and Cooper Rivers in 1680.

[46] The Spanish did, in fact, organize an attack on the infant settlement almost at once. In the summer of 1670 three Spanish ships, reinforced by Indians, headed for Charles Town, but bad weather for once worked in favor of the settlers, forcing the Spanish vessels away. Without the Spanish to assist in the attack, the Indians departed. Sirmans, *Colonial*, pp. 19-20.

any more than five quarts of pease for every man a Weeke four quarts . . . for every woman a Weeke, and three quarts . . . for every child. . . ."[47] The result of food shortages was, of course, that the proprietors were forced to provide food to the settlers on credit, a process which soon led "even the most prominent . . . heavily into debt." While there never was a "starving time" in Carolina, the settlers would not enjoy a good harvest until 1674.[48] Until then they largely depended on the proprietors and on the natives for food.

---

[47] Alexander S. Salley, ed., *Journal of the Grand Council of South Carolina, August 25, 1671–June 24, 1680* (Columbia, 1970), pp. 26-27. Hereafter cited as *Council Journal, 1671-1680*. See also Chapter Three, footnote 57 below, for a more detailed discussion of food shortages in early Carolina.

[48] Converse D. Clowse, *Economic Beginnings in Colonial South Carolina, 1670-1730* (Columbia, 1971), pp. 56-67. Clowse asserts that "the food problem persisted for at least four or five growing seasons, limiting all other work" (p. 57).

Danger of attack and scarcity of supplies were not the only sources of difficulty in the first years of settlement. Governor Sayle was neither effective nor popular. He was old, a religious dissenter, ill, and zealous in seeking to impose his own strict standards of moral behavior on the settlers. His stewardship was openly challenged by a faction led by William Owen, an egotistical Anglican who not only questioned the validity of Carolina's first election, but also argued that the governor and council were not legally competent to grant land. Owen actually staged a counterelection of his own in the province. (Men elected in this poll appear in the public records as having been elected to "Owen's Parliament.") Governor Sayle was dead by early March 1671, which abruptly ended Owen's influence in the colony. Sayle's replacement by Joseph West, however, did not end political conflict in the new community. The governor was criticized and his power challenged by a group of Barbadians who found a leader when Sir John Yeamans reached the colony that summer.Since the original commission as governor had been directed to him, Yeamans naturally assumed that he would be invested with the office once he arrived in Carolina. He was, after all, a landgrave, which made him the highest-ranking aristocrat in the colony. Yet West had been named as Sayle's successor by Sayle himself, and he argued that only the proprietors could deprive him of the governorship. Yeamans first attempted to persuade the parliament, and later the Council, that he was entitled to the position, but failed. Ultimately the proprietors did choose to defer to their own Fundamental Constitutions, when they decided that the landgrave should be the governor.

Yeamans took power in March 1672. His tenure was brief and unsuccessful. Settlers blamed him for food shortages, while the proprietors blamed him both for accumulating an ever `increasing debt and for overcharging the colonists for the supplies he secured at proprietary expense. Before their decision to replace him with West could reach Carolina, Yeamans had died. West became governor in August, 1674. This story is detailed in Sirmans, *Colonial*, pp. 26-29.

Yet in spite of such difficulties, the colony attracted new settlers. In September 1670, the *Carolina* left for Barbados, returning in February 1671, with 64 immigrants. Another ship, the *John and Thomas*, brought 42 more Barbadians to the colony at about the same time. Prior to 1672, 96 New Yorkers came to Carolina on the *Phoenix* and the *Blessing.*[49] The influx of immigrants provides perhaps the best testimony not only to the wisdom of the proprietors in using rather liberal land allowances to immigrants as a magnet to attract settlers, but to the success of the policy as well. Clearly the offer of land at attractive terms was sufficient to induce persons to venture their futures (and risk their capital) in a place whose history could not serve as a basis for promise of a prosperous future. It was, then, the land which drew men and women to Carolina, just as open land would serve to pull settlers and investors across the continent for the next two centuries.[50] It is thus important to bear in mind that one

---

[49] Waring, *First Voyage*, p. 36; Craven, *Southern Colonies*, pp. 346-47; Sirmans, *Colonial*, p. 22.

[50] This is not to say that settlers were not lured to Carolina by favorable reports about the climate, or that the proprietors' promise of religious freedom meant nothing in attracting colonists. It does seem clear, however, that the key attraction of Carolina, given early food shortages, a history of failed settlements, hostile natives allied to Spaniards, and uncertainty about the healthfulness of the place, must have been the availability of land at generous terms. In this respect, the social and political system outlined in the Fundamental Constitutions makes a good deal of sense. In offering huge estates and hereditary titles to persons of means willing to populate (at their own expense) the estates they received (at no cost to the proprietors), and in the process requiring those persons to assume communal responsibilities, the proprietors were acting in a most practical fashion. They had land. They needed people to settle it and to help keep order. The Fundamental Constitutions provided a means to achieve the desired ends with the least inconvenience and at little expense to the proprietors.

Richard Waterhouse, in "England . . . Carolina," quotes a Dublin alderman who, in 1708, wrote to South Carolina inquiring about a person who had gone to the colony "out of a humor to goe to travel, but for no other Reasson. . . ." Waterhouse also suggests that some left England for Carolina because of "Religious motives," especially in the decade of the 1680's. Nevertheless, the primary reason for migration to Carolina, according to Waterhouse, seems to have been the "concern for material prosperity." In assessing motives for settling in the colony, Waterhouse writes: "To men of all classes Carolina offered the opportunity to acquire what was denied them in England—inexpensive land" (p. 263). In discussing why Barbadians left that island for Carolina, Waterhouse notes that, "the lack of opportunity in Barbados, when combined with the prospect of owning relatively large amounts of land in Carolina, must have been important factors in influencing numbers of small landholders to move to Carolina" (p. 279).

way to assess the Carolina venture is to focus on what may well have been most important to the settlers—on the transfer of land from the proprietors to the persons who came to live in the colony. For the proprietors began only with virgin territory completely lacking European inhabitants. Without settlers their vast holdings meant nothing. Colonists came largely to secure land and to use land. Therefore, in determining just who acquired land and how it was obtained, we learn much about the early social composition of the community. In asking what the initial recipients did with their land—whether they prospered, continuing to amass property over time, or failed, losing their estates, or simply hovered motionless at one level of wealth during their lives in Carolina—we seek to determine whether the promise of the colony was realized.

Surely the Carolina colony cannot be deemed a success if we focus attention on either of two goals which motivated the proprietors. First, in spite of a growing population, and an emerging economy in which Carolinians sold furs and naval stores to England, while sending salted pork and beef, and pipe staves to the West Indies in return for sugar and rum,[51] the colony was not profitable to the proprietors.

Second, the political and social order specified so carefully in the Fundamental Constitutions never emerged in developed form, and the Fundamental Constitutions themselves were repeatedly rejected by those who lived in Carolina. While neither profit nor adoption and implementation of the Constitutions were immediate or even short-term goals of the proprietors, it is doubtful that any of them would have become involved in the creation of Carolina were these goals not deemed realizable once the colony had matured.

If the proprietors anticipated that their Carolina venture would yield significant profits, they must have experienced acute disappointment. By 1674 their initial agreement (concluded in April of 1669) to finance the colony had run its course, and since the colonists could not support themselves, the proprietors determined that it would be necessary to continue to contribute their own funds if the colony were to succeed. Thus each agreed not only to provide £100 a year for the following seven years, but also to credit "all returns and effects . . . to be received from the . . . plantacon" toward "the dischargeing the present debts oweing by the said Proprietors upon the account of the said Plantacon. . . ." In future these

[51] Clowse, *Economic Beginnings*, pp. 60-65; Sirmans, *Colonial*, p. 23. Some colonists derived profit quite early from sending captured Indians as slaves to the West Indies, a trade the proprietors considered illegal. See Clowse, *Economic*, pp. 65-66.

revenues would be employed to buy "Comodities to be sent unto the said Province for the better carrying on the plantacon. . . ."[52] As early as April 1671, Ashley, writing on behalf of the proprietors, had displayed alarm at the way in which their economic interests, "which," he noted, "are very moderate and faire," seemed to be disregarded by their own officials.[53] That December Ashley instructed a ship's captain working for the proprietors to "encourage men of Estates to remove to Carolina. But," he stressed, "forbeare to invite the poorer sort yet for a while" because they only "relye and eate upon us."[54] The proprietors' mood changed little in the ensuing years. In the spring of 1675 Ashley wrote to the colony's officials that the proprietors were both distressed and frustrated because they had wrongly assumed that "theire expenses would not be endless. . . ." They had invested, he pointed out, "a greater Summe of Money in carrying on that Plantacon and Sending . . . supplyes then they at first designed or could have imagined." Yet, he continued, the colonists had made no effort to even attempt to repay the proprietors. The result was that the proprietors were loath "to bury any more money amongst people who tooke soe little care to satisfie them" and who "intended never to live of themselves." He concluded by noting that "by the Expence of 9 or £10000 we have purchased nothing but the charge of maintaineing on 5 or 600 people who expect to live upon us."[55]

The friction generated between the proprietors and the colonists during the first years of settlement by the settlers' failure to repay debts was never really relieved. Not only did private debts to the proprietors (arising from the settlers' need to secure food and supplies from the proprietors' storekeeper on credit) remain unpaid, but quitrents proved difficult to collect. This must have been especially galling to the proprietors since they did not demand rents from the settlers at the outset, choosing instead to wait for their revenues until the colony was well established. By March 1679, the proprietors had sunk "17 or eighteene thousand pounds" into the province "by w[ch] . . . ," they asserted to the king,

---

[52] *Shaftsbury Papers*, p. 432.

[53] "Ashley to Gov. Sayle," *ibid.*, p. 311.

[54] "Ashley to Capt. Halsted," *ibid.*, p. 364.

[55] "Ashley to the Governor and Councell," *ibid.*, pp. 466-67.

"we have brought the place to a prosperous condition."[56] But prosperity did not induce the colonists to pay their debts. Not until 1694 did the Assembly pass a rent collection statute, which led to a yield of £73 for the proprietors.[57] The situation did not improve over the next 15 years. Because of continued widespread "evasion of quitrent payments, the proprietors moved," in 1709, "to curtail land sales and headright grants."[58] In a response that must have infuriated the proprietors, the Assembly enacted a law which prohibited their agents from repossessing any estate that had been held legally for more than seven years.[59]

Ultimately, the proprietors did profit from Carolina, but not those individuals who had planned, financed, and then supported the colony to its maturity. It was the heirs of the original recipients of the charter who, in 1729, sold their rights to the crown for £2500 each. In addition, they received £5000 to cover "the estimated arrears in quitrents."[60] A reliable recent estimate of the total amount expended by the proprietors on Carolina between 1663 and 1729 suggests that they had spent about £25,000 during the 66 years they held the charter to Carolina.[61]

Just as economic gain cannot be cited as an example of fulfilled proprietary goals for their Carolina enterprise, so too is it impossible to argue that the social and political order which developed in the colony was shaped by the proprietors' design as described in the Fundamental Constitutions. Carolina did display a local nobility, whose status was reinforced by control of vast properties. Certainly the policy of religious toleration dictated by the Constitutions did take hold in Carolina, and the colony surely served as a refuge for religious dissenters from many

---

[56] *Records in the British Public Record Office Relating to South Carolina, 1663-1684* (Atlanta, 1928), pp. 71-72. Hereafter cited as *B.P.R.O.-S.C, Vol. 1*.

[57] Sirmans, *Colonial*, p. 54. The beginning of quitrent collection led many colonists to buy land from the proprietors and thereby avoid the rents which accompanied land granted on the basis of headright concessions. Sirmans argues that proceeds from such land sales provided the first return to the proprietors on their investment "in three decades" (p. 54).

[58] Clowse, *Economic Beginnings*, p. 157.

[59] *Ibid.*, p. 157.

[60] *Ibid.*, p. 242.

[61] *Ibid.*

areas.[62] But aside from these two specific examples of aspects of the Constitutions which came to be reflected in the society that developed in Carolina, and, of course, a pattern of land allocation which identified certain parcels with names derived from that document (for example, baronies),[63] the proprietors' overall scheme was never implemented. The Fundamental Constitutions as a whole were never adopted, nor was any attempt made in the colony to modify customs or behavior to conform more closely to the proprietors' master design. For more than three decades the proprietors urged the colonists to adopt the Constitutions. Consistently the Assembly refused to pass the necessary legislation, and the proprietors just as consistently instructed their officials to approach "as neer as possible" the "sacred and unalterable" plan.[64] In 1698 they promulgated a revised, shortened version which, as in the past, the Assembly refused to accept. "For more than thirty years," wrote Charles M. Andrews, "these Constitutions were a disturbing factor in the life of the colonists, and the determination of the proprietors to enforce them and the unwillingness of the assembly to accept them made it difficult for anyone . . . to know just what were the laws they were expected to obey."[65]

---

[62] Sirmans, *Colonial*, p. 10.

[63] See the series of articles in the early volumes of the *South Carolina Historical and Geneological Magazine* by Henry A. M. Smith, entitled "The Baronies of South Carolina." While pieces of land were identified by the names specified in the Constitutions, Ashley's plan to divide Carolina into neat 12,000 acre seigniories, baronies, and colonies, "failed completely." Carolina terrain was too broken up by waterways to permit such neat division, and the colonists refused to be guided by a scheme they knew to be wholly impractical. See Sirmans, *Colonial*, p. 32.

[64] Quoted in Andrews, *Colonial Period*, III, p. 220.

[65] *Ibid.*, p. 222. Conflict between the colonists and the proprietors during the early years of settlement was not, of course, generated solely by financial difficulties or by the Carolinians' refusal to adopt the Fundamental Constitutions. The core of conflict between those who lived in Carolina and those who "owned" it was the proprietors' opinion that they ought to be able to shape colonial behavior since they had financed the entire enterprise, and the equally fervent belief of the settlers that no matter what their intentions or motives, men who did not live in the territory were not qualified to dictate their notions to persons whose first-hand experience suggested better alternatives. For example, the proprietors wanted Carolinians to settle in towns, but the pull of fertile land scattered across the frontier proved stronger than proprietary wishes. Settlers simply went where they believed they could best succeed. A second example of proprietary notions failing to mesh with colonial behavior involved the profitable trade in Indian slaves. The proprietors "condemned as foolish

Given this record of frustrated expectations and failed plans, instances of overt proprietary rage at the colonists are surprisingly rare. They (or at least Ashley, speaking for them) seem to have maintained genuine hope that their goals ultimately would be realized. Perhaps they drew a measure of satisfaction from their one central success—Carolina at last had been settled with Europeans who would clearly survive in the territory. Indeed, the province promised to flourish. Where Spaniard and Frenchman had failed, the Lords Proprietors succeeded. If they saw neither profit from, nor the social and political system they devised for the colony adopted in Carolina, at least they did see the place filled with Englishmen who took up the land they offered. In peopling the province and distributing land among its inhabitants, the proprietors achieved a remarkable success. It was that success in conveying land to immigrants which locates the origin of an American dream of upward mobility, opportunity, and property acquisition by the dispossessed and propertyless of the Old World in places such as seventeenth century South Carolina. This study will explore that process on a personal level for some of the first English men and women to settle in the American deep South.

Historians of early America have traditionally focused most of their attention on New England and Virginia. However, other parts of English America have never been completely ignored by historians, and a remarkable amount of work has been completed by scholars interested in the Caribbean, New York, Pennsylvania, Maryland, and the Carolinas. While there are a number of excellent studies dealing with colonial South Carolina, wide gaps remain in our understanding of the colony. We have carefully researched, well-wrought published monographs which focus on the political and religious life of the province,[66] the colonial economy,[67] and the colony's black population.[68] This literature is bolstered

---

and immoral" such activity. Colonists disagreed, since the trade was one source of profit. Equally troubling was the proprietary attempt to monopolize trade with the Westoes. Indian traders in the colony responded by undermining relations between the English and the tribe, which ultimately led to war. The consequence of this conflict was the destruction of the Westo tribe, which made the proprietary monopoly meaningless. See Sirmans, *Colonial*, pp. 32-34.

66 Sirmans, *Colonial*; Weir, *Colonial*; Brinsfield, *Religion*.

67 Clowse, *Economic Beginnings*.

68 Wood, *Black Majority*.

by unpublished dissertations on the land system[69] and on the colonial upper class.[70] Yet we know very little about the lives of early Carolina's mass of white colonists—about the men and women who came to the colony without either money of their own or ties to well-off relatives or friends in Europe or the Caribbean who would help them to succeed. If we are to comprehend fully the process of settlement in the early American South, we must examine the personal histories of individuals who, precisely because they were not members of the colonial elite (political, social or economic), never appeared regularly in the colonial records, much less in the books of historians which were written out of those records. We need, in other words, to look at persons who came to Carolina to *raise* their social or economic status. If we are to assess whether the notion of America as a land of opportunity had any meaning in the early South, if we wish to know, moreover, whether or not that image was partly created there, then we must look not at men and women who began with significant assets, or at men and women whose race prohibited them even from seeking to achieve upward mobility, but rather at persons who came with little.

Since we know virtually nothing about such persons as a group,[71] even the most basic questions need to be answered. How many such men and women came to the colony to seek their fortunes? From where did they

---

[69] Robert Kilgo Ackerman, "South Carolina Colonial Land Policies," Ph.D. dissertation, University of South Carolina, 1960.

[70] Richard Waterhouse, "South Carolina's Colonial Elite: A Study in the Social Structure and Political Culture of a Southern Colony, 1670-1760," Ph.D. dissertation, The Johns Hopkins University, 1973. The origins of the South Carolina upper class have also been discussed by Richard S. Dunn in "The English Sugar Islands and the Founding of South Carolina," *South Carolina Historical Magazine* 72 (April, 1971), 81-93. Hereafter referred to as S.C.H.M or S.C.H.G.M. for volumes published under the title *South Carolina Historical and Geneological Magazine*.

[71] Geneologists, for example, have provided marvelous highly detailed individual accounts of the lives of a number of the first English Carolinians, and of some families whose origins in America can be traced well back into the colonial era. Works which have (at least according to their titles) sought to discuss those white immigrants who, as a group, came to Carolina as servants, are disappointing. They focus almost exclusively on the eighteenth century, and ignore most questions that interest students seeking to learn about the process through which servants became free settlers in the colony. See John Donald Duncan, "Servitude and Slavery in Colonial South Carolina, 1670-1776," Ph.D. dissertation, Emory University, 1971; and Warren B. Smith, *White Servitude in Colonial South Carolina* (Columbia, 1961).

come? Did they arrive in groups? Or, was immigration an individual action? When did they choose to come—at the very outset or later? And why did they elect to immigrate at any particular time?

If such questions are of interest, still more intriguing is the possibility of determining whether the colony actually was a land of economic and social opportunity. In other words, did men and women who immigrated early in the colony's life actually advance? How many even survived? And if they lived and accumulated property, what were the boundaries which limited their accomplishments? That is, how far upward could an individual move? And what was the typical movement upward? Were there a few isolated instances of striking upward mobility which may have served to placate or co-opt a huge mass of poor disadvantaged whites who nevertheless remained content and quiet because they believed someday, somehow, they might accomplish similar feats of mobility? Or was success the norm for poor immigrants? Were such colonists correct in judging their chances to be better in Carolina than in other American settlements to which they might have migrated?

Needless to say, answering such questions presents the historian with a variety of problems. Surviving records from the early years of life in the colony do not readily yield the kinds of data that permit scholars to compile portraits of many individuals. Those persons for whom data are available frequently were not of "the common sort."[72] Nevertheless, this study is an effort to engage in that enterprise—to try to formulate (far too often in a manner which is no more than speculation) responses to such questions. It largely focuses on the lives of men and women who began in the colony at the very bottom of the white social and economic hierarchy—on those who arrived with the least social and material assets but who might have had the greatest aspirations for altering their status—in short, on the colony's first indentured servants. These people, more than any other white immigrants, came in order to better their condition at some later time. For them, immediate gain was not a goal. Their hopes were pegged on the future, on the promise Carolina offered. It is their story which will be told here.

---

[72] The problems confronted by students interested in completing demographic studies of seventeenth century Carolina are discussed rather fully in Chapter Two.

CHAPTER TWO

Carolina Servants and the Historical Record: Limitations and Possibilities

I. Limitations: Servants and the Sources

Formidable obstacles impede any investigation of social and economic mobility in seventeenth century South Carolina. Unlike other areas in America settled by Englishmen, South Carolina cannot provide its students with neat sets of manuscript records that detail births and deaths, marriages and baptisms, land owned and taxes paid. The very earliest church records in South Carolina, which historians of New England have used so marvelously, date from the second decade of the eighteenth century. Carolinians did not at first settle in towns; hence there are no town records which report land allotments or the issues that concerned inhabitants. There are no quitrent rolls, no detailed census data. No personal diaries and virtually no private correspondence have survived. There are, of course, volumes of manuscript records and a vast official correspondence, which contain all sorts of valuable data to entice the social historian. But they sometimes yield a huge amount of information on a few individuals; and more often, a very small amount about the vast majority of settlers. Demographers would find the South Carolina records from the seventeenth century alien and decidedly hostile territory.[1]

Those settlers whose dealings occupy a disproportionate amount of space in the records—about whose lives we can devise the most complete accounts—are precisely those about whom we *need* to know the least. They

[1] Many of the sources employed by demographers studying other seventeenth century colonies are available for South Carolina in the eighteenth century.

were the wealthy, the aristocrats, the men and women who came to the colony in positions of power, who brought with them the wealth and the family or business ties with their counterparts in England or Barbados which at the outset answer our questions about how they proceeded to establish themselves in the infant colony.

The group with the greatest potential for upward mobility, the ideal "test group" to examine in attempting to answer the most elemental of all questions about the nature of mobility in seventeenth century South Carolina (Was it a land of opportunity where those who started with little could in the end achieve much?)—the servants—are precisely the men and women whose activities were least likely to be recorded in official documents or referred to in the correspondence that flowed back and forth from the colony to England or the British West Indies. Yet there is enough information contained in surviving records involving the men and women who began as servants, to allow us to draw some conclusions about their lives and to arrive at answers to at least some of the questions we have about them, as well as about the opportunities for advancement offered to settlers by the colony. To be sure, all the questions we have about these men and women cannot be answered. And in many cases, limited or incomplete data force the scholar to suggest, speculate, or guess. However, it is possible to formulate reasonably sound answers to enough of our questions about such settlers that the effort is worthwhile. And the prospect of opening to view the lives of these most common of common people is tantalizing.

One other matter should be considered here. While there are insufficient data on seventeenth century South Carolina to allow a demographic study of the type completed for a number of American colonial towns, we do not require nearly such massive evidence in order to discuss mobility. In fact, an examination of mobility requires really only a few bits of evidence, and but two dates—a date at which we are able to attribute one status to an idividual, and a later date for which the same, a higher or a lower status, can be established. While such would in no way be definitive (a person could continue to move "up" or "down" after the second date, unless that were a date of death—hence the appeal of using wills or estate inventories for the second date), even such a bare outline has value when discussing those whose lives have been obscured simply because they were *so* common, or mean, or debased that they seldom managed to get into the colonial records; or because historians commonly have displayed a bias in favor of studying other, more prominent types of settlers. Yet even given the difficulties involved in securing information on servants, the South Carolina records yield, in a surprising number of cases, far more data than the required minimum. But who were these men and women identified as "servants" in the colonial records? What did the term "servant" mean?

Servant, in the usage of the seventeenth century, was an imprecise term. It denoted a variety of statuses, the most common of which signified a person who entered into a formal contractual relationship with another, agreeing to perform whatever tasks the "master" required. The master, in return, maintained his servant for the entire time the contract specified, providing at minimum shelter, food and clothing. The formal contracts, or "indentures," commonly ran from two to seven years. Such, for example, was the indenture that engaged Miliscent How to serve Captain Joseph West in South Carolina:

> Know all men that I Milicent How of London Spinster . . . doe firmely by the p[rese]nts bind and oblidge my selfe as a faithfull & obedient Serv$^{t.}$ in all things whatsoever, to serve and dwell wth. Cap$^{t.}$ Joseph West, of the s^{d} Citty of London Merchant, in the Plantac'on, or province of Carolina, according to the Lawes & Customs, and Orders for serv^{ts}., wch. are provided and settled in the s^{d} place; The s^{d} Joseph West providing for the s^{d} Milicent his Servant all such necessaryes in the time of her service and at the expirac'on of ther terme as the lawes and orders of the place doth like wise provide and oblidge Masters to performe to their serv^{ts} Witnesse my hand and Seale this pnt twentyeth day of September 1669.[2]

Miliscent signified her acceptance of the agreement by making her mark.

Servant might also denote someone who performed specific tasks, and in addition to food and clothing, received a set amount of money

---

[2] A. S. Salley, ed., *Records of the Secretary and the Register 1671-1675* (Columbia, 1944), pp. 7-8. (This is the first volume in a set of manuscript sources referred to as "Wills, Inventories and Miscellaneous Records." This particular volume, as well as a few others, is available in a published edition. In cases where I have used the original manuscript volume for a reference and whenever I cite a volume which has not been published, I shall identify it with the label "(MSV)" for "Manuscript Volume." The labels "(WPA)" and "(CWA)" refer to typescripts of some original sources. These designations are more fully discussed in the Bibliography. Milicent How, illiterate and unwed servant, married a carpenter named Originall Jackson by 1672. Earlier scholars (e.g., Langdon Cheves) speculated that she *may* have married Jackson (*Shaftsbury Papers*, p. 410 fn.). However, on a document in *Records of the Register and the Secretary 1675-1696, 1703-1709* , (MSV), p. 36, Milicent Jackson made her mark—the letter "H". The Jacksons deeded four acres for a "Church, or House of Worship to be erected" in Charles Town in January 1681. See *Records of the Register and the Secretary 1675-1696, 1703-1709* (MSV), p. 117.

either during or after the completion of the agreed upon term of service. Thus, for example, another indenture to Joseph West, this from January 1674:

> This indenture wittnesseth y^{t} Samuell Morris doth by these p^{r}sents promise . . . and Covenant With Coll -: Joseph West of the Province of Carolina to Serve him . . . for and dureing the terme of two years & three week in such servis and Imploym^{t}: as the s^{d} - Joseph West or his Assignes shall Imploy [him] . . . a board the Ketch called the ffelowship of Carolina or aboard of any other ship or vessell or upon the Land in any place so far as is agreeable to the Custome of semen w^{ch}: belong to a ship or other vessell. And in Consideration whereof the s^{d} - Joseph West doth promise to allow ye s^{d} - sam: morris sufficient meat and drinke and at ye end of one year & three week to pay the s^{d} - sam morris five pounds or the value of it in goods att Barbados, or Virginia, or Carolina, as Sam Morris shall desier it and att he Expiration of the other year to pay him five pounds more as Afores^{d}., . . .[3]

Morris was able to sign his name. He began in Carolina as a servant arriving with the first fleet, and apparently preferred working for someone else with his needs provided for, to trying to survive by planting on his own land.[4]

A working definition of *servant* is made more difficult because the head of a household commonly was referred to as the "master," while his indentured servants, slaves, employees, and even some junior family members were his "servants." Needless to say, some prospective settlers, desiring to boost the number of acres they might claim, and acutely aware that the surest way[5] to acquire specific acreage was through the headright offered for the importation of family and servants, persuaded brothers, sisters, cousins, nieces, nephews, even friends (some of whom may have been reasonably well-off) to appear on passenger lists or before colonial officials as servants. It seems reasonable to assume that many of these never performed any labor for their "master," were "out of their time" very soon after reaching the colony, and ready to make their own claim for the acreage due them for having immigrated as servants. The issue

---

[3] *Records of the Secretary and the Register 1671-1675*, pp. 53-54.

[4] He may have tried and failed, or sold his right to his 100 acre land concession upon completion of his original indenture, for there is no record of his claiming a land warrant for himself.

[5] The Proprietors did give land to those who had performed some service on their behalf for the good of the colony; for example, to those who invested heavily or who promised to recruit new immigrants.

becomes yet more complex when we encounter men and women listed as servants whose arrival *did not* generate a claim of land by their "master" for having imported them. In such situations one wonders just what the role was that such "servants" fulfilled. For example, Affra Harleston appears as a servant to Ed. Hollis and Joseph Dalton on a list of those aboard the ship *Carolina* about to leave England for the colony in August, 1669. However, she was the daughter of an Essex gentleman, and neither Hollis nor Dalton claimed land for having brought her to Carolina.[6]

Or consider Affra Harleston's fellow passenger aboard the *Carolina*, Barnaby Bull. He is listed as one of six "servants" to Stephen Bull, but Stephen never claimed a land concession for bringing Barnaby to South Carolina. In fact, Barnaby was Stephen's younger brother, and had a warrant in June 1672, for 150 acres, the concession allotted to settlers who transported themselves to the colony as free persons.[7] Given the wide range of statuses that the word *servant* denoted to contemporaries, I have chosen to use it here to signify any person whose passage to South Carolina was paid by another person; or for whose importation another person (but not, of course, a husband or father) secured a warrant for land. While it is impossible to be certain that every settler included in my sample of those who began life in the colony as servants was, in fact, a bound servant, I am confident that any error in identification is so small as to be insignificant in my analysis of the data I have compiled on these men and women. Moreover, even if not servants in the traditional sense, such men and women surely did start out at the very bottom of South Carolina

---

[6] *Shaftsbury Papers*, pp. 134, 394. Hollis never reached the colony. Dalton did, and became an early leader. He had a warrant for 1150 acres for bringing seven servants to South Carolina who appear on the passenger list with Affra Harleston, but she was not among those listed in the warrant as a basis for his claim. She married John Coming before February, 1672, so her "term" was of short duration, if she served at all. See *Records of Secretary 1692-1700* (WPA), p. 319; *Records of the Secretary 1692-1700* (MSV),, p. 230; *Records of the Secretary 1700-1710* (MSV), pp. 22-23; Misc. *Records 1682-1690* (MSV), pp. 1, 51-52; *Records of the Register 1696-1702* (MSV), pp. 102, 123; *Memorial Book Vol. 1* (MSV), pp. 324-25.

[7] See Eugene M. Sirmans, "Masters of Ashley Hall," unpublished Ph.D. dissertation (Princeton University, 1959), pp. 6, 25. Had Barnaby been a servant arriving before March, 1670, he would have been entitled to receive only 100 acres. "Instructions . . . to . . . ye Governor & Councell," July 27, 1669, *Shaftsbury Papers*, p. 121. See also Henry DeSaussure Bull, D.D., *The Family of Stephen Bull of Kinghurst Hall, County Warwick, England and Ashley Hall, South Carolina, 1600-1690* (Georgetown, S.C., 1961), p. 1.

white society, and the point of examining the servant group is not so much to see how well servants as such did, but rather to look at a group that began at the bottom of the social and economic hierarchy.[8] If, therefore, someone other than a father or husband[9] paid for the trip to South Carolina, or claimed land for doing so; or, if a person appears in the records as a "servant" and I have found no reason to question that status, I have included that person in my servant group.

Equally troublesome as are questions of status at arrival are those that involve precise identification of settlers once freedom had been attained. Specifically, it is often impossible to ascertain whether or not a given reference in the sources describes a former servant, a different person with the same name, or a child with the parent's name. Thus, is George Rewberry who claimed his first warrant for land in May 1685, the same George Rubry who arrived in the colony in June 1671, as a servant to Oliver Spencer? If so, what was he doing during the intervening years? It is unreasonable to assume that his term of service to Spencer lasted fourteen years, or exactly twice as long as the time generally accepted as the lengthiest period for which servants engaged themselves.[10] In this instance, it is possible to determine that both *Rubry* and *Rewberry* signify the same man.[11] In other cases such a determination is impossible. Thus John Cooke

---

[8] I have discarded the names of those about whose actual status I had strong reservations. If each of my "servants" did not actually perform labor "in all things whatsoever" and "serve and dwell" with a master for a period of years, I am reasonably certain that each did begin life in the colony at the lowest possible level, starting out at most with the standard land concession given newly-freed servants.

[9] Obviously some husbands did claim land concessions on behalf of wives who had arrived as servants. If the marriage took place in the colony *after* the woman had completed her term, such women have been included in my sample.

[10] Custom dictated that the longest contracts would run seven years. To resolve questions which arose involving length of service in South Carolina, on April 7, 1687, the Assembly passed "An Act for Servants . . . Arriving Without . . . Contracts" which read: " . . . all persons hereafter arriving . . . without indentures or contracts, under the age of ten years old . . . shall serve till that they arrive at the age of twenty one yeares old, and under the age of fifteen yeares, and above ten, shall serve the terme of seaven yeares, and others that arrive without indentures . . . above the age of fifteen yeares old, to serve five yeares. . . ." Thomas Cooper and David McCord, eds., *The Statutes at Large of South Carolina*, Vol. II (Columbia, 1836), p. 30.

[11] On Rubry, see Alexander S. Salley, ed., *Warrants for Lands in South Carolina 1672-1679* (Columbia, 1910), p. 84 (hereafter cited as *Warrants, 1672-79*); Alexander S. Salley, ed., *Warrants for Lands in South Carolina 1680-1692* (Columbia,

came to South Carolina in 1671 as a servant to Richard Cole. We hear nothing of him other than that his fellow servant Dennis Mahone tried to persuade him to run away, until 1705 when he, or another man named John Cooke, held a grant for 200 acres; and yet another for 350 acres six years later. There were at least two settlers named William Davice, two named Thomas Clark, two or three named John Mills, two named John Rivers, perhaps two named John Wilkinson, and two named Robert Williams. Yet only one of each pair had started as a servant. Rarely is it possible to ascertain which data in the sources apply to which person. Equally troublesome is the likelihood that information on any given servant actually applies to a child of the same name. (It was not uncommon for a daughter to be given the mother's Christian name.) As if these concerns were not sufficient to confuse the researcher, in three instances one encounters two *servants* who shared a name. Thus one Thomas King arrived in the first fleet a servant to Florence O'Sullivan, and one Thomas King arrived in 1672 a servant to Oliver Spencer. One Robert Leeds arrived in 1672 a servant to Thomas Lane, and another Robert Leeds arrived before 1677, a servant to Robert Gough. One John Willson arrived in 1672 a servant to John Strode and Company, and a second John Willson came in 1672 a servant to Jacob Wayte.[12] While it is sometimes possible to

---

Secretary 1675-1696, 1703-1709 (MSV), p. 22; *Records of the Register and of the Secretary 1711-1715* (MSV), pp. 332-33. Rewberry's warrant of 1685 does establish that he was the same person as Rubry, for he claimed 300 acres on behalf of his own arrival, that of his wife Elizabeth, and Nicholas Webb, all of whom arrived, according to the warrant, in June 1671. Since both he and Nicholas Webb were servants to Spencer, along with Webb's wife Elizabeth, since the arrival date on the warrant corresponds with the arrival date of Spencer's servants, and since Elizabeth Rewberry must have previously been Elizabeth Webb, it seems clear that Webb had died, and Rewberry, now married to Webb's wife, was claiming land on behalf of all three of them.

[12] On John Cooke, see *Warrants, 1672-1679* p. 55; *Journal of the Grand Council 1671-1680*, p. 14 (servant); *Proprietary Grants No. 1, Vol. 38* (MSV), p. 534; *Proprietary Grants No. 2, Vol. 39* (MSV), pp. 155, 171; *Abstracts of the Grants and Commissions of LDS. Props. 1692-1718, 1733-1736, 1775-1820 (2 vols.)* (MSV), pp. 223, 361, 375 (grants). On John Mills, see *Warrants, 1672-1679*, pp. 76, 77; *Records of the Secretary 1675-1696* (MSV), p. 227; *Records of the Register and of the Secretary 1711-1715* (MSV), p. 225; *Abstracts of the Grants and Commissions of LDS. Props. 1692-1718, 1733-1736, 1775-1820 (2 vols.)* (MSV), p. 254; *Proprietary Grants No. 2, Vol. 39* (MSV), p. 32. On John Rivers, see *Warrants, 1672-1679*, p. 55; *Journal of the Grand Council 1671-1680*, pp. 14, 47-79; *Recs. of the Secretary of Prov. D, 1724-25* (W.P.A.), pp. 266, 305; *Records of Secretary 1711-1719* (MSV), p. 25. On John Wilson,

attribute data about people who shared names to the proper person if one arrived free and one as a servant (it is not uncommon to find "arriving a servt." after the name in land warrants), this is virtually impossible when both arrived as servants. Since progressively smaller parcels of land were offered over time by the proprietors to servants who had gained their freedom, we can distinguish between these former servants almost exclusively when looking at their very first land warrants. Thus a servant who had arrived in 1670 might receive 100 acres at freedom, while one who came in 1671 could claim 70 acres. Subsequent warrants (unless they note the person's date of arrival, which occasionally happens), all grants, and nearly all biographical data cannot be attributed to one or the other with any degree of accuracy.[13]

Even the most thorough search for, and subsequent analysis of the data cannot eliminate totally the likelihood for error given such problems. In cases where I have been uncertain about the applicability of specific pieces of evidence to specific individuals, I have excluded them from my computations.

If the sources are inadequate, incomplete, and difficult to read (or interpret) with absolute confidence about one's conclusions, can research yield results of any significance? Is it possible, for example, to compose a picture of the social and economic consequences of the decision to enter Carolina during the first years of settlement for even a few individuals who came as servants? Can we determine, in other words, what were the actual possibilities for such men and women in the colony? What might people who came in servitude look toward as they contemplated their futures in Carolina after their terms of service expired?

---

see *Warrants, 1672-1679*, p. 76; *Records of Register F 1707-1711* (MSV), p. 115; *Records of the Secretary 1700-1710* (MSV), p. 127. On Robert Williams, see *Shaftsbury Papers*, p. 135; *Records of the Secretary 1675-1696* (MSV), p. 164. On Thomas King, see *Warrants, 1672-1679*, pp. 84, 201; A.S. Salley, ed., *Warrants for Lands in South Carolina 1692-1711* (Columbia, 1915), p. 178 (hereafter cited as *Warrants, 1692-1711*); *Records of the Secretary 1694-1705* (MSV), p. 196; *Records of the Secretary 1700-1710* (MSV), pp. 119, 184. On Robert Leeds, see *Warrants, 1672-1679*, pp. 64, 75, 148. On John Willson, see *Warrants, 1672-1679*, p. 104; *Records of the Secretary and the Register 1671-1675*, p. 63; *Warrants, 1692-1711*, p. 227; *Proprietary Grants No. 2, Vol. 39* (MSV), p. 26; *Abstracts of the Grants & Commissions of LDS. Props. 1692-1718, 1733-1736, 1775-1820 (2 vols.)* (MSV), p. 250; B.P.R.O.-S.C. Vol. 2, pp. 62, 67, 68.

[13] The difficulties involved in assessing property acquisition for such people are discussed in Chapter Six, pp. 128-129.

II. Possibilities: The Spectrum of Servant Mobility

In November 1700, Edward Hyrne wrote to his brother requesting funds to purchase a plantation near Charles Town. "Here is a man in this country," he said, "that came over a poor Servant about 18 or 20 years ago, that has gottan a great Estate . . . [and] I am credibly informed he has now about 4000 head [of cattle] besides a great number of horses, hogs, etc. and that he had last year 800 calves."[14] Surely Hyrne cited this example to impress his brother with the stunning opportunities for economic advancement the colony offered. In a land where a servant might eventually achieve tremendous wealth, the prospects for everyone must be outstanding. Hyrne, of course, had to know that not every settler, much less every servant, had amassed a fortune in South Carolina. He carefully avoided noting those who failed in their quest for wealth. But, in fact, many did fail, not only to accumulate substantial amounts of property, but even to acquire sufficient land to enable them to survive as freeholders living at a subsistence level of existence.

If great success ultimately eluded most early Carolinians, it was not so uncommon that Hyrne's example to his brother was seriously misleading. Enough settlers in the seventeenth century did advance socially and economically to warrant a degree of optimism about one's chances sufficient to attract men and women to venture lives and capital in the colony. Hyrne might have chosen among a number of former servants in selecting a classic success story to relate for his brother.

Great Mobility: Rowser, Cattell, and Raven

Richard Rowser came to South Carolina from Barbados in 1671 a servant to John Maverick.[15] He must have been dutiful and a willing worker, for soon after his arrival the Grand Council noted "how industrious and useful" he and a fellow servant had been "in this

[14] Letter of Edward Hyrne to his brother; Nov. 19, 1700, in possession of G. R. Mackie, Ontario, Canada. I am grateful to Mrs. Agnes L. Baldwin for providing me with a copy of this document. See also Mabel L. Weber, "Hyrne Family," *S.C.H.G.M.*, XXII (Oct., 1921), 101-118; and "Historical Notes," *S.C.H.G.M.*, XXVI (July, 1925), 172-173, which says Ed. Hyrne was in Carolina in 1701.

[15] *Shaftsbury Papers*, pp. 271, 341.

Collony."[16] He completed his term of service to Maverick by the Fall of 1674, and set to work as a free person, starting with the land concession offered by the Lords Proprietors to all immigrants, whether servant or free. Before his death in 1683 he had accumulated at least 630 acres.[17] Sarah Rowser, wife of his son William, and presumably heir to Richard's original estate, at her death in 1723, owned property valued at more than £778 including seven slaves.[18]

As impressive as were the achievements of Richard Rowser, even more stunning was the success of John Cattell, who arrived in Carolina in August, 1672, as a servant to Thomas Butler.[19] Starting in 1674 with a 70 acre land concession from the Proprietors as his "freedom dues," Cattell, by buying and selling land and presumably holding most of it long enough to grow crops and graze cattle, accumulated a huge estate before his death in 1710.[20] While it is impossible to determine exactly the extent of his property,[21] it included 27 slaves[22] and well over 2000 acres of land. He was elected to serve in the Commons House of Assembly from

[16] *Council Journal, 1671-1680*, p. 7. Rowser and Philip Jones each were rewarded with ten acres by the Council.

[17] *Warrants, 1672-1679*, pp. 83, 211. He had grants for 630 acres. See *Misc. Records 1682-1690* (MSV), p. 63; *Proprietary Grants No. 1 Vol. 38* (MSV), p. 219. His wife Mary had a warrant for an additional 70 acres recorded on Nov. 1, 1683, which indicates Richard probably died before that date. On Dec. 4, 1683, "Came Mary Rowzer & Entered her cavet & Prayed letters of administration upon ye Goods & Chattells Lands & Tenemenets of Rich Rowzer late of this Province Planter deceased. . . ." *Records of the Secretary 1675-1695* (MSV), p. 196.

[18] *Records of the Secretary of the Province C, 1722-1724* (MSV), pp. 76 (will), 135 (estate inventory).

[19] *Warrants, 1672-1679*, pp. 49, 82.

[20] *Warrants, 1672-1679*, p. 82; *Records of the Register 1709-1712* (MSV), pp. 165-69.

[21] Since one of his four sons was also named John Cattell, land grants for that name could apply to either.

[22] *Records of the Secretary of the Province H, 1730-31* (WPA, Vol. 62B, 1729-31), p. 853.

Berkeley and Craven counties in 1700.[23] Cattell's descendants were among the most prosperous Carolinians. His son Peter left an estate valued at more than £15,391, which included 800 head of cattle and 60 slaves.[24]

A third example of striking upward mobility among persons who began life in South Carolina in servitude is of interest because sufficient details of the servant's life have been recorded to allow us to gain some sense of the means employed by early Carolinians to achieve wealth and prominence in the colony. John Raven[25] came to Carolina as a servant to Hugh Carteret, arriving in April, 1672. While no record has survived of his acquisition of land for his own immigration, he probably did claim his "freedom dues," for in 1683 he is referred to as a "victular," which implies he had acquired cattle or hogs that he probably grazed on his own land.[26] The next year he claimed a warrant for 50 acres on behalf of his wife Ruth, whose arrival in 1682 entitled her to receive that amount of land as her headright.[27] We hear little of the Ravens until 1692 when the Grand Council listened to the complaint of Elizabeth Jones against "her Master John Raven." Raven obviously had been successful enough in his business to acquire a servant of his own, and one reason may have been that he demanded a great deal of those whose labor he controlled and spent as little as possible on their maintenance. For Elizabeth Jones had

---

[23] His holdings probably were far more extensive. This computation does not include his purchase of 1450 acres in March, 1696, nor does it include any grants in 1704 or thereafter, since 1704 is the date of the earliest grant for any of his children. See Public Record Office, London, CO 5/398, AM. & W. *Indies, Grants Made in Province (South Carolina) 1674-1765*, pp. 9, 16, 17, 18, 20; 25, 34 for 1704 and 1705; *Records of the Register and the Secretary 1675-1696, 1703-1709* (MSV), p. 489, for purchase of 1696. See also Walter B. Edgar, ed., *Biographical Directory of the South Carolina House of Representatives*, *Vol. 1*, *Session Lists*, *1692-1973* (Columbia, 1974), Session Lists for Commons House, Fifth Assembly, 1700-1702.

[24] *Records of the Secretary of the Province H, 1730-31* (WPA, vol. 62B, 1729-31), pp. 532-527. Peter died in June 1730. He had served as a member of the Grand Jury before 1725; B.P.R.O.-S.C. *Vol. 11 (1723-15)*, pp. 223, 229-30. His brother William served in the Commons House 1716-17, 1720-21; and as a Justice of the Peace; B.P.R.O.-S.C. *Vol. 7 (1717-1720*, pp. 9-11; *Memorial Book Vol. 1* (MSV), p. 182.

[25] Also referred to as John Ravens in the records.

[26] *Records of the Register 1696-1703* (MSV), pp. 80-81, land purchase by John Raven and Phillip Williams, "both of Charles Town . . . victulars."

[27] *Warrants*, *1680-1692*, p. 148.

run away from her Master, and the Council was forced to command her to "Returne to and Continue with . . . [him] and behave her Selfe. . . ." But the Council simultaneously ordered "that the Said John Raven doe alsoe observe his part of [providing her with] . . . Sufficient Cloathing, Meatt and drinck and moderatt Correction onely . . . and [take the time] to teach [her] . . . what he is obliged to doe. . . ."[28] Clearly, having been a servant did not dictate that once free, one would use his own servants mildly and compassionately. Raven's concern to protect his own interests—the Council had, after all, ordered a supplier of food to feed a member of his own household adequately—ultimately yielded the results he desired. He managed to acquire a sufficient number of cattle and hogs to justify registering with the government a brand to identify them as his property.[29] He purchased vast amounts of land, sold a little his second wife had inherited from her deceased husband,[30] served as a trustee of his church,[31] and was elected to the Commons House of Assembly.[32] He died some time between 1715 and 1719.[33] His son, John Raven, Jr., was a Captain (in the militia), served in the Commons House and on the Grand Jury, and

---

[28] Alexander S. Salley, ed., *Journal of the Grand Council of South Carolina, 1691-1692* (Columbia, 1907), pp. 34-35. Hereafter cited as *Council Journal, 1692*.

[29] *Records of the Secretary 1709-1725* (MSV), second page from back of volume. Nov. 27, 1695, "This day came John Raven of Colleton County & recorded his marke for Cattle & hoggs as followeth one slitt in ye Right Eare and in ye left his Brand marke being I:R."

[30] *Records of the Register & of the Secretary 1711-1715* (MSV), pp. 297-300, May, 1711. Raven and Elizabeth "his wife, late Elizabeth Beadon Relict and Executrix of George Beadon" sell 69 acres, part of 150 she had inherited, for 103 pounds 10 shillings current money. "Current money" was a term used to describe foreign coins in South Carolina, which circulated widely given the perennial shortage of English specie in America. The most recent student of colonial South Carolina's economy estimates that "current money" was valued at about 62 percent of sterling. See Clowse, *Economic*, pp. 145-147.

[31] *Records of the Register and of the Secretary 1712-1713* (MSV), pp. 60-62.

[32] *Session Lists*, 1695, 1702-3, 1703-5, 1707-8.

[33] *Recs. Secy. Province, 1714-17* (WPA), Vol. 64, pp. 305-8, records land purchase by him, Nov. 20, 1715. *Recs. Secy. Province B, 1722-16* (WPA), Vol. 65, pp. 209-10, records gift of Elizabeth Raven "widow" to her son, May 20, 1719.

proved title to 3758 acres of land, of which 2300 came directly from his father.[34]

Moderate Mobility: Boswood, Edwards, Smith, and Mahone

Needless to say, most of those who arrived in South Carolina as servants did not do as well as Rowser, Cattell, or Raven. Indeed, it is unlikely that many came to Carolina as servants with serious hopes of becoming spectacularly wealthy. Few would have experienced severe disappointment or believed they had been seriously misled in formulating their expectations, when they failed to achieve the success enjoyed by the most upwardly mobile of former servants. Probably most would have been quite content to reach a level of wealth well below that enjoyed by such men. Aspirations which drew people to Carolina as servants very likely defined "success" as ownership of sufficient property to insure that their families would be decently clothed and fed, with enough wealth left over to provide for some luxuries.

But, in fact, quite a few servants were able to do much "better" than that—to achieve a level of wealth distinctly below that which was defined by the lives of Cattell, Raven, and Rowser; but still superior to the measure of success most servants must have envisioned when they decided to migrate. Samuel Boswood displayed such mobility. He reached Carolina from Barbados in February, 1671, along with six other servants to Major Thomas Gray.[35] Within four months he was free of obligations to Gray, had purchased a town lot, and apparently was practicing a trade—he is identified in the land sale as a "taylor."[36] At about the same time he was able to pay for the passage to the colony of his wife and two daughters, whose arrival in June, 1671 allowed him to claim a land

---

[34] *Memorial Book Vol. 5* (MSV), pp. 122-23; *B.P.R.O.-S.C. Vol. 11 (1723-25)*, pp. 223-30; *Session Lists*, 1720-21.

[35] *Warrants, 1672-1679*, p. 28. The warrant noted that Gray's seven servants arrived in February and June, without specifying which arrived when. But Boswood purchased land on his own account in May 1671, indicating he was free by then. See *Records of the Secretary and the Register 1671-1675*, p. 5.

[36] *Records of the Secretary and the Register, 1671-1675*, p. 5. Boswood paid three pounds sterling for a lot on Albemarle Point, a choice location in the middle of the little settlement.

concession from the Proprietors of 240 acres.[37] He soon had sufficient funds to pay for the passage of a servant, which allowed him to claim an additional 70 acres.[38] Boswood was prospering. In 1678 he paid £30 sterling for "one Negro woeman slave by name Sara"[39] and six years later he claimed 50 acres from the government for having imported "one Negroe man named James."[40] Boswood probably pursued a number of paths to prosperity. His land surely was worked by him or those whose labor he controlled; he consistently is referred to as a tailor; he occasionally sold parcels of land, and he may have engaged in the practice of making loans.[41] In fact, James Moore "Captain," "Esquire," "Gentleman," Proprietor's Deputy, and future governor of the colony seems to have been in debt to Boswood for a substantial amount. The exact extent of his estate at his death in 1691 is not known.[42] But he had controlled warrants for 620 acres, had purchased more than 180 acres, had sold more than 130 acres, had claimed the right to 40 acres, and held grants for 220 acres.[43]

---

[37] *Warrants, 1672-1679*, p. 13. He made the claim about a year after they arrived, for his warrant is dated June 7, 1672. He may, however, have occupied the land prior to securing a warrant to have it surveyed.

[38] *Warrants, 1672-1679*, p. 19. Warrant dated July 9, 1672, servant Ann Workeup arrived August, 1671.

[39] *Records of the Register and the Secretary, 1675-1696, 1703-1709* (MSV), p. 91. May 20, 1678.

[40] *Warrants, 1680-1692*, p. 165. Dec. 12, 1684. James arrived in September.

[41] On land sales by Boswood, see *Records of the Secretary and the Register 1671-1675*, pp. 27-28; *Warrants, 1680-1692*, p. 99; *Records of the Register and the Secretary 1675-1696, 1703-1709* (MSV), pp. 175-76; on debts to him, see *Records of the Secretary and the Register 1671-1675*, pp. 34-35; *Records of the Secretary 1675-1695* (MSV), p. 6. *Warrants, 1680-1692*, pp. 192-93, is a series of warrants for land assigned to Boswood by Capt. Moore, probably to settle a debt. In 1680 he traded two "heifers halfe gon in calfe" for 30 acres which indicates he was using the land he possessed. See *Records of the Register and the Secretary 1675-1696, 1703-1709*(MSV), pp. 147-48.

[42] *Records of the Secretary 1675-1695* (MSV), p. 459, August 5, 1691. Governor Sothell named the administrators of the estate of "Samuell Boswood Taylor decsd. . . ."

[43] See *Records of the Secretary and the Register 1671-1675*, pp. 5, 27-8; *Warrants, 1680-1692*, pp. 165, 192-93; *Records of the Register and the Secretary 1675-1696, 1703-1709* (MSV), pp. 147-8, 171, 175-6; *Proprietary Grants No. 1 Vol. 38* (MSV), p. 58; *Records of the Secretary 1675-1695* (MSV), p. 2.

Like Boswood, Christopher Edwards came to South Carolina from Barbados, but he arrived in the "first fleet" in 1670. He must have been a good worker, for his master, Richard Deyos, refused to fulfill the conditions of their agreement, attempting to hold Edwards in servitude after his term had expired. But in June 1672, three witnesses testified before the Grand Council that "they were privie to the contract between Richard Deyos and Christopher Edwards, his servant . . . [who] was to serve . . . the terme of two yeares . . . to commence from the time of his arrivall." Hence, he had fulfilled his obligation to Deyos "the 17th day of March last past" and, the Council ordered, Edwards was now not only a free man but could immediately "take warrants for the land due him."[44] Nine days later Edwards had a warrant for 20 acres "for his present planting" and in September he claimed 170 acres on behalf of the arrival of his wife and daughter. In January 1673, he received a warrant for 80 additional acres, the rest of his 100 acre headright."[45] In 1677 he sold one tract of 80 acres, a second of 50 acres, and referred to himself as a "Planter."[46] The next year he and his wife had a warrant for yet another 100 acres which may have allowed them to sell off other property in 1680.[47] Christopher, Anne, and their son Francis were dead by 1692, for in June, William Cockfield, a former servant himself, petitioned the Council for the goods and was granted administration rights over the estate of "ffrancis Edwards Decsd orphan & son of Christopher Edwards decsd."[48] While the Edwards family may not have left much property for Cockfield to use, having sold off land periodically, in the course of their 20 years in the colony they had controlled at minimum nearly 400 acres.

---

[44] *Council Journal, 1671-1680*, p. 34.

[45] *Warrants, 1672-1679*, pp. 15, 32, 58.

[46] *Records of the Register and the Secretary 1675-1696, 1703-1709* (MSV), pp. 81, 101.

[47] In 1690 Edwards and "Anne his wife" concluded two land sales, one of 50 acres to Sam Boswood (*Records of the Register and the Secretary 1675-1696, 1703-1709* (MSV), pp. 175-76), and one of 66 acres to Thomas Hurt (*Records of the Register and the Secretary 1675-1696, 1703-1709* (MSV), p. 124).

[48] *Council Journal, 1692*, p. 42; *Records of the Secretary 1675-1695* (MSV), pp. 410, 466-7. Cockfield had maintained Francis for an unspecified period prior to June 21, 1672, when he petitioned the Council.

Abraham Smith came to South Carolina from England in the first fleet, a servant to Colonel Joseph West.[49] He had completed his term of service by 1677 when he claimed his right to 100 acres.[50] A year later he claimed an additional 270 acres, "in ye right of his wiffe," which suggests he married well. For somehow Hannah Smith had, through inheritance, gift, or purchase, acquired the right to many acres of land beyond those due her because of her own arrival in the colony.[51] The next year Abraham and Hannah had a warrant for an additional 70 acres,[52] and purchased ten acres for £12.[53] They may have had more ready cash than most Carolinians, since Abraham, in addition to working their land, practiced a trade. He consistently is referred to as a bricklayer. Like Boswood and Edwards, Smith proved willing to sell property.[54] Before his death sometime between 1684 and 1694,[55] he held grants for at least 200 acres and warrants for 440 acres.[56] After his death Hannah secured at least 100 acres more.[57] She also was named an heir to Margarett (Miliscent) Jackson, who

---

[49] On the ship *Carolina* passenger roster he is cited as a servant to Will: Bowman. However, West claimed land for having brought him to the colony. *Shaftsbury Papers*, p. 135; *Warrants for Lands in South Carolina 1672-1679*, p. 63.

[50] *Warrants, 1672-1679*, p. 141.

[51] *Warrants, 1672-1679*, p. 186.

[52] *Warrants, 1680-1696*, p. 6.

[53] *Records of the Register and the Secretary 1675-1696, 1703-1709* (MSV), pp. 89, 90.

[54] Misc. *Records 1682-1690* (MSV), pp. 165-6. Smith sells 100 acres for £20, Dec. 11, 1684.

[55] Last reference to him living is December 1684. Misc. *Records 1682-1690* (MSV), p. 166; first reference to Hannah Smith widow is August 1694. *Proprietary Grants No. l Vol.* 38 (MSV), p. 152.

[56] *Records of the Register and the Secretary 1675-1696, 1703-1709* (MSV), p. 185; *Proprietary Grants No. l Vol.* 38 (MSV), p. 66; Public Record Office, London, Co 5/398, *Am. & W. Indies, Grants made in Province [South Carolina] 1674-1765*, p. 4; *Calendar of State Papers, 1677-1680 (Vol. 10)*, p. 1638.

[57] *Proprietary Grants No. l Vol.* 38 (MSV), p. 290; Public Record Office, London, Co 5/398, *Am. & W. Indies, Grants Made in Province [South Carolina] 1674-1765*, p. 9; *Proprietary Grants No. l Vol.* 38 (MSV), p. 152; *Records of the Register and the Secretary 1675-1696, 1703-1709* (MSV), p. 314.

(with her husband Original) had been the Smith's neighbors, and who may have been a fellow servant with Abraham to West.[58]

Boswood, Edwards, and Smith may have sold some property because they needed money. It is more likely that they sold land to turn a quick profit, perhaps a huge profit. Since the proprietors did not offer to sell land to the settlers until the mid 1680's,[59] the only source of it to settlers, other than by claiming acreage on the basis of persons brought to the colony at the expense of the claimant, or through direct grant by the proprietors in return for some service, was by purchase from someone who already owned property in South Carolina. If one wanted to acquire land contiguous to that which he already possessed, and if he lived in an area where unoccupied or unallocated acreage was scarce, he was virtually forced to secure it by purchase from his neighbors. Hence, large profits could be made by those fortunate enough to have arrived in Carolina early, and who had received property which was well situated in terms of access to shipping by lying on a major river, or through its proximity to land owned by a settler eager to expand his own estate. And former servants, especially if they had arrived early, probably were just as likely as any settler to have such desirable parcels of land in their possession.

Examine, for example, the career of Dennis Mahone,[60] who reached the colony in 1670 with the first fleet as a servant to Richard Cole. He was not happy living under the control of another man, for late in 1671 he was hailed before the Council, which noted that he had

> been formerly guilty of running away . . . and departing out of this Collony to attaine the protection of the Crowne of Spaine . . . and upon his penitency and amdnm.t of [his behavior] . . . had his punishm.t due for the same suspended; yett the s^d Dennis Mahoon little regarding his Allegiance to o^r · · · King and his fidelity and submission to [the] Lords Proprietrs still prosecuting his Evill Intencons aboot the tenth day of October last endeavoured to perswade and entice some of his fellow Serv^{ts} . . . to run away . . . And . . . being . . . found guilty of the same . . . [it is ordered] that the said Dennis Mahoon shall forthwith be stript naked to his Waste & receive thirty nine lashes upon his naked Back.[61]

---

58 *Records of the Register and the Secretary 1675-1696, 1703-1709* (MSV), p. 117; *Records of the Secretary 1675-1695* (MSV), p. 55.

59 Clowse, *Economic Beginnings*, pp. 4, 77-8.

60 Also cited as Mahoone, O'Mahone, etc.

61 *Council Journal, 1671-1680*, p. 14.

Presumably the Council, given Mahone's attitude toward servitude, deemed it wiser to inflict physical pain than to extend his term of service, since that punishment might only tempt him to further exploits in the direction of St. Augustine. By August 1672, Mahone was free and possessed his first warrant for 100 acres.[62] Two years later he had found a wife and had another warrant, this for 200 acres.[63] He probably did some farming, tended a small herd of cattle and hogs, and had saved at least £7 sterling by 1678 when he handed that amount to John Hooper in return for 140 acres.[64] Exactly 11 months later he sold the same tract for £17, 10 s.[65] Two years later, in June, 1681, Mahone concluded a second land transaction—he sold 50 acres, "fower calves & three . . . steers five sows one boare & [torn] negro man by name Cato" to a recent immigrant for £100. What is instructive is that he had purchased the property (but perhaps not the stock) less than a month earlier from Edmond and Hannah Fogete for £10 sterling.[66] The Fogete's reaction to the transaction is unrecorded. Mahone was dead 18 months later. His will notes that a number of persons were in debt to him; it distributes five grown cows, four calves, his clothing, and his hogs; but it fails to mention the acreage he owned.[67]

---

[62] *Warrants, 1672-1679*, p. 33, August 30, 1672.

[63] *Warrants, 1672-1679*, p. 80, July 25, 1674.

[64] *Records of the Register and the Secretary 1675-1696, 1703-1709* (MSV), pp. 66-7. Mahone is identified in the sale as "Planter" Aug. 10, 1678. See also "*Last Resort*" (MSV), pp. 229-32; *Memorial Book Vol. 1* (MSV), pp. 196-97.

[65] Since Mahone paid sterling for the land, his profit may not have been so great. For the records fail to note whether Reuben Willis, the purchaser, paid Mahone in sterling or in "current money." In either case, Mahone turned a nice profit on the sale. *Records of the Register and the Secretary, 1675-1696, 1703-1709* (MSV), p. 104; "*Last Resort* " (MSV), pp. 220-32; *Memorial Book Vol. 1* (MSV), p. 195.

[66] Misc. *Records 1682-1690* (MSV), pp. 318-20.

[67] *Records of the Secretary 1675-1695* (MSV), pp. 186-7. Will dated December 10, 1682. He was dead before February 6, 1683. See *Records of the Secretary 1675-1696* (MSV), p. 23. Settlers who used land during their careers in Carolina but did not include it in their wills, are discussed more fully below. See Chapter Five, pp. 107-109.

Basic Mobility: Horton, Orill, et al.

Most servants, of course, never achieved the success enjoyed by Boswood, Edwards, Smith or Mahone, yet secured their freedom, claimed land, built homes, and married. Such, for example, was John Horton, who was brought to South Carolina in March, 1674, along with three other servants, the wife, and four children of his master John Fallock.[68] By August 1677, Horton had married and claimed warrants for 170 acres as the proprietors' concession for himself and his wife Mary.[69] In late summer, 1681, they acquired a town lot in Charles Town, and built a house.[70] There Horton began to work as a carpenter—he was skilled. John and Mary might have prospered, but he died less than one year later. His inventory has survived and tells us that in five years, working for himself, John Horton had accumulated property valued at a little more than £48, which included, aside from his home, five pair of underwear, four old shirts, three very old coats, two guns, four head of cattle, and one sick servant maid.[71]

Or consider what we know about the career of Philip Orill,[72] who arrived in the colony from Barbados or Bermuda in August 1671, along with John Coming's five other servants. Like Mahone, Orill was not a contented servant. In June 1672, Coming's wife Affera,[73] filed a complaint with the Grand Council against two of her servants

> & more especially against . . . Phillip Orill for threatening to overset the Boate wherein she was . . . and giving the provisions allowed him and his fellow servants to the Doggs and threatening to run away to the Indians & divers over gross abuses & destructive practices. . . .

---

[68] *Warrants, 1672-1679*, p. 142.

[69] *Warrants, 1672-1679*, p. 142.

[70] *Records of the Register and the Secretary 1675-1696, 1703-1709* (MSV), p. 138. Lot No. 39, August 22, 1681.

[71] *Records of the Secretary 1675-1695* (MSV), pp. 6 (death), 109 (bond of administrators), 110 (inventory of estate).

[72] Also cited as Onill, Orell, Orrill.

[73] Perhaps a former servant; see above, p. 33.

Orill received 21 lashes "upon his naked back" for his conduct.[74] A free man by January 1677, Orill and a friend purchased 80 acres from Christopher Edwards. Three months later they sold 15 acres at a great profit.[75] The following month Orill claimed his 70 acre headright as "one of ye freemen of this province."[76] We hear nothing more of Phillip Orill until June of 1684, when he sold what was apparently the last 15 acre parcel of land left from the acreage he had acquired from Edwards seven years earlier. There is no surviving record of how he and his friend disposed of the other 50 acres, or of his fate after 1684.[77]

Other servants failed even to achieve as much as Orill. The records are spotted with references to servants who came to the colony, served out their time, claimed their "freedom dues" and then disappeared. Perhaps they simply existed in the colony, living at a subsistence level, quietly trying to survive. It is tantalizing to speculate about their lives, but data from which answers to our questions could be fashioned simply do not exist. Occasionally, however, we get a glimpse of these people—sufficient to substantiate that they did, in fact, survive in the province, but very rarely how they maintained themselves.

Thus, for example, Otho Christopher came to South Carolina a servant to Thomas Butler in November 1672. The records are completely clean of any reference to him, with one exception. In August, 1682, Otho Christopher was listed as one of six carpenters who spent ten days repairing a ship owned by Stephen Bull. He was alive, he was working, he was in South Carolina, ten years after his arrival as a servant. How he

[74] *Grand Council Journal* (MSV), p. 31; *Council Journal, 1671-1680*, pp. 33-34.

[75] *Records of the Register and the Secretary 1675-1696, 1703-1709* (MSV), p. 81 (purchase); *Records of the Register and the Secretary 1675-1696, 1703-1709* (MSV), pp. 46-47 (sale). They paid Edwards £3, 8 s. for the 80 acres on January 14, 1677. They sold 15 acres of the parcel for £10 "lawfull money of England" (sterling) April 27, 1677.

[76] *Warrants, 1672-1679*, p. 135; May 19, 1677.

[77] His partner John Bezant had died before 1684, apparently leaving the land to Orill, for Orill had clear title to it. He received £12 sterling for the 15 acres, meaning that Edwards' original tract had yielded £22, plus 50 acres. Misc. *Records 1682-1690* (MSV), pp. 127-18, June 14, 1684.

spent the ten years, or how, much less if, he survived after that, we do not know.[78]

Or, one might wish to speculate about William Cockfield, who arrived in the first fleet as a servant to Paul Smith.[79] He was free before October 1673, when he claimed his 100 acre concession. The records are silent about him until 1692, when he was appointed the administrator of the estate of Christopher Edwards' son Francis, whom he had supported for an unspecified period of time. He then once again disappears from our view.[80] We know only that he survived at least until 1692, probably by farming his 100 acre freehold.

More common, however, are the cases of men such as William Bevin, John Cole, and John Fraiser. Bevin was one of 12 servants brought to South Carolina by Florence O'Sullivan in the first fleet. He was free by July 1672, when he had a warrant for his 100 acres. He never reappears in the records.[81] Cole came to the colony from Barbados in February 1670, with two years, six months, to serve his master Thomas Gray. He claimed 70 acres in May 1674. We know nothing more about him.[82] Fraiser was a servant who also arrived in the first fleet. He had a warrant for his 100 acres in July 1675. In December of that year a land sale conducted by others notes the nearby land of "John Frazer Planter." Like Bevin and Cole, Fraiser failed to leave any record of himself other than that he survived his term of service and went on to claim a small piece of land as a free person.[83]

---

78 *Warrants, 1672-1679*, p. 49; *Records of the Secretary 1675-1695* (MSV), p. 101.

79 George Beadon received the land concession for Cockfield and three other servants, as the administrator of Smith's estate. *Warrants, 1672-1679*, p. 48.

80 *Records of the Secretary, 1675-1695* (MSV), pp. 318, 410, 466-67. *Memorial Book Vol. 1* (MSV), pp. 126-30, 356, note that Moses Cockfield "yeoman," sold and traded land in Berkeley County in 1706-07; and that John Cockfield and Rachel, his wife, also of Berkeley County, sold land to William Bull in 1722. There is no reference to William Cockfield.

81 *Warrants, 1672-1679*, pp. 37, 104, 21.

82 *Warrants, 1672-1679*, p. 85; *Shaftsbury Papers*, p. 253.

83 *Warrants, 1672-1679*, p. 98; *Records of the Register and the Secretary, 1675-1696, 1703-1709* (MSV), p. 55.

Such, then, in the broadest sense were the varieties of mobility experienced by servants who arrived in South Carolina during the first decade of settlement. These brief biographies do not aim to provide a definitive description of what happened to all servants in the colony. Nor do the career summaries do more than suggest a few of the many paths servants pursued in their quest to realize their dreams of success. Not everyone who moved rapidly and far upward in the society conformed to the patterns of mobility defined by Cattell, Raven, and Rowser. Needless to say, some servants followed different paths to moderate wealth from those staked out by Edwards, Boswood, Smith, and Mahone; much less to the level of relative security achieved by Horton and Orill. Most important, it is essential to recognize that, given the overall incompleteness of the records which have survived, even those who from our vantage point appear ultimately to have attained less than a secure position as free and independent persons, may well have enjoyed a higher standard of life than some who seem to have prospered. For we have at best poor data on which to base our judgments, much less reliable measures to employ in assessing what those data mean. Few who arrived in the colony during the first decade of settlement left wills, and fewer wills than were actually written have survived in the records. Even worse, only a small fraction of these are accompanied by an estate inventory and appraisal. While all kinds of discrete facts about individual colonists are scattered in the manuscript volumes, only seldom can they be put together for any single person in a way that will allow us to assess his or her holdings at any moment, or to calculate property controlled at time of death.

III. Land Acquisition as a Measure of Mobility in Early Carolina

Given such difficulties when dealing with individuals, systematic analysis of lager groups presents tremendous problems. If we know, for example, that John Horton possessed four shirts, and enjoyed the services of one old sick maid servant, we do not know, in aggregate, how these measures of success compare with similar data on other former servants. The one commodity about which data have survived for a sufficient number of people who came to South Carolina between 1670 and 1680 to permit comparative analysis, at what admittedly is an unsophisticated level, is land. Extensive and comprehensive records of the warrants for land settlers acquired have survived. These are sufficiently accurate that scholars can rely confidently on them as a basis for discussion of comparative mobility. In addition, the warrants are supported by a good deal of data on the actual grants made in Carolina.

Two serious problems obstruct our ability to use the surviving data on land acquisition as we would like. First, land warrants represented only the *right* to possess a specified number of acres—they did not convey title to property. If, for example, a recent immigrant had paid for his own passage to the colony, he would have the right to claim a specified number of acres as his headright, and additional acres on behalf of the arrival of others he brought with him. He would thus receive a warrant for that amount of land, and in the vast majority of cases would immediately take possession of it. If he followed the procedure outlined by the proprietors, he would then arrange to have it surveyed (for which he paid a fee), the Surveyor General would return a copy of the survey to the authorities, and they would then issue a formal grant for the property. But especially in the earliest years of settlement, few settlers adhered to this procedure. Instead they simply used their initial warrant to establish their claim to property, and avoided the required subsequent steps necessary to secure a grant. Custom assured them that their claim to the land was secure, and they thereby delayed the payment of surveyor's fees. Even more important, they avoided obligating themselves to pay the quitrents the proprietors planned to begin collecting in 1689 from all who had received grants of land in the colony. Clearly settlers, among them some of the most prominent inhabitants, were content simply to hold their land by force of a warrant to it, re-recording that warrant if necessary, to avoid the monetary obligations imposed by completing the process required to secure actual title to it. Thus, the volumes of warrants are filled with duplicate documents—one encounters a huge number of warrants for which there are identical counterparts dated several years later.[84] Most colonists

---

84 E.g., Florence O'Sullivan "Capt.," Surveyor General, probably dishonest, surely a poor or lazy surveyor, entered a warrant for 1900 acres for his own passage plus that of 12 servants on the first fleet. This was dated (recorded) September 6, 1672. He was surely using the land before then. *Warrants, 1672-1679*, p. 37. On September 14, 1675, the warrant reappears. *Warrants,1672-1679*, p. 104. O'Sullivan's intent clearly was to retain legal possession as long as possible simply through keeping his warrant to the land in force, but not to secure a formal grant for it, which would have made him liable for quitrents after 1689.

I am indebted to Dr. R. Nicholas Olsberg, then supervising publications at the South Carolina Archives in Columbia, for spending several afternoons with me in July, 1973, during which we worked through the problems of understanding the system of land distribution in force in the earliest years of settlement.

held warrants for far more acreage than they ultimately secured through grants. We can reasonably assume, but we cannot be certain, that their warrants represent the acreage they actually used. Acreage identified through warrants in the proprietary period almost never conforms with acreage identified through grants. Frequently, especially among former servants (those least likely to have the cash necessary to cover the expenses of surveying and recording fees, much less the ability to obligate themselves to annual land taxes), there exists no grant for any of the land attributed to their possession by the records of warrants.

The second major problem in using land as a measure of mobility is that we have scanty data to use in computing what any given piece of

---

St. Julien R. Childs has offered an alternative explanation for the existence of multiple warrants for specific parcels of property. "Many warrants," he writes, "were issued more than once because the surveyor to whom they were originally directed had been superseded in office before he made the survey. . . . As surveyors continued to change, duplication of the warrants does not show fraud as some writers have thought." Childs, "The First Carolinians," S.C.H.M., 71 (April, 1970), 101.

The best evidence that my interpretation is valid comes from the personal histories of settlers such as James Bryan, one of Colonel West's servants, who came to Carolina with the first fleet. Bryan's only grant for land is dated June 1709. In late summer of 1694, when they wrote their will, James and Susanna Bryan left "all our Estate . . . which we shall be possessed on att ye time of our Decease" to their son-in-law. Yet at that moment they had no real property they could pass on because none had been granted to them. Their will was registered in 1709, exactly the time they acquired their solitary land grant. It seems clear that the Bryans had been using land they held by virtue of their headright concessions for many years, but only chose to have it formally granted to them at the time they registered their will, in order to be able to leave it to their heirs. See *Proprietary Grants No. 1, Vol. 38* (MSV), p. 35; *Records of the Register of the Province F 1707-1711* (MSV), p. 80.

The system, functioning as the colony's leaders intended, is illustrated in *Grant Book C [Register 1694-1707, Secretary 1722-1740]*, (MSV), p. 152. Thomas Hurt recorded two warrants on March 7, 1674, one for 128 acres, the second for 370 acres. On June 27 Stephen Bull, Surveyor General, returned a survey for 498 acres. Hurt received a formal grant for 498 acres on April 15, 1676. Hurt provides us with an excellent example of the potential for being misled by too great a reliance on the records of warrants and grants as indicators of a settler's actual property holdings. For in addition to the land he secured by virtue of warrants issued in accordance with the headright system, Hurt purchased from private settlers at least 303 acres before January 1680. This land never appears under Hurt's name in the colonial records of warrants issued and grants made. We can only wonder how many settlers acquired acres by direct purchase from or trade with their fellow colonists through transactions which were not recorded, or, if documented, were registered in volumes that are now lost. See *Records of the Register and the Secretary, 1675-1696, 1703-1709* (MSV), pp. 124-26.

property was worth. The records are filled with land transactions that provide only the range of values attributed to certain numbers of acres. Even various pieces of land which, from our perspective, seem to have been equivalent (town lots, parcels on the same river), brought widely different prices at virtually the same time. The situation is further complicated by inconsistencies in the recording of prices paid—land was sold or traded for all sorts of goods ranging from crops to livestock to rights to the labor of servants and slaves—all of which themselves had a wide range of values both over time and at any given moment. Still more troubling, when land was sold for cash and the price paid was recorded, we frequently have no reference to the kind of money involved; whether, for example, the transaction was concluded for sterling or "current money."[85]

Given these problems, I have cited the most accurate measure of value available. But I have also noted the total amount of land any individual or family seemed to control. Since for every warrant there does not exist a corresponding grant, I have noted, where possible, both warrants and grants; and have assumed that no grant was made without a prior warrant (hence, I have never added the acres identified in warrants to those specified in grants to arrive at a total amount of property acquired by any individual). And I have commonly stressed that the people in my sample of early Carolinians accumulated "at least" a certain number of acres in those instances in which I cannot be certain about the correspondence of warrants to grants held by the individual.

In order to present a picture of the achievements of early Carolinians that as closely as possible approximates the reality they created, I have followed one other practice throughout this work. All of my data are derived from a small aggregate number of individuals. And in most instances, when data are presented, I base my discussion on evidence drawn not from the entire group of early Carolinians considered here, but rather from a portion of that larger group. For example, I can measure land accumulation only for that portion of the servant population which survived servitude, acquired real property, and had such accomplishments recorded in records that have survived. I can consider the impact on mobility of literacy, date of arrival in the colony, or gender, only for the minority of my sample for whom I can determine literacy, date of arrival, and land accumulation. The point is that, by definition, the numbers presented here are derived from small groups of people.

---

[85] See footnote 30, *supra*.

In such situations data from only one or two individuals can dramatically bias results obtained when one looks for averages. In a small sample, a single person who achieved far more or far less, or who lived much longer or died much earlier than everyone else in the group will, if his or her example is included when a mean is calculated, shift the result to a level which fails to represent as accurate a portrayal of what actually occurred as would be obtained if it were discarded. Mathematicians label such extreme examples in small groups *outliers*, and accept two ways of dealing with them. *Winsorization* involves taking "the smallest and largest observations" and giving them "the value of their nearest neighbors." A second procedure, *trimming*, involves omitting a set percentage of a sample at both the high and low extremes—for example, discarding the top and bottom 10% of any small group. The result obtained when this is done provides a clearer sense of the reality experienced by most of the persons in a sample.

In this study whenever numbers are presented in an effort to show what early Carolinians achieved and how their achievements were affected by such factors as literacy, date of arrival, or gender, I have provided *two* sets of figures. I always state the mean derived from a consideration of every individual for whom measurable data exist. I also provide a mean computed after the 10% of outliers at each extreme have been eliminated—a mean derived from a consideration of the middle 80% of the sample. I have Winsorized no data in this work.[86]

---

[86] I am grateful to Professors Robert McDowell, Chairman, and Edward Spitznagel, Dept. of Mathematics, Washington University, for their help in dealing with the problems generated by studying data from small groups. See also Wilfrid Dixon and Frank Massey, *Introduction to Statistical Analysis*, 3d ed. (New York, 1968), pp. 329-33, 488-89, 500-01.

CHAPTER THREE

Servants and Servitude in Early Carolina

I. The Significance of Servants in the Population of Early Carolina

Between 1670, when the first fleet reached Carolina, and the end of 1679, at least 241 men, women and children arrived in the colony as servants. Doubtless a greater number set out for Carolina as servants, but some surely failed to reach the colony because they died or, as did one servant in the first fleet, ran away at a stopover port while traveling to Charles Town.[1] A large majority of these servants, nearly three-quarters of them, arrived in Carolina before 1672. This is, of course, not surprising, since at the outset many investors in the colony—both those who immigrated and those seeking land but hesitant to settle at once—relied on the importation of large numbers of servants to secure extensive land warrants. Moreover, the proprietors insisted that lands dispensed to actual or potential settlers be adequately peopled. They sought both the income and the security that would derive from as rapid and massive an influx of inhabitants as possible. They did not intend to see their vast domains in America lie idly, or to allow their holdings to be threatened by the Spanish or the Indians through underpopulation. Nor were they about to permit an adequate population for a limited area to become insufficient

[1] Joe Reed, Steward to Hambleton on the *Carolina*, ran away when the ship stopped in Ireland to secure additional settlers. *Shaftsbury Papers*, pp. 135-6, 154, 157.

by being spread too thinly over widely scattered locations separated by wilderness.[2]

Thus, the original "Barbados Concessions" of 1663, concluded between the proprietors and a group of wealthy Barbadians who were contemplating settling in Carolina, specified that lands granted would be held "upon ye condicon . . . of continewing one able man serv^{t} or two such weaker servts . . . on every hundred acres . . . . In failer of w^{ch} . . . there shalbe three years given . . . for there compleating ye s^{d} number of persons or [the proprietors will arrange for the] . . . sayle or other disposure of such part of there lande as are not soe peopled within . . . three yeares. . . ." The stricture was repeated three times, just to be certain the proprietors' intentions were clear.[3]

Many, therefore, established their claim to land in the colony by sending servants to live on and work the property before immigrating themselves. Some merely desired to have their servants prepare their land for cultivation by clearing it of woods, and erecting homes they might occupy once they arrived. Others may never have intended to live in South Carolina, seeking instead to hold their property permanently through the presence on it of their servants, and deriving only whatever economic gain could be achieved through the labor of people on land held by absentee owners. Thomas Clutterbooke, for example, resided in Barbados in 1672. But he possessed 670 acres in South Carolina by virtue of having helped finance the exploratory voyage conducted by Captain Hilton in 1663, and for having sent two servants to the colony in 1671. While his servants toiled on land they did not own, Clutterbooke remained at home in Barbados.[4] In September 1671, the Grand Council had stressed that seamen on the proprietors' ship *Blessing* were entitled to land concessions in South Carolina. Since the proprietors insisted that land dispensed be adequately peopled, and since seamen, by definition, could not reside continuously on their property, the Council determined that by securing servants to inhabit their holdings, the sailors could insure that their property rights would not be threatened.[5] Acutely aware that "any plantacon soe graunted [which in] . . . ye space of three yeares be

---

[2] Clowse, *Economic Beginnings*, pp. 47-49.

[3] "Barbados Concessions" in *Shaftsbury Papers*, pp. 29-49, especially pp. 46-48.

[4] *Warrants, 1672-1679*, p. 15.

[5] *Council Journal, 1671-1680*, p. 4.

neglected to be planted wth a sufficient Number of Sarv^{ts}" would be lost to the proprietors, those seeking to insure retention of lands they had received in the colony imported as many servants as they were able to locate and afford. Thus, of the 239 adult servants whose arrival in South Carolina can be dated, fully 170 reached the colony in 1670 and 1671, while only 69 were brought by new settlers or by those already residing in the colony from 1672 to 1680.[6]

The most recent and authoritative estimates indicate that the early population of Carolina consisted of roughly half Barbadians and half immigrants from England.[7] Among servants, however, Englishmen outnumbered Barbadians by nearly two to one. Of course, since the origin of only 124 of the servants can be ascertained, perhaps if more complete information were available, the ratio might change. In any case, among servants arriving in South Carolina between 1670 and 1680 whose origins can be traced, 80 came directly from England while 44 came from the West Indies, mainly from Barbados.

There was, to be sure, a measure of bias against Barbadian servants among South Carolina's early settlers of English origin, which might explain why proportionally only half as many servants came from Barbados as did free persons. Perhaps this was an offshoot of more general resentment by some for what they felt was the excessive influence of Barbadians over the colony's life.[8] In any case, Governor West, writing Ashley in March 1671, noted: "I hope yor Honn^{rs} are thinking of sending a

---

[6] I have selected 1672 as a cutoff date because the number of servants arriving in that year, 16, represented a drastic decrease from the number imported in 1670 and 1671. The decline continued thereafter.

[7] "By the second summer of settlement," writes Peter H. Wood, "almost half the whites and considerably more than half of the blacks in the colony had come from Barbados." *Black Majority*, p. 24. John Locke, Ashley's secretary, noted in a summary of correspondence that in a letter to Sir Peter Colleton, John Coming had written that "the Barbadians endeavour to rule all" in Carolina. The original letter is lost, but dated from the Fall of 1671. *Shaftsbury Papers*, p. 347. Wood suggests that the Barbadian influence in the colony distressed the proprietors, and led them to make overtures to prospective settlers in New York, Virginia, New Jersey, and New England. Wood, *Black Majority*, p. 24.

[8] In May 1674, the proprietors, writing to officials in the colony, noted that under the governorship of Sir John Yeamans (1672-74), it seemed to many that a major goal had been to have "our own plantation soe ordered that in Reputation people and Improvementt itt might arrive att no other pitch then to be Subservient . . . to the Interest of Barbados." *Shaftsbury Papers*, p. 436.

supply of Serv^{ts} from England, for some of these [already sent] wilbe out of their time the next yeare, and wee find that one of our Serv^{ts} wee brought out of England is worth 2 of ye Barbadians for they are soe much addicted to Rum, y^{t} they will doe little but whilst the bottle is at their nose."[9] For whatever reason, the best data available show that most of South Carolina's early servants came to the colony from England.[10]

Given the proprietary insistence that land allotted by adequately peopled, a land policy which determined that acreage would be dispensed mainly on the basis of immigration, and the fact that in the early years of settlement, virtually all enterprises required an extensive amount of labor, it is not surprising that so many servants were imported during the first years of settlement. The one monograph that focuses specifically on white servitude in colonial South Carolina accomplishes little beyond establishing that servants did exist in the colony, and largely ignores the seventeenth century.[11] In fact, during the first year of settlement the servant population dwarfed the free white population, and throughout the first decade of colonization servants comprised a significant segment of white society.

Some numbers make the point. Writing to the proprietors soon after the start of actual settlement, Joseph West noted that "As for our Gouerno^{r} [Sayle] hee is very aged, and hath much lost himselfe in his Governm$^{t:}$ and would have cal'd a Parliam^{t} amongst us allthough wee could not make 20 ffreemen in the Collony, besides the Councell. . . ." The situation changed very little in the following months, for in March 1671, William Owen wrote, "we are about 200 and od soules here

---

[9] *Shaftsbury Papers*, p. 299.

[10] It is also worth considering that England probably had a far larger number of inhabitants who were likely to accept indentured servitude in South Carolina than did Barbados. Those emigrating to Carolina from Barbados generally had sufficient capital to start out as free persons. England, on the other hand, had a large supply of poor men and women for whom the costs of servitude were likely outbalanced by the ultimate rewards of "sufficient meate, drincke, apparell washing and lodging. . . ." See *Records of the Secretary and the Register 1671-1675*, p. 28.

[11] Warren B. Smith, *White Servitude in Colonial South Carolina* (Columbia, 1961).

alreadie of whom there be abouts 40. or 50 freeholders. . . .[12] Thus, initially the proportion of servants to free persons was between four and five to one. That ratio probably held a little less than a year later when Joseph Dalton informed Ashley that "it appears that 337 men [71 women] 62 children or persons under 16 years of age is the full number of persons who have arrived in this Country in and since the first fleet out of England to this day. . . ." However, since some had died and others run off, Dalton pegged the actual population at 406.[13] This count was largely substantiated by a Spanish soldier, Camuñas, who had visited in the colony for eight days. In July 1672, he reported to officials in St. Augustine that upon close observation he had noted 250 men able to bear arms, plus others he did not see.[14] As noted earlier, in 1675 Ashley, disappointed at high costs and low returns, in a decidedly nasty letter to the governor and council, remarked that the proprietors had "by the Expense of 9 or £10000 . . . purchased nothing but the charge of maintaining on 5 or 600 people who expect to live upon us."[15] Already the number of servants imported had begun to decline in relation to the number of free persons arriving, and even that number was not great. By 1680 the total population numbered only between 1000-1200 persons, an increase due to "individual immigrants dribbling into the province" plus gains from births.[16] Sizeable numbers did come to the colony as part of what one scholar has called "group migrations" during the next two years, the population doubling in that span of time, and increasing by 1690 to between 3500 and 4000

---

[12] Joseph West served as Governor 1671-72. See "West to Proprietors," Sept. 1670, *Shaftsbury Papers*, pp. 203-24; and "Owen to Robert Blayney," Mar. 22, 1671, *Shaftsbury Papers*, p. 302.

[13] "Dalton to Ashley," Jan. 10, 1672, *Shaftsbury Papers*, pp. 381-82.

[14] St. Julien Ravenel Childs, *Malaria and Colonization in the Carolina Low Country, 1526-1696* (Baltimore, 1940), pp. 133-34.

[15] "Ashley to Governor and Council," June 10, 1675, *Shaftsbury Papers*, p. 467.

[16] Clowse, *Economic Beginnings*, p. 73. A tract published in Dublin in 1683 asserted that "within these 2 years there was not above 200 Men and now [men] are judged to be one thousand." See John Crafford, "A New and Most Exact Account of . . . Carolina. . . .," pp. 4-5.

persons.[17] It is likely that very few of these newcomers were servants, since an authoritative count of the population made by the governor and council in 1708 establishes that by the start of the eighteenth century white servants had come to comprise but a tiny fraction of the colony's population. Dated September 17, 1708, the report claims 9580 people as living in South Carolina. Of these, only 120 appear to be servants. Black slaves, however, are computed to number 4100, with 1400 Indian slaves counted. The free population totaled 3960. By 1708, therefore, not only did South Carolina have a slave-based economy and a population in which slaves outnumbered all whites (servant and free) by a ratio of about four to three, but there were almost nineteen free adults in the colony for every servant. The reporters mentioned that the colony's white population had declined during the preceding five years, and offered some data on that decrease. Citing "the Late sickness brought here from other parts . . . & small supply from other parts [immigration]," they declared that the free population had fallen by 140, and the servant population "for the aforesaid Reasons & having completed their servitude" had fallen by 80. Thus in 1703 there had been 200 servants working for a white adult population of 2400, which yields a ratio of 12 free adults for every servant.[18]

We know that black slaves dominated the labor force of Carolina by 1700. Given the heavy influence of Barbadians in the colony well before that date, and the extensive use of slaves on the sugar plantations in Barbados (thus insuring that many of South Carolina's early settlers were not only familiar with, but biased in favor of slave labor), it is reasonable to inquire why slave labor failed to dominate the economy of South Carolina from the outset of settlement.[19] The question is intriguing since using slaves would have yielded to Carolina's first settlers exactly the same benefits they derived from servant laborers. Slaves surely would have performed hard work in an economy which, especially during the

---

[17] Clowse identifies three groups which added significant numbers to South Carolina's population between 1680 and 1681: French Protestants, disaffected Scots, and English dissenters (the largest group). Clowse, *Economic Beginnings*, pp. 73-75.

[18] "*Governor and Council to Proprietors*," Sept. 17, 1708, *B.P.R.O.-S.C. Vol. V, 1701-1710*, pp. 203-24. For an extensive as well as excellent discussion of the process by which blacks came to dominate the labor force between 1680 and 1700, see Wood, *Black Majority*, chapters 2 and 3.

[19] On the use of slave labor in Barbados, see Wood, *Black Majority*, pp. 45-46.

first years, imposed heavy labor on the settlers. Masters would have received exactly the same land concessions from the proprietors for importing slaves that they received for bringing white servants to the colony.[20] Presumably, at the outset of colonization slaves were just as acceptable to the proprietors as were servants in fulfilling the requirements dictating that lands granted be adequately inhabited. Only later—when the numbers of blacks had increased dramatically—do we encounter statutes which insist that there be a certain number of whites in residence on every plantation with a heavy black population.[21]

If, therefore, black slaves would have satisfied the requirements which motivated settlers to secure white servants, why did the first colonists fail to use slaves, choosing instead to rely on servants? The question is especially interesting given the fact that slaves' labor would be

---

[20] The "Barbados Concessions" specifically mention that by importing slaves, masters would be entitled to receive land (*Shaftsbury Papers*, p. 43, item 7). However, some doubt about the matter is evidenced by the fact that the proprietors wrote Governor Yeamans during the winter of 1671-72 to point out that, "We find you are mistaken in o[r] Concessions that we have not made provision of land for Negroes for by saying that we grant 150 acres of land for every able man Servant in that we meane Negros as well as Christians and the same in the other perporc'ons w[ch] you may cause to be layd out to those who carry Negros." *Records of the Secretary and the Register 1671-1675*, p. 12. The "Concessions" had offered less land for the importation of slaves than for adult male servants. Originally slaves brought their owners the same number of acres they received for women and children, since these "weaker" servants contributed, in Peter Wood's words, "less to the strength of the outpost" than did white males who could bear arms and be trusted to use them on the settlement's enemies. Now the proprietors, perhaps responding to the fact that many Barbadians considering emigration already owned slaves, and seeking to make Carolina attractive to them, offer as many acres for the importation of a slave as they do for a servant. See Wood, *Black Majority*, pp. 15-20.

[21] The preamble of "An Act to Encourage the Importation of White Servants into this Province" (1716) reads: "Whereas sad experience hath taught us that the small number of white inhabitants of this Province, is not sufficient to defend the same even against our Indian enemies, and whereas the numbers of slaves are daily increasing in this Province, which may likewise endanger the safety thereof, if speedy care be not taken to encourage the importation of white servants. . . ." The act went on to require owners of ten slaves to acquire one white servant. Cooper and McCord, eds., *Statutes*, Vol. II, pp. 646-648. As early as 1698, however, the assembly offered a bounty of 13 pounds for every white male adult servant (except Irish), and 12 pounds for every white male servant under 16 years of age. Every master who owned six black slaves was to take one white servant. *Ibid.*, pp. 153-54. A similar act was passed in 1712. *Ibid.*, pp. 385-6.

available to the master for a far longer period than that of servants, whose "time" might embrace a span as short as perhaps only one or two years. Some have speculated that the key factor was cost—slaves simply were too expensive for most of the early colonists given the limited resources they commanded. But it seems that other factors may have been important in keeping Carolina's first settlers from meeting their labor needs by securing slaves. First, even though Barbadians were quite familiar with Negro slavery, and had employed black slaves with great economic success in the island, some whites may quite simply have considered blacks undesirable in the new colony. They may have feared or disliked blacks because of purely racist attitudes or feelings which we know were widespread in England during the colonial era. Second, at the outset of settlement it was not clear to anyone just what kind of economy would develop in South Carolina. Settlers, both on their own and at the proprietors' urging, experimented with a wide variety of crops in an effort to discover just what would flourish in Carolina's climate and soil. Colonists engaged in a diverse range of activities as they attempted to ascertain what kinds of endeavors would yield profits. Therefore, given these uncertainties, some who might have been able to afford the capital outlay required to buy slaves must have hesitated simply because they could not be certain that those activities which ultimately would prove profitable could utilize slave labor. Moreover, even if slaves could be used in pursuits that turned out to be suitable to Carolina's environment, potential masters may well have pondered whether the long-term costs of maintaining slaves, as well as their high initial cost, would make them a better source of labor than white indentured servants.[22] Because nearly all of the tasks involved in erecting the colony demanded heavy labor, it was reasonable to engage servants for a limited amount of time, until the likely direction of economic activities could be determined.

Since no Englishmen previously had lived in the area on a permanent basis, the environment and its healthfulness posed a question no one was able to answer. Slaves simply might die off in Carolina, and a

---

[22] Winthrop D. Jordan's works, *White Over Black: American Attitudes Toward the Negro, 1550-1812* (Chapel Hill, 1968), and *The White Man's Burden: Historical Origins of Racism in the United States* (New York, 1974), have established the widespread prejudice against blacks which characterized English attitudes towards Africans during the colonial era. On the continued experimentation carried out by Carolina's first settlers as they attempted to learn what crops would thrive in the colony, see "Ashley to Governor Lynch of Jamaica," October 29, 1672, *Shaftsbury Papers*, pp. 414-15.

dead slave cost more than a dead servant—a crucial consideration in a settlement which had very little specie. Barbados, on the other hand, had been settled for a long time and had a well-established economy focusing on sugar production. Slaves had survived in the climate well enough and had been able to work hard enough to make them an attractive commodity. Their use in the sugar industry was an established and lucrative fact. More important, there was only a limited number of slaves available for English use in America (the English colonies, after all, competed with those of other European nations for slaves) and South Carolina lost out to Barbados in competition for them. The Spanish colonies sought slaves and had cash with which to pay for them. So did Barbados. The result was that the eagerness with which colonists of various nations sought to buy slaves drove the price upwards, probably out of the reach of Carolina's early settlers.[23] Potential slave buyers in South Carolina probably hesitated also because they knew that slaves were far more likely than servants to flee the colony, and a runaway servant meant less of a loss than a runaway slave.[24]

One final point—perhaps the single greatest need for any infant settlement in the wilderness is people, but not just any kind of people. While slaves would fulfill that need expressed in terms of a labor source, they would fail absolutely to fulfill that need expressed in other terms. The colony desperately needed people who could be relied upon to assume the burden of defense. White servants could be armed and trusted not to turn against their temporary masters in a conflict because they shared with their masters a common loyalty to the English government, as well as a common vision of the future. White servants could look forward to land, freedom, and full participation in the emerging society. Black slaves, of course, could never do so. Even in a conflict which might divide the colonists along class lines, white servants at least *might* fight to maintain the interests of those "above" them precisely because they had reason to believe that some day they would be members of a dominant class. Even if this were a dubious proposition, it was clear that slaves could never internalize or act upon such notions. As we have seen, military preparedness was a central issue of life in early Carolina. Indeed, one of the first settlers remarked, "We are here settled in the

[23] For the argument that early Carolinians chose servants rather than slaves due to the high cost of slaves and the limited capital available to make such purchases, see Wood, *Black Majority*, pp. 48-50.

[24] *Ibid.*, pp. 50-51.

very chaps of the Spaniard."[25] Concerns about adequate defense against the Spanish and potentially hostile Indians continued to occupy the attention of the settlers over time—few during the first years in Carolina felt entirely secure in their occupation of a small parcel of territory in a vast and possibly hostile wilderness.[26] In such an environment servants made more sense than slaves as a source of labor and a basis for acquiring land.

Slaves failed to fulfill early South Carolina's population needs in another sense as well. Slaves could never become full participants in the society or in the economy. They could never acquire land, which meant that the proprietors would never derive rent revenue from them. Their owners surely would spend money in the colony to purchase the food and clothing they *needed*, but it was unreasonable to assume that any owner would spend much more than the minimum which subsistence required, especially in the early years when money and commodities usable as barter were in short supply. Servants, however, would some day become free, own land, engage in farming it, establish themselves as tradesmen, or pursue any of a variety of tasks essential to the general well-being of the government and the inhabitants. Freed servants certainly would spend more on their own and their families' maintenance than owners would spend on their slaves. Freed servants would participate in every aspect of the colony's life; slaves would perpetually remain only a labor force. Thus did a wide variety of factors conspire to exert a determining influence in the decision to import white servants rather than black slaves during the early years of settlement.

Needless to say, once the initial sense of insecurity had passed, cash crops were discovered, and questions about the healthfulness of the climate were resolved, South Carolinians turned with great speed to slaves as a source of labor. Servants, at the outset so central to the social and economic life of the colony, quickly became so scarce that the colony's officials adopted legislation to increase their numbers, a certain signal that they had ceased to occupy a numerically significant position in South Carolina.[27]

---

[25] "Joseph Dalton to Ashley," Sept. 9, 1670, *Shaftsbury Papers*, p. 183.

[26] See, e.g., *Shaftsbury Papers*, pp. 179, 346, 374, 395, 407, 464.

[27] See note 21, *supra.*

II. Characteristics of Carolina's Servants

Who were these 241 people who came to the colony as servants before 1680? The most basic description involves gender—206 were males while 35 were females. This staggering sexual imbalance is perfectly comprehensible given the immaturity of the settlement and the role servants fulfilled—servants performed labor, and during the early years of settlement labor was needed. Men, quite simply, could be expected to perform more hard work for longer periods of time than could women. Of the 170 servants arriving before 1672, 147 were males and 23 were females; among those arriving between 1672 and 1680, 58 were males and 12 were females. (There is no clear arrival date for one male, hence the 240 total rather than 241.) Thus, in the first two years of settlement, for every female servant imported, more than six males were imported. This ratio declined somewhat to one female for every four to five males during the last eight years of the decade, indicating that the colony was moving very slowly toward social maturity. If, as Joseph Dalton had asserted, in January 1672 there were 337 men and 71 women in the province, after deducting the servants, there were about 190 free males and 48 free females[28] residing in South Carolina, a sex ratio among free adults of roughly four males for every female. Obviously the free population was far more likely to exhibit a more even sex distribution than the servant population, but it is clear that men far outnumbered women at the outset, and for a number of years thereafter. By 1703 the ratio among all adult whites was roughly 1.5 males for every female,[29] a clear indication that by the start of the eighteenth century South Carolina displayed perhaps the most important aspect of a firmly established community. For only in new societies intended to endure do men import women of the same race to serve as wives and mothers. In areas where men do not intend to make permanent homes, where their goal is to make as much money as rapidly as possible and then return home, the sex ratio commonly is heavily biased in favor of males.

---

[28] Since we cannot ascertain exactly how many of the servants had gained their freedom by January 1672, it is impossible to be precise. Nor can we be certain that Dalton's numbers themselves reflect more than a close estimate of the actual population.

[29] "Governor and Council to Proprietors," September 17, 1708, *B.P.R.O.-S.C. Vol. V, 1701-1710*, pp. 203-04.

If most of the servants shared the same gender, they also probably came from similar backgrounds in England or Barbados. The evidence needed to establish what they did prior to emigrating exists for only a small fraction of the sample. In all likelihood, people would not agree to work for someone else and thereby submit to that person's absolute control if they could exercise other options which, if not economically more advantageous, at least did not involve loss of freedom. The servants, therefore, who did give up freedom and agree to perform hard work, surely did not come from well established families. The only guarantees South Carolina's first servants received in return for their labor and freedom were that they would be provided with passage to the colony, food and clothing, and enough land once free to at best support themselves. None questioned that opportunities for economic and social advancement did exist, but the probability of becoming moderately well-off, much less of securing real wealth, was not sufficiently high to lure many to the colony as servants who already enjoyed even moderate security somewhere else.

There were, to be sure, some servants who failed to conform to such a pattern. While evidence exists which allows us to determine that "servants" such as Affra Harleston and Barnaby Bull cannot legitimately be thus labelled for purposes of investigating mobility among people who started at the very bottom, surely there were others who entered the colony as "servants" solely for the purpose of increasing their "master's" initial land concession; or who were labelled servants quite honestly by seventeenth century standards but who, in fact, were skilled people whose role was not to perform labor, but rather to attend to their "master's" health or business affairs. At least one servant later practiced medicine, but it is not clear whether he had any formal training for his "profession" or if he had been a medical practitioner prior to coming to South Carolina,[30] much less his exact role as a servant. Other servants seem to have acted as business agents on their master's behalf, and apparently were entrusted with the responsibility of executing mercantile transactions which had a bearing on the success of their master's enterprises. John

---

[30] James Williams who, with his wife Martha, arrived as servants in the first fleet. A land warrant dated December 5, 1675, reads in part, "You are forthwth to cause to be laid out for James Williams 200 acres of land for himselfe and Martha his Wife arriveing Serv^{ts}. in the first ffleet. . . ." *Warrants, 1672-1679*, p. 91. In March 1683, he is cited as James Williams "Chirurgian." *Warrants, 1680-1692*, p. 94; the title is repeated in *Warrants, 1680-1692*, p. 185. In September 1698 he is cited as "Doctr. James Williams." *Warrants, 1692-1711*, pp. 153-54.

Farrington, for example, a servant to Lt. Colonel John Godfrey, seems to have been given the responsibility for arranging shipment of "two barrills of Rum quantity Seaventy foure gallons and one barrill of Sugar" from South Carolina to Virginia.[31] Other servants came to the colony already able to perform highly skilled work—they practiced a trade which meant they were more than mere laborers. In December 1670, John Foster and Thomas Gray entered into a contract to transport goods and servants to Carolina from Barbados. Of the nine servants identified, four clearly were practicing a trade prior to their arrival in the colony as servants, for between the servant's name and the time he is to serve, an occupation is cited. There were two sawyers, one carpenter, and one "Tayler."[32] There is no doubt that other servants who appear in the records after attaining freedom, and are identified as skilled tradesmen, brought their skills with them to Carolina.[33]

Of course, not many servants were tradesmen, or came to the colony with skills. Early in 1672 Joseph West wrote Ashley, and Locke's memorandum of the letter says that West "Desires yt ye servants hereafter sent may be husbandmen or trades man the last that were sent

---

[31] If he did not exercise absolute authority in the matter, he surely had responsibilities greater than merely loading the cargo aboard the "good Sloope Mactauck," for he signed the required agreement between Godfrey and the ship's officers. *Records of the Secretary and the Register, 1671-1675*, p. 48. (There is, of course, a possibility he merely witnessed the agreement.)

[32] "Articles Between Foster and Gray," Dec. 23, 1670, *Shaftsbury Papers*, pp. 253-54.

[33] E.g., Thomas Archcraft, who arrived a servant in 1671, was a gunsmith, but not a good one. A year after his arrival the Grand Council was forced to threaten, then place him in custody, because of delays and shoddy work. Citing "complaints of diverse persons" who have had "their armes lying along time in the hands of Thomas Archcraft Gunn Smith" waiting to be repaired "and by noe means can gett them dispatcht" and considering that all arms "should be allwayes ready & well fitted for service," the Council ordered that Archcraft apply himself to the work, and commanded that he "shall not worke upon any other worke untill he hath finished the s^{d} Armes [nor] . . . make any Indian Hatchetts for any person . . . wthout speciall lycence" from the Governor and Council. Archcraft apparently did not comply, for about eight weeks later the Council noted the "dayly" complaints against Archcraft who "by his faire pretences . . . hath gained any defective armes into his custody [and] . . . either, alltogether neglects, the mending of them, or else returnes them as ill, sometimes worse than when he received them." He was ordered to "remaine in the Marshall custody, untill he has sufficiently fixed up all the defective Armes he hath received. . . ." *Council Journal, 1671-1680*, pp. 7-8; 51-52.

being bad."[34] On the other hand, while most who came to Carolina were surely poor and without a trade, even though the need for servants was tremendous, those who did come in the first decade were not the meanest people available. There is no evidence that the slums and prisons of London and Barbados disgorged their occupants in the direction of South Carolina.[35] Those who came as servants entered their contracts as free persons.[36] Their immigration was not a punishment inflicted upon them (or

---

[34] *Shaftsbury Papers*, p. 387.

[35] For suggestions that prisoners became servants in America, and specifically in Carolina, see: Warren B. Smith, *White Servitude*, pp. 3-4; Theo. D. Jervey, "The White Indentured Servants of South Carolina," S.C.H.G.M., XII (Oct., 1911), 163-71 (list of convicts imported from Bristol 1726-1728, p. 171); Wood, *Black Majority*, p. 42, fn. 28 (see note 37 below for discussion of this.); John Donald Duncan, "Servitude and Slavery in Colonial South Carolina, 1670-1776," Ph.D. dissertation, Emory University, 1971, p. 52, states that convicts "appear to have been sent" as servants to Carolina in the 1680's; he notes that political prisoners were sent in the eighteenth century (p. 56), and cites an attempt "as early as 1687" by English officials to send convicted criminals as servants to the colony. (The attempt failed because Carolinians refused to accept such immigrants [p. 66].)

For the view that servants were, if not well-off, at least from the "middling" classes, see the classic article by Mildred Campbell, "Social Origins of Some Early Americans," in James M. Smith, ed., *Seventeenth Century America: Essays in Colonial History* (Chapel Hill, 1959). Wesley Frank Craven, *White, Red and Black: The Seventeenth-Century Virginian* (New York, 1977), accepts Campbell's view of servants as coming from a variety of classes, and opposes the view that criminals came (or were sent) in the seventeenth century as indentured servants (pp. 5-7). A heated discussion of Campbell's original article filled the pages of the *William & Mary Quarterly* in 1978-79. See "'Middling People' or 'Common Sort'?: The Social Origins of Some Early Americans Reexamined," by David W. Galenson, and "Mildred Campbell's Response," in *William & Mary Quarterly*, XXXV (July 1978), 499-540; Galenson, "The Social Origins of Some Early Americans: Rejoinder," and "Mildred Campbell Replies," *William & Mary Quarterly*, XXXVI (April 1979), 264-86. While Galenson and Campbell disagree over the precise composition of the servant group as identified in lists of servant registrations in England in the second half of the seventeenth century, it is clear that both scholars accept a view of servants as a mixed group of men and women from a variety of backgrounds. The argument concerns the definition of status for servants whose occupation was "not given" on the surviving documents, and the methodology employed in arriving at such a definition. See also Galenson, *White Servitude in Colonial America: An Economic Analysis* (Cambridge, 1981), pp. 34-50.

[36] There is evidence that a small number of servants were brought to the colony under false pretenses. For example, early in 1679 one Robert Kincade was ordered to be set free and to be paid back wages by his master because "it appears [servitude] was

an alternative to imprisonment), but rather, they came because they wanted a chance to exert themselves in a setting where their efforts might yield social and economic gains in their own lives, and the lives of their descendants.[37]

---

onlie Imposed upon him by the Artifice & fraud of Randall Evans, Marriner." Evans was himself a former servant and must have enticed Kincade to Carolina and then sold his "contract" in order to secure cash, a land warrant, or both. *Records of the Secretary 1675-1695* (MSV), p. 53.

[37] Peter Wood suggests that "there is little doubt that some who arrived on indentures had criminal records." He cites a memorandum of 1697 about female prisoners "now lying in Newgate" who had been offered to Carolina. However, Wood does not mention that although these prisoners were offered to *several* colonies, only the Leeward Islands proved willing to accept them. I have encountered no evidence which suggests that prisoners were sent to Carolina as servants in this era. See Wood, *Black Majority*, p. 42, fn. 28, and *B.P.R.O.-S.C. Vol. III*, pp. 204-06. Needless to say, more than a few servants were, to use West's word, "bad." One servant, wrote the Council to the Proprietors, named Richard Crossland (or Crossley) was in fact "one whom his Mr. Sett ffree, for his Idlenesse." (March 21, 1671) *Shaftsbury Papers*, p. 292. Not every servant accepted that status as a temporary condition which would later serve as a springboard to upward mobility. Note, for example, the "Articles of Agreement Concluded made and agreed the 29th day of September 1682 Betweene Mathew English of Carolina Victualler & Robert Midling of the other pte Labourer." English was a former servant and was illiterate. Midling's background remains a mystery, but he could read and write. "It is mutually convenanted and agreed on by and between the p^{ties} by these p^{s}sents: and the said Robert Midling doth covenant promise to and wth the s^{d} Mathew English his Exorts administ^{s} to and with them by these p^{s}ents that he the s^{d} Robert Midling doth and shall well and truely serve the s^{d} Mathew English his Exorts Administrat^{s} in all or any manner of Service that the s^{d} Mathew English shall or may employ him in *during the whole terme and time of his Naturall life* for which the s^{d} Mathew English doth covenant promise to and with the s^{d} Robert Midling to finde him the s^{d} Midling Sufficient meat drinke Washing Lodgeing and apparroll dureing the whole time afore$^{sd.}$ . . ." *Records of the Secretary 1675-1695* (MSV), p. 123 (emphasis added).

Richard Waterhouse has suggested that among those coming to Carolina from Barbados, "Many . . . who emigrated as indentured servants may have been the sons and daughters of small Barbadian landholders. There was no future for them in indenturing themselves to Barbadian planters, because there was no land available to be granted them there when they had finished their time." "England, the Caribbean, and the Settlement of Carolina," *American Studies*, 9 (December 1975), p. 279. Earlier Waterhouse stated that of those who came to Carolina as servants from England, "No doubt the majority . . . were recruited from that class of landless and semi-landless cottagers, labourers and servants which constituted half the population of Restoration England" (page 261).

In fact, a surprising number came to the colony with at least a rudimentary education. Since it is unlikely that many adult servants mastered reading and writing skills while serving their terms, literacy rates among servants most likely measure abilities acquired before their immigration. They thereby are very instructive when assessing the backgrounds of these men and women. The best study of literacy in early America establishes that the ability to sign one's name (the only yardstick available for measuring reading and writing skills) signifies the ability to read. Moreover, it is probable that fewer colonists could sign their names than could read. "Scholars agree," writes Kenneth Lockridge, "that the level of signatures runs below but closely parallels reading skills and runs above but roughly parallels writing skills. . . .The most precise *absolute* definition which could be placed on signatures is that they correspond to the actual level of fluent reading."[38] The ability to sign documents, as opposed to making a mark, can be measured for 58 male and two female servants. While neither woman could sign her name, 31, or more than half the male servants, were able to do so. Although it is highly doubtful that this percentage would hold true were we able to examine documents requiring a signature from all 241 servants,[39] it seems a significant segment of the servant population demonstrated a higher level of education than that commonly associated with thoroughly disadvantaged people, especially when those people were living in the seventeenth century.

---

[38] Kenneth A. Lockridge, *Literacy in Colonial New England: An Enquiry into the Social Context of Literacy in the Early Modern West* (New York, 1974), p. 7.

[39] The ways in which literacy rates as measured here relate to mobility and the biases inherent in such an examination, are discussed later. Here it is sufficient to point out that merely by participating in any kind of transaction (a will, a land sale) which required the parties involved to sign their names, a former servant was displaying a degree of "success" or of endurance not enjoyed by most other servants. Hence, such a former servant might be more likely to demonstrate literacy. It is worth noting, however, that some of my data on literacy are taken from surviving contracts for servitude, which would not be subject to the kind of bias associated with land sales.

In three instances the servant under consideration exhibited both the ability and an inability to sign his name. I have counted all three as literate, assuming that the failure to sign a name indicated either physical weakness due to illness, or feebleness associated with old age.

III. Conditions of Servitude

Nearly all of the 241 servants whose lives are examined here came to South Carolina as individuals, unencumbered by family ties. Only 5% came with a husband or wife, only one came as a child with his parents. Thus, during the first ten years of settlement, only six servant couples immigrated to the colony, three arriving before 1672, one in 1672, and the other two thereafter. All of the factors which worked to bias the servant population in favor of males, similarly worked against the appearance of married couples in the colony. Since servants were meant to work, and men were obviously more desirable than women as heavy laborers, we find few servant couples arriving at any time during the first decade.[40]

Although 95% of all servants engaged as individuals to serve a master, very few were alone as servants once they reached the colony. It is possible to determine the number of servants possessed by the master of 215 of the servants in the sample. Only 17, or about 8%, of the 215 worked alone as the single servant "owned" by their master. Forty-one of the servants, 19% of the total, had either one or two fellow servants to share the burdens imposed by their masters. But since acreage held and worked varied in direct proportion to the number of servants imported, it may well be that those working for masters who controlled only a few other servants worked at onerous tasks on a less regular basis than those whose masters owned a huge amount of land through the headrights they gained for bringing in many servants. And it is reasonable to assume that masters who possessed only a few servants shared their lodgings with their laborers, as well as their meals. On larger estates, even if the master resided on the premises, it is unlikely that he ate the same food or slept under the same roof as his servants. Surely the tasks performed by servants who had only one or two companions were more varied than were those of servants working in groups large enough to permit some regularized division of labor. Twenty-two percent, or 48 servants, worked

---

[40] The servant couples were: William, Ann, and William (Jr.). Jones (1673); Robert and Mary Thomas (1671); John Thomas and wife (1677); Nicholas and Elizabeth Webb (1671); Richard and Susan Wells (1672); and James and Martha Williams (1670). Two brothers seem to have arrived and worked together as servants. Thomas and William McLaughlin reached the colony in May 1679, as servants to Jona Lynch. Both were free by 1684. See *Warrants, 1672-79*, pp. 143-44.

alongside three or four fellow servants, while 47%, or 100 servants, worked alongside five or more people who shared their status.[41]

Most servants apparently were content with their lot. Instances of overt disobedience are rare, and surely would have been recorded had they been sufficiently serious to warrant harsh penalties.[42] On the other hand, only two of the servants[43] were so good that they received formal official recognition (and rewards) for their loyal service. In all likelihood, most servants probably were not happy to be doing another's work and subject to another's will, but the future promised sufficient rewards that they quietly endured whatever agonies they felt.

Of the 241 servants in South Carolina between 1670 and 1680, only nine believed that their existence was so intolerable that they either ran away or were hailed before the authorities for contemplating flight from the colony.[44] Only three, all servants to Affra Coming, frightened their "owner" by threats to such a degree that they were forced to undergo the rigors of an appearance before the Council, and only two were labelled felons.

Perhaps disobedience was rare because servants knew that punishments meted out by their superiors could be harsh. We know nothing of either the crimes committed by, or the sentences imposed on the two felons, only that the Council held a special session in July 1673, to hear the case.[45] Better evidence has survived on the other servants who came before the body. Michael Lovell and John Chambers appeared

---

[41] In some cases servants worked alongside slaves (at least eight servants worked for masters who also owned slaves). I have not included the slave population in the number of servants controlled by any given master. In only five cases does the number of slaves owned seem to have a serious bearing on the overall breakdown I have offered here. William Sayle's four servants worked alongside his four slaves, which surely lessened the burdens imposed on the servants (*Warrants, 1672-1679*, p. 52), and John Hopkins' mistress owned eight slaves in addition to her one servant. *Ibid.*, p. 112.

[42] The Grand Council, whose journals are intact, served as the body before which cases of servant disobedience, as well as cases of abuse of servants by masters, were heard. Thus, any serious offenses by servants are probably known.

[43] Richard Powser and Phillip Jones, *Council Journal 1671-1680*, p. 7.

[44] The case of Raven's servant, Elizabeth Jones, has been considered earlier; it is therefore not discussed further here.

[45] *Ibid.*, p. 61. They were Sam Lucas and Thomas Laford.

along with Philip Orill before the Council in June 1672, accused of threatening their mistress. While Orill received 21 lashes for his "gross abuses" and threats,[46] Lovell and Chambers merely were warned, and "advised . . . to render a more dutifull obedience to the lawfull Commands of their said Mistresse upon payne of condigne punishment" in the future.[47] Runaways received a variety of penalties for their actions—if they were caught. Bryan Fitzpatrick would have faced harsh treatment for "a very ill office done . . . upon an Indian" in the summer of 1671 which, when the Governor seemed determined to investigate "the truth and man'er how the Indian's life was taken away," led to his flight from the province. About a year after his actions the Council noted that he "hath departed this province with an intent to go to the Spaniards . . . [and since] he as yett hath gott no further then St Helena," two colonists were sent to capture and return him to Charles Town for punishment. There is no question that the penalty contemplated by the Council was stiff, for if Fitzpatrick resisted, the hunters were "then to maim, destroy or kill him as they shall find best to agree with their owne safety."[48] Those sent to capture the departed servant failed either to bring him back or to harm him. Fitzpatrick found sanctuary with the Spanish in St. Augustine, reported on the strength of the English in Carolina, and served as a gunner at the fort which protected his former masters' enemies.[49]

Dennis Mahone wanted to flee, but he did not have Fitzpatrick's success. Late in 1671, he appeared before the Council which, before imposing its sentence, declared that he, "among others having been formerly guilty of running away . . . and departing out of this Collony to

---

[46] See above and *ibid.*, pp. 33-34.

[47] *Ibid.*, pp. 33-34.

[48] *Shaftsbury Papers*, pp. 352, 336-39, 411. The Council did discuss in January 1672, the case of "some persons namely James Willoughby and Thomas Munkister upon an Indictm^t··· for running away from this Collony. . . ." Neither seems to have been a servant. Nor were Richard Batten and William Loe, who not only ran away, but also stole "a Negroe belonging to Capt: Nathanieel: Sayle, & diverse other goods belonging to other persons" in February 1673. In September 1673, the Council noted that "as of late divers obstinate and evill disposed persons have run away," and sent "a small party of men" to capture them. It is thus clear that not only servants, but some who arrived as free persons as well, could develop tremendous antipathy for the colony. See *Council Journal, 1671-1680*, pp. 47, 54-56, 63-64.

[49] Childs, *Malaria*, p. 134. Fitzpatrick greatly overestimated the strength of the settlement, inflating the population well above its actual size.

attaine the protection of the Crowne of Spaine . . . intending thereby the destruction of this settlem$^{t.}$ and upon his penitency and amendm^{t} . . . of life had his punishm$^{t.}$ due for the same suspended; yett . . . little regarding his Allegiance to o^{r} . . . King and his fidelity and submission to Lords Propriet^{rs}. still prosecuting his Evill Intencons about the tenth day of October last endeavoured to perswade and entice some of his fellow Serv^{ts} · · · to run away and depart this Collony And . . . being . . . found guilty of the same, . . . shall forthwith be stript naked to his waste & receive thirty nine lashes upon his naked back." John Cooke, the servant Mahone had sought to induce to flee with him, was not punished, which means either that it was his first offence, or, more likely, he had informed the authorities of Mahone's plans.[50]

In January 1672, the Council discussed the situation of John Ratcliffe, a servant who, like Mahone, had tried to lead two of his fellow servants to freedom. The two[51] apparently did not heed Ratcliffe's advice, for they do not seem to have been punished. Ratcliffe, however, "hath for some time past remained in Irons in the Marshalls Custody." Moreover, Indians had "pursued him & brought him back" and now they had to receive compensation for their actions on behalf of the Master and the government. Ratcliffe's term of service was extended 16 months to meet those costs, but he did get out of the marshall's custody.[52]

The only other runaway case which was sufficiently important to require the Council's attention involved two servants who had fled and been captured. Richard Nicklin and John Rivers "now prisoners" had been "sentenced to death for contriveing to run away from this Province. . . ." But the Council, displaying an awareness of larger considerations than merely punishing a criminal offense, was willing to be lenient, for it "conceaved . . . that the death of the s^{d} persons may not only lessen the strength of the province but perhaps may not . . . be a matter so well approved on abroad." Since servants were useful not only because they worked, but also because they could be relied upon to assist in defending

---

[50] *Council Journal, 1671-1689*, p. 14.

[51] Richard Bardiner and William Davice.

[52] It is interesting to note that the Council offered to reduce the additional time imposed on Ratcliffe if he or someone acting on his behalf would pay the costs of his capture. In fact, his master paid, and the 16 months plus five he had been absent were added to the years he owed his master. *Ibid*, pp. 22-23, 50; *Shaftsbury Papers*, pp. 373-74.

the province from its enemies, and because the officials were eager to induce large numbers of people to come to Carolina as servants, the Council ordered that the two "be allowed opportunity of submission and prayer for mercy," especially since "the crime . . . for which they are sentenced to dye was founded only on discourse, and never came to act." Rivers and Nicklin eagerly grasped the opportunity offered, acknowledged that they had "deservedly received the sentence of death," that they had "come to a better understanding of their errors," stressed that they were "in a condicon farr from any suitable preparacon to encounter the terrors of death," swore that they were "earnestly desirous to amend their lives," and were anxious to be "examples of yor hon^{rs}: clemency and mercy." The sentence was reprieved but their pardon was withheld "for a time" in order to encourage them to live up to their words of contrition.[53]

---

[53] *Council Journal, 1671-1680*, pp. 47-49; *Shaftsbury Papers*, pp. 413-14. Clowse, *Economic Beginnings*, p. 53, suggests that servants who were punished for misdeeds "typify the sort of indentured servant who had been unsuccessful in England and became a liability in America." However, while their masters may have considered them a liability, there seems to have been little correlation between trouble experienced as a servant and later achievements. That is, as suggested earlier, Mahone and Orill enjoyed a good deal of success once freed. Chambers received a sizeable land grant (270 acres plus 36 acres) and was a carpenter. Lovell was a sawyer and owned property in Charles Towne. On Orill, see *Warrants, 1672-1679*, p. 135; *Records of the Register and the Secretary 1675-1696, 1703-1709* (MSV), pp. 46-7, 81; *Records of the Secretary 1675-1695* (MSV), p. 1; Misc. *Records 1681-1690*, pp. 92, 197; *Warrants, 1680-1692*, pp. 4, 10; C.S.P. *1677-1680 (Vol. 10)*, p. 547; P.R.O., CO 5/398, p. 1; *Proprietary Grants No. 1 Vol. 38* (MSV), pp. 16, 59; *Records of the Register and the Secretary 1675-1696, 1703-1709* (MSV), pp. 94, 171; *Records of the Secretary 1675-1695* (MSV), pp. 219-20 (will). On Lovell, see *Warrants, 1680-1692*, p. 66; P.R.O., CO 5/398, p. 4; *Proprietary Grants No. 1 Vol. 38* (MSV), p. 60; *Records of the Register and Secretary 1675-1696, 1703-1709* (MSV), pp. 107, 174; *Records of the Secretary 1675-1695* (MSV), p. 187; Misc. *Records 1682-1690* (MSV), pp. 170-71; *Records of the Register 1705-1709* (MSV), p. 250. It is thus clear that some of these disobedient servants did go on to become stable and dependable contributors to the emerging Carolina society.

In September 1671, West wrote Ashley and noted that a prominent colonist had recently been sent by the governor overland to Virginia. West expressed concern over the trip because the colonist who had been sent, Dr. Henry Woodward, was the colony's most effective Indian agent and "Interpreter." Not only was his presence considered necessary, but the trip might prove dangerous, and West feared for his safe return to the colony. Equally troubling, however, were the journey's implications regarding stability among the province's servant population. For, as West suggested, "if he arrives safe in Virginia," he would establish a path runaway servants might follow

Needless to say, there must have been numerous cases of servant resistance which never received recognition (and inclusion in the records) by the Council. However, had such cases been serious, surely they would have required official action; and it is probably safe to assume that given the relatively low frequency with which servants came before the Council to receive punishment for offenses, in general the level of contentment among the servant group was high enough, and the certainty of punishment strong enough, to preserve peace between servants and masters.

Other factors worked to develop the sense of well-being servants maintained about themselves. Acutely aware of the colony's need for white immigrants, laborers, and potential full participants in the social, economic, and political life of the settlement, Carolina officials consistently stood ready to enforce the contractual or customary provisions which guaranteed that servants would be fairly used by their masters. Disobedient servants knew that they would have to deal with a Council with which resided the power and willingness to inflict severe punishment on them for their actions. Similarly, masters who contemplated abusing their servants knew that the Council would act on behalf of any who were badly treated. Servants knew this as well, and proved willing to seek the Council's intervention to preserve their rights frequently enough to allow the government to maintain its image as protector of servants at a level of visibility which well served its goals of making the province seem an attractive place to potential servants. The colony's officials had forced John Raven to treat his servant Elizabeth Jones decently. They had determined in a formal hearing that Christopher Edwards had fulfilled his contract with a master reluctant to free him. They had freed another servant because he had been defrauded.[54] They ordered one master who refused to pay the costs involved in laying out a ten acre lot for his freed servant to do so. And they found a new home for a servant whose original master could not "maintaine [him] with . . . necessary provisions, and clothes."[55] If

---

to escape from Carolina. West noted that "we have lost two allready." *Shaftsbury Papers*, p. 338.

[54] Robert Kincade, set free February 13, 1679. See earlier and *Records of the Secretary 1675-1695* (MSV), p. 53.

[55] *Council Journal, 1671-1680*, pp. 16-17. Complaint of Susanna Kinder against Florence O'Sullivan, December 1671. On January 28, 1683, Christopher Field appeared before the Council and "made complt. that his said Master could not at present" clothe or feed him adequately. The Council may not have done Field a great service by

such cases in which the Council acted to protect servants from cruel, dishonest, or impoverished masters were as rare as were cases of servants abusing their masters, the cause in all probability was that both masters and servants knew that to avoid trouble with the Council, their actions had to fall within certain bounds. When individuals in either group exceeded the limits of behavior defined as acceptable, none doubted that there was a sympathetic group ready to hear complaints, or that it would willingly exercise the power it possessed to enforce decent conduct in the province. The aim was both to preserve peace and to insure that potential immigrants knew beforehand that their interests would be protected if they chose to settle in the province. Even if that strategy did not induce huge numbers to come, it at least minimized the actual hardships masters might have inflicted on their bondsmen, as well as the number of cases in which discontented servants abused the persons or property of their masters, or fled. Thus, by what seems to have been scrupulous attention to the dictates of justice, by preserving the image of being willing both to mete out harsh punishment and to be merciful, and by being attentive to the needs and treating the interests of both masters and servants in an even-handed manner, the Council encouraged some to import servants and others to accept servitude. The Council, in other words, fostered trust.

Consider the case of Richard Nicklin and his master Joseph West. Even though he had been hailed before the Council in October 1672 for planning to run away, sentenced to death, and then pardoned—even though, in other words, he had been in trouble—Nicklin did not hesitate to seek the protection of that body when he believed he had been badly served by his master. Nearly one year after his humble petition for mercy had been accepted, Nicklin "came . . . before the Grand Council and made complaint that he had already served Coll: Joseph West the terme of two yeares which was his contracted time of servitude and thereupon ought to be free; and upon heareing of the matter on both sides alleadged and the certainty of the said terme . . . on neither hand fully appearing," the Council determined that Nicklin should serve West one more year, "and if the said Coll: West doe not in the meane time prove the said Richard Nicklin is to serve longer, then . . . [he is] to be free after the expiracon of the said yeare, or if . . . Richard Nicklin can prove he had but two yeares to serve that then the said Richard Nicklin shall have sufficient satisfaccon [pay] for the said third yeares service." Thus did the Council attempt to

---

selecting O'Sullivan to receive his labor in return for "finding him sufficient victualls and clothes for his better preservacon. . . ." *Ibid.*, p. 52.

keep both parties from feeling that their interests had been ignored. If a servant formerly sentenced to death could receive such a fair judgement, did not that establish that any servant might expect to receive equal satisfaction? Nor could the master complain, for his rights also had been carefully guarded.[56]

But what worked more than anything else to make life as a servant tolerable was the promise of freedom and land in the future. Land was most important, for unless a person possessed property, freedom would have had no meaning. Surely some men were able to support themselves nicely by practicing a trade, but even sawyers, joyners, and tailors seem to have sought and used the land they were able to acquire either to supplement their incomes or to serve as their major source of income, much less to provide them with food. Few settlers, rich or poor, failed to hold and use land during the early years of settlement. At the outset, given the unsophisticated nature of the economy, the uncertainties involved in determining just which pursuits would yield profits, and actual or feared shortages of food,[57] virtually every settler recognized that economic

---

[56] *Ibid.*, pp. 62-3.

[57] In the early years of settlement, concerns about the ability to feed the inhabitants were expressed frequently. For example, the Council wrote the proprietors in 1670, "Wee haue not aboue one months' prouision in the Collony. . . . Our necesityes are soe great that wee must [buy them on your account elsewhere] . . . or else dessert the settlement." *Shaftsbury Papers*, p. 175. They did secure supplies, but soon wrote again saying that "we could hardly get another supply before the former was gone." *Ibid.*, p. 178. The same month one colonist wrote that "our Prouision failed us." *Ibid.*, p. 187. Early in 1671 the Council, though delighted at the arrival of two ships which delivered in excess of a hundred new settlers, expressed fears that there would not be sufficient food in the province to sustain them; they went on to note that the colonists already resident in Carolina were "weake by reason of scarcity of provisions." *Ibid.*, pp. 282-83. At one point, after the food supply had diminished drastically, the Council wrote that the settlers were reduced to eating only "a pint of pease a mann a day." *Ibid.*, p. 288. Even the supposedly wealthy Barbadians, Locke noted, "as well as the rest [of the colonists] want provisions." *Ibid.*, p. 350. As late as 1672 officials continued to fear that the supply of food was inadequate. Locke wrote that "Provisions like to be scarce before ye next crop," and that to counter the threatened shortage the Council had ordered the settlers to plant "2 acres per head." *Ibid.*, p. 387. In 1673 food was so scarce, the Council asserted, that "none appeare to spare any" food to maintain an Indian prisoner awaiting trial. *Ibid.*, p. 422. In such an environment every settler wanted enough land to be able to feed himself, or to produce sufficient products to allow for the purchase of food. Part of such food shortages may, of course, have resulted precisely because the colonists turned to pursuits other than planting in an effort to identify lucrative enterprises. But whatever the cause of food shortages, the desire for land must

security, if not wealth, depended on access to land. And, in fact, once Carolinians located products which commanded markets and reasonable prices—cattle and hogs to feed colonists elsewhere in America, and wood for barrels in which those colonists could pack their own products—the sensed need for land became even more acute.[58] In any case, all perceived that to insure their independence, to keep from being forced to give up a degree of freedom in order to earn a fixed wage or to receive sustenance, land was essential. Especially for freed servants who by definition started out with little or no capital, the only way to begin—to accumulate the money which might serve as the basis for other more lucrative enterprises—was to obtain land and work it.

Thus the key component among the various factors which coalesced to preserve contentment among servants was the land policy administered by the proprietors' agents in South Carolina. The regulations governing distribution of land put into force at the outset of settlement remained in effect well beyond the years when servants composed a substantial segment of the immigrant population, until 1679,[59] and were neatly summarized in the initial set of instructions annexed to the commission provided by the proprietors for the colony's first governor.[60] Of the 15 specific segments into which these instructions are broken down, three deal

---

have intensified throughout the province as settlers sought to ensure that they would not be forced by want of food to give up their independence. For whether used to plant crops, graze herds, or supply timber, land was viewed as essential to any person seeking to survive in Carolina as a free person.

[58] An excellent discussion of the economy prior to the discovery of rice as a major source of income for Carolinians is Clowse, *Economic Beginnings*, chapters 2 and 3. The extent to which the early settlers turned to cattle grazing both to meet their needs for food and to provide a commodity for export, drove the proprietors to write the colony's leaders in May, 1674: "In your letters you have been frequent in the mention of a Stock of Cattle, but not having paid us for tools and clothes, how do you think that we should be at so far a greater charge in cattle? You say it will enable you to pay your Debts, but do you not think if wee bring cattle thither wee who doe not want ground can not keep them & Make the profit of our charge and venture as well as others especially it being our designe to have Planters there and not Graziers for if our Intentions were to stock Carolina att that Rate, we could doe better by Baylife and Servants of our own, who would be more observant of our orders than you have been. . . ." *Shaftsbury Papers*, pp. 437-38.

[59] They finally were altered May 19, 1679. See B.P.R.O.-S.C. *Vol. I*, pp. 82-4.

[60] July 27, 1669. *Shaftsbury Papers*, pp. 119-23.

with the headrights immigrants could claim. To those who arrived prior to March 1670,

> [A]ll free persons above the age of sixteene yeares [would receive] 150 Acres of land for themselves & 150 Acres more for every able man Servt they bring wth them or cause to be transported into the . . . Collony. And 100 Acres for every Woman Servt and Man Servt under 16 yeares of age. And 100 Acres to any Servt when out of their time. . . .

Those arriving after March 1671, would receive 100 acres:

> And 100 Acres more for each man Servt they bring . . . , and 70 Acres for each Woman Servt or Man Servt under sixteene yeares of age. And to every serv^{t} that shall arrive before ye time last menconed, seaventy acres to his or her proper use for them & their heirs forever.

Those reaching Carolina before March 1672, would receive "seaventy acres, and 70 Acres more for each man Servt. . . . And 60 acres for each woman Servt or child." Servants arriving before that date were to receive seventy acres "for ever when there time of servitude is expired."[61] While servants could not become rich by working the acres thus allotted them, they could survive as free persons. And for most of them, even a small parcel of property in a tiny settlement in the wilderness represented at least a chance, which was enough to lure them to South Carolina. But what factors worked to make masters support the institution of servitude and maintain their servants? Exactly what, in other words, did masters gain from their servants?

It is possible to outline, in a rough way, the hard economic benefit masters derived from their servants. As noted earlier, servants were a boon to the colony in a variety of ways, but it is important to consider what individual masters received from individual servants in more precise terms than merely noting that servants provided labor—an asset, to be sure, but not a wholly satisfactory form of description, especially since some data do exist which allow a more detailed approach.

Obviously—and surely prominent in the minds of settlers contemplating importing them—servants represented land. The problem is not how much land, for we know that at prescribed times certain kinds of servants netted a specific number of acres for their masters. The problem involves establishing a value for those acres. Attempting to formulate reliable land values by looking at land sales—what real settlers paid for actual properties—might yield the most desirable results. Unfortunately, as noted earlier, in any given year parcels of land which from our vantage

---

[61] *Ibid.*, p. 121.

point seem to have been identical (town lots, pasture land, wooded acreage, property fronting on navigable rivers) sold for widely varying prices. Only infrequently do documents that describe land sales, or even the actual sales contracts, reveal the extent and type of improvements, leaving us incapable of determining, for example, that one farm sold for a higher price than another of the same size because it contained a larger or sturdier house or barn. Land transactions were recorded in a standard format, which generally included only a traditional clause assuring the purchaser that he would receive title not only to the land but also to all improvements on it.[62]

Since reliable prices for land cannot be gleaned from records of private land sales, the best yardstick for measuring the real values of unimproved acreage is the price put on such land by the proprietors themselves. Unfortunately, their land distribution policies during the decade of the 1670's did not allow for direct purchase of land in the colony by the settlers. Instead, the proprietors relied on the system of headright concessions, and on direct grants as rewards for services to them

---

[62] The "standard" clause, repeated consistently in records of land conveyances with only minor variations, reads: " . . . with all and Singular the houses, Edifices, buildings, Gardens, Orchards backsides, feedings wayes passages watercourses woods and underwoods . . . and all and Singular other the profitts Comodities and appurtenances whatsoever. . . ." This from a land sale by Sam Boswood to Paul Grimball, May 29, 1682, in *Records of the Register and the Secretary 1675-1695, 1703-1709* (MSV), pp.175-6.

The wide variation in property prices can best be illustrated by a glance at several land sales. On February 11, 1699, John Chaplin sold 56.5 acres on Weipootew Creek for £12 sterling. *Records of the Register 1696-1703* (MSV), pp. 285-86. On August 10, 1678, John Hooper sold Dennis Mahone 140 acres for £4 sterling. One month later the buyer sold the same land for £6 sterling. *Ibid*.., pp. 122-23. On November 21, 1674, James Powell sold the rights to 70 acres (his headright) for £10 sterling. *Ibid*., p. 85. On May 22, 1677, Mathew Smallwood sold 15 acres on Wandow River for £7 (probably current money), but three years later purchased three "small islands all of them together conteyining eightie acres of land scittate upon . . . [the same] Wandoe River" for £22 (current money?). *Ibid*., pp. 48-9, 157-58. The impact of inflation on land values can be illustrated by looking at the prices paid for town lots in Charles Towne over time. In November 1684, Michael Lovell sold his town lot for £25. Misc. *Records 1682-1690* (MSV), pp. 170-71. In 1704 John Cattell paid £183 for only part of a similar lot. His son, John Jr., sold the same lot for £343 six years later. *Records of the Register 1709-1712* (MSV), pp. 161-69. Unfortunately, data which would permit us to assess the significance of such variables as the type of improvements on any given piece of property, much less its "quality," are not extant.

or the colony, to convey land from their hands into those of the colonists.[63] Not until the middle of the following decade did they devise a formula for selling land. When they did, they pegged the price at 12 pence per acre.[64] Later, under Governor John Archdale, who came to the colony in 1695, the price at which settlers could purchase land from the proprietors was set at £22 current money per 1000 acres.[65] Thus, depending on his or her year of arrival, age, and sex, a servant netted for his master land valued at about £5.[66]

If a master imported his servant from Barbados and made all the arrangements himself (as opposed to securing a servant from a ship's captain engaged in the sale of laborers for profit), the cost of transportation to Carolina was probably £2.[67] If the servant came to the colony from England, however, the cost of passage was more than double that charged for the trip from Barbados. A reasonable estimate of the fare, which varied according to the individual ship, the profit sought by the captain, and the quality of food and accommodations, would be about £5, or roughly equal to the value of land received in return for paying the charges involved in sailing from England to America.[68]

---

[63] Clowse, *Economic Beginnings*, p. 46; Robert K. Ackerman, "South Carolina Colonial Land Policies," Ph.D. dissertation, University of South Carolina, 1965, pp. 16-17, 34-39 (esp. pp. 36, 39).

[64] Proprietors to Joseph West . . . Governor," March 13, 1685, *B.P.R.O.-S.C. Vol. II*, p. 29.

[65] Cooper and McCord, eds., *Statutes*, Vol. II, pp. 96-104. It is also possible to estimate the value of the crops produced on land in the colony. In their letter to West, the proprietors asserted that "the produce of lesse then a quarter of an aker will pay the rent of 100 Akers." Since the rent commanded by them was one penny per acre, the produce of 100 acres would have yielded, by their estimate, 166 pounds. *B.P.R.O.-S.C. Vol. II*, p. 29.

[66] Here I have used 100 acres as the average acreage received by a master as a headright on servants, and the 1685 price of 12d., or one shilling per acre.

[67] See partnership of William Davis and William Brockus, January 3, 1680, in which passage for two servants is quoted as £2 for each (one a male and one a female servant). *Records of the Register and the Secretary 1675-1696, 1703-1709* (MSV), pp. 113-14.

[68] Smith, *Colonists in Bondage*, pp. 35-6; Galenson, *White Servitude*, pp. 230, 250.

But masters had to outfit their servants as well as pay the costs of transportation to the colony. Since individual preferences regarding the clothing one's servants needed could cause the actual costs involved to vary somewhat, only a general estimate is in order. Five pounds is the sum cited by Abbot E. Smith, an authoritative source on servitude in colonial America.[69] "Thus it would seem," Smith writes, "that the cost of procuring a servant, equipping him, and getting him [from England] to the colonies, was about ten or twelve pounds for the individual going to his own plantation. . . ."[70] However, if a Carolinian secured his servants from Barbados, the cost must have been only seven to nine pounds, all other factors being equal.

If the land acquired for bringing servants to the colony was worth roughly half of the costs incurred in the course of transporting and clothing them, what was the value of the labor they promised to perform? The most precise estimate comes from a record of a Council meeting during which a runaway case was heard. Six pounds eight shillings had been expended in the course of capturing the man, and part of the additional time he was required to serve as his punishment was specified to reimburse his master for that amount of money. Of the 21 extra months service demanded of him, 16 months equalled the six pounds eight shillings, which comes to eight shillings for every month's labor.[71] Using this value as a standard, a "typical" male servant's labor was worth £4, 16 s. a year, almost exactly the remaining half of an English servant's original cost to his master. Hence, a master could expect to break even if such a servant lived and worked for only one year; if his servant came from Barbados, the master could plan to profit from the situation well before then. Assuming that a servant's labor was, in fact, worth nearly £5 a year to his master, the potential for profit was obviously substantial.[72] And if the

---

[69] Smith, *Colonists in Bondage*, p. 36. Smith cites two sources, one writing in 1672 and one in 1689, who estimated outfitting costs at £5.

[70] *Ibid.*, p. 37.

[71] Case of John Ratcliffe. *Council Journal, 1671-1680*, pp. 22-23; see also footnote 52, *supra*.

[72] A number of estate inventories contain values of servants controlled by the deceased. I have used the Council's value rather than those gleaned from inventories since it is impossible to ascertain the "desireability" of servants so valued, or to assess the accuracy of the appraisers. In any case, the estate inventory of "John Smyth . . . Esqr. Decsd." contains one servant with 19 months to serve valued at £2, and two

servant were skilled, his labor would be even more valuable; however, the cost of acquiring his services surely would have been greater.[73]

---

servants with 19 months to serve valued at £8. *Records of the Secretary 1676-1695* (MSV), p. 21 (Feb. 13, 1683). The estate inventory of Richard Bancks values the "rights of servitude in foure servants"—a man and a woman "both sick: a certaine time on y^{m} yett unexpired" at £19; and "two young men servants" also with unspecified time still to serve, at £25. *Ibid.*, p. 85 (July 30, 1681). If the values attributed in the Smyth inventory reflect the actual value of servants to masters, a servant would have had to survive and work for from one-and-a-half to two years in order to cover his initial cost. Such values compare nicely with the estimates of net annual earnings offered by Galenson for servants in the eighteenth century. See Galenson, *White Servitude*, p. 108.

[73] In these computations I am assuming that those assigning values were stating the *net* value of the servant after the costs of his maintenance had been deducted. For surely it was taken for granted that a servant's worth must be the difference between his output and the costs his master incurred in feeding and clothing him.

CHAPTER FOUR

From Servitude to Freedom I: Servants and Survival in Carolina

I. Servant Disappearance: Desertion, Departure, Disease and Death

Of the 241 servants arriving in South Carolina before 1680, at least 102 appear in the records as free persons.[1] Thus, about 58% of those identified as servant-immigrants left no surviving record of their fates. It is therefore essential to bear in mind that analysis of servant mobility in early South Carolina is irrevocably biased at the outset *in favor of showing upward mobility*. That is, any former servant about whom data exist which can be considered in a discussion of mobility (for whom the required second date appears), by definition represents a greater degree of mobility merely through his or her documented *survival* than do well over half of the people in the total sample. Among the 147 male servants

[1] I have not counted people who appear for the first time as free persons more than seven years after their arrival in the colony, unless there is good reason to believe that the name identifies the same person who came as a servant. Probably some of those excluded were, in fact, former servants included among the 241 who entered the colony between 1670 and 1680, but it is equally likely that such references identify a different person with the same name. There is some chance of error even among the 102 I count (one male survived whose arrival date is unclear, thus the total of 102 rather than 101, the sum of numbers cited in the rest of this paragraph which specify survivals among males who arrived at various times), for frequently only one reference exists to establish a person's endurance. In such cases it is impossible to insure absolute accuracy. I am confident that any errors of this sort cancel one another, leaving a fairly accurate total. But as in other sections of this essay where numbers deriving from head counts are cited, at best I can be certain of providing a reliable *estimate*.

arriving prior to 1672, 60, or almost 41%, survived and stayed in the colony as free settlers. Of the 58 male servants who came after 1672, 30, or almost 52%, survived and became free settlers. Among all males, 90 of 205,[2] or nearly 44%, ultimately became free residents of the colony. For women the numbers are significantly lower than for men. Of the 35 female servants arriving prior to 1680, only 12, or a little more than 34%, survived and became free persons. Among females arriving before 1672, only seven of 23 reappear in the records as free, or a little over 30%. Of the 12 female servants entering the colony after 1672, five, or almost 42%, ultimately became free residents of South Carolina. Thus, women in each category, as well as overall, did not "survive" at as high a rate as did men. However, it is clear that for both men and women servants, if one arrived after 1672 his or her chances of enduring in the colony were greater than if he or she had immigrated during the first two years of settlement.

How can we explain this high disappearance rate—the failure of 58% of the servants to leave any record that they lived long enough to acquire the land due them, and to fulfill the larger society's expectations that servants, once free, would become full participants in the social, economic, and political life of the colony? If all they did was die off or depart the colony once free, or turn into restless, homeless, unruly, idle, dangerous men and women, then it would have made sense to cease bringing in servants, and instead to turn for labor to slaves who, if they could not some day become full partners in the society, at least promised to be controllable—and profitable. This suggests an intriguing possibility, but one, unfortunately, for which the evidence is scanty. Recent scholarship concludes that Carolinians turned rapidly to black slavery when they located a cash crop which would thrive in the soil and climate, and which slaves could produce profitably; when they accumulated sufficient capital to compete with alternative markets in Spanish America and the other British colonies for slaves; and when they were reasonably certain that the environment was sufficiently healthful that they would not see their costly slaves die off, before yielding some return to them (or, conversely, that it was so unhealthy *only* blacks could survive as laborers). There is no doubt that all these factors were telling in leading Carolinians away from servitude and toward slavery late in the seventeenth century. However, if servants, once freed, failed to take up land and become full partners in creating the society everyone wanted to erect, and instead either moved on

[2] Here I have eliminated the one male child who arrived as a servant with his parents.

to other colonies, or, worse, stayed in the province as unsettled, undependable, unruly, unpropertied people whose lack of commitment to stability and permanence threatened the peace and livelihood of everyone else, then it is reasonable to add one additional factor to those which commonly are fit together to fashion an explanation of why slavery emerged when it did in colonial South Carolina.

Each instance of servant disobedience, laziness, or crime contributed to the formulation of an image of servants in the minds of Carolinians which, when compared to that maintained of black slaves, must have made slaves seem more attractive as a way of meeting the colony's labor requirements. And Ashley probably represented not merely his own point of view, but that of many others when late in 1671 he instructed an agent to "forbeare to invite the poorer sort [of immigrants] yet a while, for wee finde our serves mightily mistaken in endeavouring to gett a great Number of poore People there it being substantiall men and Theire Familyes, that must make the Plantation which will stock the country with Negroes, Cattle, and other Necessarys, whereas others relye and eate upon us." Surely, if the proprietors were becoming increasingly distressed by the growing number of "poore People," sensed the need only for "substantiall men," and, moreover, specifically called (in 1671) for Negroes, the prospect of a further increase in the ranks of poor whites (newly-freed servants would occupy social and economic positions near the bottom) did not generate enthusiasm. Even less attractive, then, would be the notion of continuing to meet the need for labor through immigration of servants, much less increasing it. An obvious and available way to obtain labor, yet forestall the growth of the group Ashley labelled the "poorer sort," was to replace servants with slaves.[3]

[3] This suggestion is the same as that formulated by Edmund S. Morgan in his discussion of the emergence of Negro slavery in Virginia. See his *American Slavery, American Freedom: The Ordeal of Colonial Virginia*, (New York, 1975). For concerns expressed by Carolinians about servants as potential thieves, see *Shaftsbury Papers*, p. 358; as "bad," see *ibid*, p. 387. Ashley's remarks are in "Ashley to Capt. Halsted," Dec. 16, 1671. *Ibid*, p. 364. As late as November 1695, colonial officials noted the inability of freed servants to become full participants in the society. Governor Archdale received a petition from the Commons House which noted that even though the price of land had been lowered, the people's needs and the proprietors' expectations were not thereby fulfilled, "ffor their are a considerable number of planters, Servants that Dayley become free . . . that are not able to purchase Lands and the Rich Onely are capable . . ." of doing so. *South Carolina Commons House Journal, Nov. 20, 1695-Nov. 28, 1695*, p. 7. This volume is part of the series of Alexander S. Salley, ed., *Journals of the Commons House of Assembly, 1692-1735*, 21 vols. (Columbia, 1907-1946).

Studies of status mobility and property accumulation among those arriving as servants in early Maryland[4] point out that more than 40% of that group failed to reappear as free persons. Speculating on the fate of these servants, one author notes that "some may have been sold out of the province before their terms were completed, and some may have run away, while others may have left . . . immediately after becoming freemen. A majority probably died while still servants. . . ." However, the author is optimistic about those who did leave the colony without acquiring land, pointing out that "there is no reason to believe that those who left were any less successful than those who remained."[5]

Among South Carolina's first servants, it is not possible to determine with precision what percentage of those who failed to appear in the records as free persons left the colony, what percentage died, what percentage ran away, or what percentage remained in the colony but neglected to do anything that would have necessitated having their names recorded in sources which have survived. It is possible, however, to suggest possibilities, and to derive a rough estimate based on contemporary accounts.

It is not likely that very many servants ran away without having their flight recorded—runaway cases were rather fully described in the public record, and trials before the Council of captured runaways do exist. There is no reason to believe that some cases would be reported and others fail to receive notice. Nor is there substantial reason to believe that those who departed the colony once they had gained their freedom enjoyed levels of "success" elsewhere equivalent to, much less greater than their fellow former servants who remained in South Carolina. For it is very difficult, after considering the various reasons which might have motivated freed servants to leave the colony, to conclude that many did so with serious expectations of achieving more than they would have had they stayed. In Carolina they had friends, knowledge of what pursuits would prove

---

[4] Russell R. Menard, "From Servant to Freeholder: Status, Mobility and Property Accumulation in Seventeenth-Century Maryland," *William & Mary Quarterly*, Third Series, XXX (January, 1973), 37-64. Lorena S. Walsh, "Servitude and Opportunity in Charles County, Maryland, 1658-1705," in Aubrey C. Land, Lois Green Carr, and Edward C. Papenfuse, eds., *Law, Society, and Politics in Early Maryland* (Baltimore, 1977), p. 115, suggests that "two-thirds or more of the servants who entered Charles County" disappeared.

[5] *Menard, "From Servant to Freeholder," p. 40.*

profitable, and the right to acquire land. Even if they sold that right,[6] they were not likely to have much capital left over to start out somewhere else once they had expended the amount required to travel to their destination and maintain themselves while in transit. Nor could the amount they received for selling their rights to land have netted enough to buy a much larger parcel elsewhere, or to finance some business enterprise. Since virtually all types of skilled tradesmen were in great demand in South Carolina during the early years of settlement, it is not likely that any such recently freed servant, even if poorly informed, would believe his or her opportunities were greater in a different colony. All this is not to say that no freed servants actually departed the colony and subsequently achieved levels of upward mobility equal to or greater than those attained by former servants who remained. It is to say that reason, simple inertia, the geographical isolation of the colony, and uncertainty about starting fresh on unfamiliar terrain all worked to prevent such emigration.

There is, on the other hand, one bit of evidence which indicates that in spite of such considerations, freed servants may in fact have chosen to leave South Carolina. The evidence relates directly to survival rates for servants arriving before and after 1672. Of the 170 adult servants arriving prior to 1672, only 67, or slightly over 39%, stayed to reappear in the records. Of the 70 adult servants who came after 1672, 35, or 50%, endured to become free settlers. By 1672, after more than two years of settlement in the colony, much more was known about what Carolina actually was, and what it would likely become in the future, than was known about either before that date. Thus, there was far greater potential for serious disappointment with the place itself and the kinds of people who chose to live there among those who arrived earliest than for those who came after 1672. Men and women who immigrated at the outset were, therefore, far more predisposed to leave once freed, no matter what their prospects elsewhere, than were those who came after many of the questions everyone had about the nature of the colony had been resolved. Servants choosing to immigrate after 1672 arrived better informed than those coming earlier, since the earliest servants, along with everyone else who came at the very outset, could have had only hopes about possibilities—at the start there simply was no reality to examine prior to reaching a decision about immigration. At least part of the difference in survival rates between those

---

[6] See *Records of the Register and the Secretary, 1675-1696, 1703-1709* (MSV), p. 85, for an example of a sale of the right to acquire property, as opposed to the property itself. This former servant, James Powell, remained in the colony.

servants coming to the colony at earlier versus later dates may well be due to a higher rate of departures based on disenchantment with what they encountered in the colony among those who arrived prior to 1672.

Another possible course of action for newly-freed servants was to sell the rights to the land due them prior to taking possession of it. The only examples of this in the records come from persons who chose to remain in the colony, and either went to work for wages or practiced a trade which required some skill. Thus, James Powell, "Taylor," noted in November 1674, that by virtue of his arrival in South Carolina as a servant he was entitled to claim 70 acres, but that he had sold his rights to the property to John Barton for £10 sterling.[7] It is likely that some former servants did sell their land rights and then quit the colony. Or they may have chosen to remain as laborers, yet not find their way into the colony's official documents, thereby becoming part of the large group of whom we know nothing more than that they were servants in the colony.

Other former servants, entitled by the proprietors' concessions to acquire land, apparently never did so. The most sensible explanation is that they sold their rights to such property. Thus, Edward Dale never claimed his headright, even though he was referred to as a "planter" in 1677 when he purchased 40 acres.[8] Michael Lovell never took the warrant for land due him for arriving as a servant. He did, however, have a trade (being labelled a "sawyer" in 1672, and consistently thereafter) which he presumably preferred to planting crops or raising cattle.[9] John Dawson never claimed his land concession by taking out a warrant. But he, too, had a trade, appearing as a "turner" to whom was owed 16 s. for work he performed on the ship *Blessing*.[10] Nor did Otho Christopher secure a warrant for the land due him. Instead he became a carpenter once free of his obligation to serve a master.[11] And two former servants, rather than working the land to which they were entitled, chose to go to sea, signing

[7] *Ibid.*, p. 85. Powell later did acquire land, jointly with Barton, which he held at least until 1684. *Ibid.*, pp. 82-83; Misc. *Records 1682-1690* (MSV), p. 123; *Proprietary Grants No. l, Vol. 38* (MSV), pp. 12-13.

[8] *Records of the Register and the Secretary 1675-1696, 1703-1709* (MSV), p. 59.

[9] *Ibid.*, p. 174 (1681); Misc. *Records 1682-1690* (MSV), pp. 170-71 (1684); *Shaftsbury Papers*, pp. 394-95 (1672).

[10] *Ibid.*, p. 329.

[11] *Records of the Secretary 1675-1695* (MSV), p. 101.

contracts as mariners for fixed wages.[12] Although such examples are few, they do establish that former servants did engage in pursuits, once free, which did not involve using the land they could have acquired. While only one actual sale of rights to land by a former servant can be documented, doubtless men such as Dale or Lovell did *in fact* do so, but either failed to record the sale or recorded it in documents which have been lost. Surely other former servants similarly sold their rights to land and moved on without leaving a trace of their fates. But there is insufficient evidence even to allow us to venture a guess at the frequency with which such sale-departures occurred. Conversely, it is quite possible that such persons remained in South Carolina fulfilling a variety of roles (a few may even have enjoyed real success) but failing to take any specific action that would have been recorded. If they did, probably they became un- or semi-skilled laborers if males, or wives if females.

Since no church records exist from the earliest period of South Carolina history, there is no comprehensive account of marriages in the colony. This may well explain why such a high percentage of women servants do not appear later as free persons. Only if they secured a warrant for land and subsequently married, or if their new husband claimed a warrant based on their arrival rights, or if in the course of some later business transaction (such as a land sale) their pre-marital identity was revealed, can we ascertain their servant origin in the colony.[13] Because there was an overwhelming shortage of "eligible" women in Carolina, the prospects for rapid upward mobility for such females through marriage to an established settler were great. It is therefore unlikely that very many freed women servants believed that their opportunities would be greater in some other location. This is especially true since during these years, South Carolina, as one of the newest and the most immature settlements, presented perhaps the most strikingly imbalanced population in English

---

[12] Samuel Morris and John Reese. *Records of the Secretary and the Register 1671-1675*, pp. 53-4; *Records of the Secretary 1692-1700* (MSV), p. 274.

[13] This can be tricky, as shown earlier in my discussion of the identity of Miliscent How–Miliscent Jackson. The Christian name was the same, but the basis for my conclusion that the surnames identify the same person was the fact that in a land sale Miliscent Jackson made her mark in the form of the letter "H"—hence How. Frequently I have been tempted, when locating free married females with Christian names identical to those of some "missing" servants, to decide that I had discovered the likely fate of that servant. In each case, however, I have been unable to establish that such was, in fact, the case. It is *probable* that a very high percentage of "missing" female servants did marry and simultaneously disappear from our view.

America. But by seizing the opportunities for marriage which the colony offered, female servants simultaneously altered their one feature which allows us to identify them—their surnames. Thus, the most thorough analysis possible can at best merely result in a statement of what *probably* happened to them. In terms of the discussion here, such female servants must remain among the huge group who simply disappeared.

There was, to be sure, one other fate which might befall servants and cause their failure to reappear in the records as free persons—death. Exactly the same factor which prohibits scholars from analyzing marriages—the absence of vital records commonly preserved by churches—prevents a definitive appraisal of mortality in seventeenth century South Carolina. We can, however, engage in informed speculation as to the probability of death as the reason for disappearance among those who began in the colony as servants.

During the first decade of settlement South Carolina never acquired the kind of reputation attached to Virginia in its first years—no one seems to have considered the colony a death trap. In fact, even admitting that many early reports from the colony were written by persons with a vested interest in attracting new settlers, and therefore were likely to describe the place in as glowing terms as possible, the data we have on the climate and general healthfulness of the colony at the outset of settlement (the years during which the men and women considered here arrived and completed their terms of service) are generally very positive. Good reports in accounts intended for public dissemination obviously must be considered in that light; however, private reports to the proprietors are somewhat more reliable, or at least less likely to be blatantly misleading.[14]

Among the earliest descriptions of the area which would later be colonized derive from the voyage Captain Hilton completed in August, 1663. He reported that "the land we suppose is healthful; for the *English* that were cast away on that Coast in *July* last, were there most part of that time of year that is sickly in *Virginia;* and notwithstanding hard usage, and lying on the ground naked, yet had their perfects healths all the time. The

[14] Even those reporting to the proprietors had an interest in making the colony appear as healthy as possible, of course, since if the proprietors lost confidence that settlement could take place and their colony prosper, they might well be deterred from providing the funds and the supplies needed to preserve what had already been developed. Every settler had an interest in attracting new colonists because new arrivals purchased goods from those already residing in the colony, and increased the demand for land which thereby raised the value of property already dispensed.

Natives are very healthful; we saw many very Aged amongst them. The Ayr is clear and sweet, the Countrey very pleasant and delightful."[15] The first settlers were nearly as impressed by Carolina as Hilton had been. Three reports soon after the first fleet reached the colony agree that settlers might look forward to good health there. In September, 1670, the Council informed the proprietors that "blessed be God we haue not lost aboue foure of our people who dyed vpon distempers usual in other parts, soe far may be yor Honors be further convinced of the healthfulnesse of the place."[16] Three days later Stephen Bull wrote Ashley that the colony surely "will come to Matury wee conceive this to be as healthfull A place as ever was settled wee have lost butt fower p'souns since wee satt downe heere & those was sickly p'souns & in A declininge condicion of health before wee landed. . . ." But Bull went on to note that "there is some p'souns that have had the feaver and Ague butt we observe little mortality in the distemper neither is the distemper neere soe high as is vsuall in other Places. . . ."[17] Two days after Bull wrote, William Owen informed Ashley that once the current season passed, during which "the Countrey is close, pertaking of all ye damps, vapours, and exhalacons," the health of the settlers would be even better than it had been. Owen also noted that the prospects for Englishmen coming directly to Carolina without prior "seasoning" in the colonies were excellent, for, he said, of the four whose deaths had been reported, "there dyed but one person of all them that cam out of Engld and he of a Lingring and a Consumption distemper."[18] Early in November a report proclaimed that all the Barbadians who "departed aboute 12 months paste . . . for the settling of [Carolina] . . . are in very good health, . . ."[19] which was confirmed in a letter to the proprietors from Barbados two weeks later.[20]

In March, 1671, West asserted that although "we have been something weak handed and our men have been sickly and weak," the illnesses were not serious, for "wee have not had one Dyed out of our

---

15 *Shaftsbury Papers*, p. 24.

16 Sept. 9, 1670. *Ibid.*, p. 180.

17 Sept. 12, 1670. *Ibid.*, p. 193.

18 Sept. 15, 1670. *Ibid.*, p. 197.

19 "Barbados Proclamation," Nov. 4, 1670. *Ibid.*, p. 210.

20 "Sir John Yeamans to Proprietors," Nov. 15, 1670. *Ibid.*, pp. 218, 221.

Family sinc^{e} wee came into ye countrey; wch I looke vpon as a great mercy from God. . . ."[21] Later that month the Governor of Bermuda wrote the proprietors and expressed delight at the reports he had received "of the health of the People."[22] West's second letter of the month, this to Ashley, repeated his earlier assertion that only one had died in his family, or company, and went on to note that "Our Servants haue bene sickly as well as others but now they are . . . healthfull." But even so, he requested that a doctor, "and a chest of good medcines" be sent to the colony, because, he stressed, "those few people y^{t} haue dyed amongst us, I believe most part for want of good looking after...."[23] About the same time, an anonymous correspondent noted not only that the colony was healthful, but also that "not one Master of a ffamily since ye Settlem^{t} hath died here excepting o^{r} good Aged Gouerno^{r} . . . who was at least 80 years of age—not one man now in ye Collony there being about 200 . . . is at all distempered wth any sickness."[24] In late summer Locke noted that while Carolina "begets a good Stomach, . . . the new comers [were] all sick of the bloudy flux" from eating unripened corn.[25] A year later Locke again mentioned that all in the colony were "in health,"[26] and in May, 1673, he received word that the settlers "sing the same song they did from the beginning, a very healthy, a very pleasant & fertill country, but great want of victuall, cloathes & tools. . . ."[27]

Thus, reports dating from the very first years of settlement, when servant immigration was greatest, testify that though settlers did fall ill,[28]

---

21 "West to Sir Peter Colleton," March 2, 1671. *Ibid.*, p. 272.

22 "Sir John Hayden to Proprietors," March 17, 1671. *Ibid.*, p. 280.

23 "West to Ashley," March 21, 1671. *Ibid.*, p. 299.

24 "An Old Letter," probably 1671. *Ibid.*, p. 309.

25 "Carolina Memoranda," 1671. *Ibid.*, pp. 348, 350.

26 "Carolina Memoranda," March, 1672. *Ibid.*, p. 386.

27 "Sir Peter Colleton to Locke," May 28, 1673. *Ibid.*, p. 423.

28 In May, 1682, Thomas Newe wrote his father in England from Carolina. Although he confessed that, as a recent immigrant to the colony, he was not yet thoroughly familiar with the place, "one thing I understand (to my sorrow) that I knew not before [which is that among new settlers], the most have a seasoning [period during which they succumb to illness], but few dye of it." New apparently did not adjust to the

they also recovered, that most did not fall ill, and that the colony could quite legitimately be labelled a healthy place. Later, of course, we know either that the level of healthfulness declined drastically, or that observers began suddenly to produce accurate reports of a situation which had existed previously.

In any case, it is abundantly clear that by the middle of the second decade of settlement, South Carolina was rapidly acquiring a reputation for being anything but healthful, and that well before 1700 the lack of good health among the colony's inhabitants not only worked to deter immigrants from coming, but also seems to have influenced some settlers to depart for new and presumably more benign environments. The first outbreak of malaria sufficiently widespread to be labelled an epidemic occurred in 1684. In 1697-98 smallpox reached epidemic proportions; a year later and again the following year yellow fever took a terrible toll among the settlers. In January, 1700, the council wrote the proprietors that "a most infectious, pestilentiall & mortall distemper" had killed more than 160 persons in Charles Town in only two months.[29]

A promotional tract, probably written by Thomas Ashe in 1682, while acknowledging that Carolina's settlers during the torrid months of July and August "have sometimes Touches of Agues and Fevers," stressed that they were "not violent, of short continuance, and never Fatal. English children there born," he went on, are commonly "strong and lusty, of sound Constitutions, and fresh ruddy Complexions." The following year, John Crafford's " . . . New and most exact account of . . . Carolina . . ." stressed that "Portryal is the choyest place in Carolina" and not only displayed "very rich soyl, and good clymate" but also that it was "a most healthy Country."[30] Ashe's and Crafford's glowing reports, along with others intended to attract settlers, may have been a response to a general decline in the esteem in which the proprietors' colony was coming to be

---

environment as well as "the most," for he died before he had been in the colony a full year. Alexander S. Salley, ed., *Narratives of Early Carolina* (New York, 1967), p. 183.

[29] Joseph Ioor Waring, *A History of Medicine in South Carolina, 1670-1825* (Columbia, 1963), p. 371. Elder William Pratt wrote in his journal in 1698, "A letel after [January] . . . ther was many dyed with the smal pox that distemper groing mor mortal then before." Salley, *Narratives*, pp. 199-200.

[30] Thomas Ashe, "Carolina, Or a Description of the Present State of that Country," in Salley, ed., *Narratives*, p. 141. John Crafford, *A New and Most Exact Account of the Fertiles and Famous Colony of Carolina (On the Continent of America)* (Dublin, 1683), p. 7.

held. Already in 1679 they had commented on the apparently widespread unfavorable accounts of Carolina being circulated by former settlers whose disenchantment with the colony had led to their departure,[31] but related emigration solely to economic failure, and in any case ignored the possibility that those who had failed in the colony and carried back to Europe or to other parts of America negative tales about life there, might simply have been too sick to perform the labor required to sustain themselves. Yet the same year Ashe's pamphlet appeared, the proprietors displayed acute awareness of the potential health hazards in their colony. Their "Instructions for granting of Land in Carolina," dated November 21, 1682, pointedly stressed that in choosing sites for the port towns of two new counties, the locations should be "farr from Marshe swamps or standing Waters,"[32] which even in the late seventeenth century were recognized as areas to avoid if one wished to retain his health. In fact, experience in Charles Town, situated in precisely such an environment, dictated the stricture against choosing similar locations for new centers of population.

By the summer of 1684 even those with the deepest desire to visualize the colony in as positive a manner as possible could not escape the fact that settlers were dying in Carolina. In June the proprietors wrote that "Wee are by all people Informed y^{t} it hath no good Water in it and all people that come to the province and Landing there & the most falling sick it brings a Disreputation upon the whole Country. . . ."[33] The following spring they told the governor and their deputies that "Wee are very sorry for ye great Sickness you have been troubled wth wch wee Impute chiefly to the unhealthy Scituation of Charles towne." Indeed, by 1684 the town had acquired a one-word description, "Sickly," which everyone, from the colony's most ardent promoters to its most severe detractors, agreed aptly described the place. Apparently even those who

---

31 "Proprietors to Governor and Council," May 19, 1679. *B.P.R.O.-S.C., Vol. I*, pp. 83-84. The proprietors noted that those who, due to their own idleness or foolishness, "findeing themselves disabled to plant quitt the place and to excuse their owne Ill husbandry lye the blame on the Countrey and the nature of the Soyle to the Discouragement of others. . . ."

32 William J. Rivers, *A Sketch of the History of South Carolina to the Close of the Proprietary Government by the Revolution of 1719 with An Appendix Containing many Valuable Records hitherto unpublished* (Charleston, 1856), pp. 399-400.

33 *B.P.R.O. - S.C. Vol. I*, p. 293. The proprietors suggested that a new location be chosen for a port town for the colony further up the Cooper River.

did not live in the town were falling ill, for the proprietors suggested that the epidemic's spread may have been caused by "bringing downe the people of the Country to keep guards there in the unhealthy months." Reiterating a plea heard often during these years, the proprietors urged that a new site be located for the chief urban center of their province, and directed that the Council and "all other Courts . . . from ye 10th of June to ye 10th of October" be adjourned so "that men might not be Compelled to come in ye sickly months into that unhealthy place where there is no good water."[34]

In 1686, a ship carrying immigrants to Carolina lost its passengers to a vessel bound for Maryland when they learned from one of the crew that in Charles Town during the previous summer "half the town had deserted or died." The sailor related his account only after the future settlers heard from the master of the Maryland-bound vessel "that two years ago he had carried to Carolina . . . thirty-two persons from Plymouth, all very vigorous, that he went back there eleven months later and that he did not find but two alive. . . ." As if that were not a sufficient deterrent to settling there, he continued "that there was not an acre of good land in all the south of Carolina."[35] A year later a resident of Boston recorded a report of Carolina provided by two former residents. "In the first place they say that they have never seen so miserable a country nor an air so unhealthful. They have fevers all year long from which those attacked seldom recover. . . . Moreover, the heat there is so intense that it is almost unbearable, and this infects the water, and in consequence diseases are caused, there being no other drink there. They also bring tidings that, before their departure, a vessel came from London with 130 persons . . . of whom 115 are dead, all from malignant fevers which spread among them."[36]

The drastic decline in the healthfulness of Carolina continued well into the eighteenth century. In 1706 yellow fever struck the inhabitants; in 1709 influenza and malaria broke out; in 1711 they reappeared, but were

---

34 "Proprietors to Governor and Deputies," March 13, 1685. *B.P.R.P.-S.C. Vol. II*, pp. 35-36.

35 Quoted in Childs, *Malaria*, pp. 244-45.

36 *Ibid.*, p. 249. Childs cautions that "rumor commonly magnifies the violence of epidemics" and that such reports "doubtless exaggerated the death rate . . . and the number fleeing from the pestilence, but there is no reason to doubt that malaria was prevalent. . . ." (pp. 250-51).

joined by the even more deadly smallpox and yellow fever; in 1712 influenza again struck; in 1715 dysentery afflicted the settlers; in 1717 influenza made yet another appearance; in 1718 smallpox and yellow fever took a heavy toll.[37] While such diseases struck especially hard at recently-arrived white settlers, even "seasoned" whites suffered tremendously. It may well be that among the forces which motivated Carolinians to turn to black slave labor and away from the continued importation of white indentured servants, susceptibility to the diseases so prevalent in the colony was crucial. Astute observers recognized that blacks were able to continue to work hard in a climate which generated fevers sufficiently virulent to paralyze white workers, if they survived at all.[38] Needless to say, the discovery of rice as a cash crop which could be successfully cultivated and which was likely to yield high returns to its producers, also played a central role in the transformation of Carolina's population from mostly white to mostly black, but blacks were chosen to produce rice specifically because they endured the rigors of the required labor, as well as the environment's inflictions, far more successfully than did whites.[39] The standard source on agriculture in the southern colonies asserts that "the prevailing belief in the colonial period [was] that white men could not endure the conditions of labor required by the [rice] industry—the necessity of working continually in the hot, pestilential swamps, the laborious processes of clearing land, digging and cleaning ditches, preparing and cultivating land entirely by hand labor, and harvesting, threshing, and pounding [the crop]."[40]

If the prevalence of disease in Carolina played a central role in lowering the number of white servants imported into the colony, did it similarly reduce the number of servants who survived to claim land and begin life as free persons? The data we have confirm that some servants

---

[37] Waring, *History*, p. 371.

[38] Among the best sources for the continued afflictions suffered by eighteenth century Carolinians are the letters and journals of the clergymen sent to the colony by the Society for the Propogation of the Gospel in Foreign Parts. See, e.g., Frank Klingberg, ed., *The Carolina Chronicle of Dr. Francis LeJau, 1706-1717* (Berkeley, 1956); and *Carolina Chronicle: The Papers of Commissary Gideon Johnson, 1707-1716* (Berkeley, 1946).

[39] Wood, *Black Majority*, pp. 80, 83-84, 90-91.

[40] Lewis C. Gray, *History of Agriculture in the Southern United States to 1860*, Vol. I (Gloucester, MA, 1958), p. 283.

did die prior to achieving freedom. But during the first decade of settlement, when a vast majority of the white servant population arrived, the colony seems to have been relatively free of catastrophic epidemics. Doubtless, many former servants were struck down by diseases which appeared after they had become free. But it is not possible to argue that the disappearance of 58% of those who arrived as servants before 1680 can be explained by the prevalence of fatal diseases in the colony. Such did appear in Carolina, but the first recorded epidemics date from the middle of the 1680's, well *after* virtually all of those in the servant sample would have been eligible to claim their land concessions and thereby appear in the provincial records as free men and women.

In January 1672, Joseph Dalton reported to the proprietors that 337 men, 71 women, and 62 children (under age 16) had immigrated to the colony. Of these, he said, 43 men, two women, and three children had died; an overall death rate of slightly over 10%.[41] Among adults, the death rate, presumably due to diseases contracted in Carolina, was 11%. Men, however, had died at a rate of nearly 13%; while women had died at a rate of only a little less than 3%.

There is no reason to believe that the death rate increased very much before the onset of epidemics near the end of the century.[42] Hence, even if settlers continued to die off at the same rate they had during the first two years of settlement, when, presumably, no one was "seasoned" and everyone in the colony was as susceptible as he or she ever would be to the diseases engendered by confronting the Carolina environment, one can assume that of the 115 male servants who failed to reappear as free men, the disappearance of about 47 can be attributed to death.[43] Of the 23

---

[41] *Shaftsbury papers*, pp. 381-82.

[42] The smallpox epidemic of 1697-98 alone killed between two and three hundred settlers, out of a white population of less than 2500. See Clowse, *Economic Beginnings*, p. 105.

[43] I have made this estimate by assuming that the death rate of about 13% of the male population every two years held constant over time. Thus, 6.5% died each year. The "typical" male servant spent about four years in servitude before appearing in the records as a free person. For the purpose of making this calculation I have simply grouped all 205 male servants into one body, and treated them as all arriving together with terms to serve of four years. After one year 6.5% of them, or 13, would presumably have died, leaving 192 male servants with three years each to serve. After another year 6.5% of these 192 servants, or 12, would have died, leaving 180 alive each of whom had two years left to serve. A year later 6.5% of these men would be dead,

females on whom no data other than that they came as servants exist, the numbers we have suggest that only two may have died.[44]

It is impossible to estimate whether the bias in favor of higher mortality rates displayed in the percentages employed here (based on deaths among a totally "unseasoned" sample[45]) is offset by the likelihood that some of those persons who were alive when Dalton submitted his figures soon thereafter succumbed to illness, or that his data were incorrect (either unintentionally, or because he wanted to make Carolina appear as attractive as possible). The most striking aspect of all this is the clear implication that the huge disappearance rate among female servants probably was not due to death prior to the end of their terms of service. This bolsters the thesis that so few female servants appear later as free women precisely because they had married, altered their names, and thereby eliminated the possibility of identifying them as former servants. Needless to say, if their lives were shorter than those of men because they died at childbirth, and their chances of appearing at a later date in the provincial records thereby lessened when compared with those of males, that would surely indicate that they had survived to become free (and marry). In any case, for both men and women, death cannot be taken as the primary reason for the disappearance of well over half of the servants arriving prior to 1680. The best evidence we have is that 68 of the 115 male, and 21 of the 23 female servants about whose fates we know nothing, disappeared not because of death, but rather, because they either departed the colony or, more likely, because they stayed and failed to perform any action which was recorded in records which have survived. It is essential to recall that, especially among male servants, resistance to disease was probably lower than among the free male population because they must have worked longer and harder at more onerous tasks than did their masters and other free men. Nevertheless, testimony from

---

leaving 169 alive, each with one year to serve. When 6.5% of these men had died, 158 newly freed former servants would be left. Therefore, a total of 47 would have died if 6.5% of the male population passed away each year.

[44] I have employed a similar procedure here, assuming that 1.5% of the 35 female servants died each year.

[45] This, of course, would maximize the overall mortality rate. However, *all* servant immigrants arrived "unseasoned" to the Carolina environment, and hence, these death rates would tend to apply to them with greater precision than they would to a sample which included settlers who had resided in the colony for various lengths of time.

contemporaries as to the level of health experienced by Carolina's first settlers, as well as estimates of mortality rates based on Dalton's report, strongly suggest that at least a majority of male servants, and a far larger percentage of female servants, did survive long enough in the colony to fulfill their terms of servitude.[46]

II. Servant Survival: Terms of Service and Life Expectancy

If a person arrived as a servant in South Carolina during the first decade of settlement, it seems reasonable to conclude that his or her chances of surviving at least long enough to achieve freedom were relatively great. Two central questions, however, must be resolved if the implications in that assertion are to be understood fully. First, exactly how long did male and female servants in the colony actually serve; and second, how long did they live? For merely to survive the contracted period of servitude would hardly be a satisfactory reward for immigration. Nor would such a pattern serve to induce others to come. However, if many former servants were able to survive long enough after achieving freedom to establish themselves as independent settlers, and if even a few were able to succeed notably—to acquire greater wealth than most Carolinians no matter what their origins had been—then the promise of Carolina could with justification be said to have been realized. Then the contracts servants entered into would have been fulfilled to the satisfaction of all parties. For implicit in such agreements was an understanding that white servants would receive in return for their labor and loyalty not only food, clothing, lodging, and a bit of land; but in addition that, with their freedom they would have both the time and the opportunity to exercise their skills and their energies on their own behalf in an environment in which their efforts would in all probability yield security, contentment, and continued independence.

---

[46] It is instructive to note, when considering mortality rates in early Carolina, that Thomas Nairne's ". . . Letter from South Carolina . . .," written in 1710, in outlining for prospective Swiss settlers what they ought to expect to encounter in the colony, proposes (based on his experience) that Europeans, in predicting what their fates will be, should "suppose of themselves to be diminished by Death ten in an hundred." Thomas Nairne, "A Letter from South Carolina . . ." (second edition), London, 1718, p. 53.

Formal indentures specified terms of service generally between two and seven years in duration. The government ultimately set seven years as a maximum term for those servants arriving without contracts. A clearer sense of how long servants typically remained unfree results from analysis of the length of time required for servants to appear as free persons—to establish themselves on the land promised to all immigrants by the proprietors, to sell or trade that land for the capital or tools necessary to become self-sufficient by practicing some trade, or in the case of women, to marry.[47]

Of the servants about whom data exist which allow us to establish that they did survive to become free settlers, 84 appear to have served from more than one to less than seven years. Doubtless, nearly all of the others served a period which fell between these limits, but for them the evidence is not sufficiently explicit to allow an accurate determination to be made.[48] Of these, 84 servants, 27, or 32%, lived in Carolina from one to two years before appearing as free persons. Thirty-eight, or 45%, required from three to five years to do so. The remaining 19, or 23%, needed between six and seven years to complete their terms and establish themselves as free settlers with land, a trade, or a husband. The average time span between arrival and definitive freedom for all these people was a little longer than three and one-half years.

These 84 servants, like the total servant population, were mostly males. Seventy-two, in fact, were men; and their average length of service works out to have been nearly 3.6 years. The 12 females averaged more than 4.3 years of servitude prior to establishing themselves as free persons in the colony. The difference makes sense, for if, as the data on sex ratios for the entire group make clear, male servants were, given the economic immaturity of the colony, far more highly valued than were female servants, it seems reasonable that in order to attract as many male servants as possible, their terms would have been somewhat shorter in duration

---

[47] Since very few actual contracts between masters and servants have survived, any effort to gauge the time between starting as a servant and becoming a free person based on such indentures might yield results which fail to reflect the reality servants experienced. Here I have chosen to base my discussion on the time between arrival in Carolina as a servant and first appearance in the records as a free person. I have discarded all those whose terms of service measured in this manner were less than one year or greater than seven years.

[48] Here, again, I have excluded the one child who came as a servant along with his parents. They served two years, as surely he did.

than would be those required of "less desirable" women. More intriguing are the data on differences between average terms of service in different time periods. For both males and females, it is clear that time spent in servitude was significantly shorter for those immigrating during the first two years of settlement than for those who came between 1672 and 1680. The 51 male servants arriving prior to 1672, for whom we can gauge the length of their terms, averaged 3.47 years between arrival and freedom. The 21 who arrived between 1672 and the end of the decade display periods of service which averaged 3.8 years. The six females arriving prior to 1672 served an average of 4.2 years; those coming later spent an average of 4.5 years in servitude. Overall, considering males and females together, servants entering Carolina between 1670 and 1672 retained that status an average of 3.54 years. Those who came between 1672 and 1680 remained servants an average of 3.96 years.[49] The most logical explanation for the increase in the length of terms of service over time is that at the very outset of colonization, when land concessions based on the headright system were most generous; and when the labor requirements of clearing land, erecting edifices, and planting crops were greatest; servants, and especially male servants, were tremendously valuable to actual or potential colonists. To many it must have seemed perfectly reasonable to require at the outset of settlement a shorter period of work from a servant than would be demanded in later years, in order to induce him (or her) to go to Carolina. A policy of shorter terms for servants coming in the first years made sense not only because they netted their master larger amounts of land and

[49] My research thus contradicts the assertion of Peter Wood and others that competition for servants among various colonies as well as individual colonists worked to decrease terms of service over time. See Wood, *Black Majority*, pp. 40-41, in which Wood cites Harlow's *History of Barbados* to show that "the usual term in Barbados dropped from 5-7 years before the Restoration to 3-5 years after, with bargains for as little as one year's labor being struck in certain instances. Carolina contracts diminished similarly. . . ." Wood's assertion may be accurate for some later date, but it does not reflect the situation in Carolina during the first decade of settlement. Later, perhaps to attract additional whites as the black population multiplied radically, terms for short periods may have become increasingly popular, but Wood does not pursue this line of argument. In fact, when the government set statutory limitations on terms of servitude for those arriving without contracts, the periods of service specified were not noticeably shorter than those I have encountered during the 1670-1680 period. Thus, the 1687 statute pegged terms for those under ten at eleven years (until they reached 21 years of age); for those between 10 and 15 at seven years; and for those older than 15 at five years. See "An Act for servants . . . arriving without indentures . . ." Cooper & McCord, eds., Statutes, Vol. II, p. 30.

might have to work harder than servants who arrived later, but also because, since no one knew very much about the place the whole proposition promised to be pretty risky. Especially those with much capital to invest must have been eager to secure as many servants as possible, no matter how short a term of service they received in return for covering expenses. Due to the proprietors' unwillingness to sell land, the only way to secure vast properties was to send out large numbers of people (unless, of course, a person merited some reward from the proprietors). Once the size of land concessions had diminished, and settled life had begun to take shape, somewhat lengthier terms quite naturally should have been required by masters of their servants, and that is precisely what seems to have occurred.[50]

Precise resolution of the other central problem—how long did these men and women live—is impossible. In only one instance among the entire sample of 241 servants are we able to ascertain the exact age of a servant. We know that Sam Boswood was 29 years old in 1676, five years after his arrival as a servant.[51] Since he reached Carolina early in 1671, he would have been 24 when he started out in the colony. In all probability Boswood was older on arrival than most servants. In early Maryland, for example, the median age of male servants when they immigrated was 19.[52] While doubtless many Carolina servants came in their teens, and a few others arrived in middle age, for purposes of discussion it is useful to assume that an average age for new servants in the colony was about 20. Employing that age as a base, it is possible, by examining references to deaths (wills, estate inventories, orders from colonial officials to appraise property owned by recently deceased settlers, claims by individuals of rights to such property, and later references in all kinds of documents to

---

50 Here, since I have been dealing with rather small sample groups, I have calculated the average terms for males and females in each category when the top and bottom five, and then 10% of the sample were discarded. The numbers compute in virtually identical fashion in both cases, and the trends are similarly alike. Interestingly, the only group which displays any significant change when those serving the longest and shortest terms are not included in the calculation is female servants arriving after 1672. When either five or 10% of the sample is excluded, the average term works out to be five instead of 4.5 years.

51 *Records of the Secretary, 1675-1695* (MSV), p. 62.

52 Menard, "From Servant to Freeholder . . . ," 47. Craven, *White . . . Black*, p. 7, says most Virginia servants were "at least" eighteen, perhaps twenty on average.

persons "now dec.[sd]") to suggest in what is admittedly a most general way, the ages to which former servants lived.

Evidence exists upon which can be based a reasonably accurate estimate of the death dates of 30 males[53] who arrived as servants between 1670 and 1680. The average time between date of arrival and date of death for this group computes to 20.7 years. Thus, if each had been 20 years old when he came to Carolina, he would have died at about age 41. Moreover, since the average term of service for males was a little more than three and one-half years, if these 30 are representative of all servants, a male choosing to immigrate as a servant during the first decade of settlement might expect to enjoy slightly more than 17 years as a free settler once his term had been completed. When the 10% who lived longest, and the 10% who died soonest after their arrival are excluded; that is, when the middle 80% are considered, the results shift in favor of a slightly shorter average life span—to 39.6 years. Of the entire group of 30 men for whom we have death dates, 17 lived 20 years or longer after their arrival, while only 13 died before they had spent at least two decades living in the colony. Five lived 30 years or longer in Carolina, while only four lived fewer than ten years after their arrival.

If, rather than basing such estimates solely on those for whom it is possible to ascertain the time between arrival and actual death, also included are former servants who definitely were alive in certain years, but for whom date of death cannot be established, the average life span exhibited by servants would lengthen. In a few cases we know that former servants were alive long after their arrival in the colony. Robert Hunt, for example, reached Carolina some time before 1672. He received a land grant in 1697, which is the last we hear of him.[54] Edward Perry who arrived in the autumn of 1675 received numerous parcels of land after 1696, and was referred to as "Esquire" in 1705. We do not know when he died.[55] Thomas Steere, who came in 1671, was still alive in 1702, as was James Williams who arrived in the first fleet. We know when neither

---

[53] Virtually no evidence exists on the death dates of former female servants.

[54] *Grant Book C [Register 1694-1707, Secretary 1722-1740]* (MSV), p. 168; *Abstracts of Grants & Commissions of Lds. Proprietors 1692-1718, 1733-1736, 1775-1820* (2 Vols.) (MSV), p. 69.

[55] *Ibid.*, pp. 55, 162, 208; *Records of the Register 1705-1709* (MSV), pp. 87-88, 96-97; *Grant Book C* (MSV), p. 203; *Misc. Records 1682-1690* (MSV), pp. 337-38.

died.[56] Needless to say, such examples were surely offset by the large number of servants who must have died quite rapidly after their arrival in Carolina, and of whom we have no later record precisely because they failed to survive long enough to acquire land.

---

[56] *Grant Book C* (MSV), p. 203; *Abstracts of Grants & Commissions of the Lords Proprietors 1692-1718, 1733-1736, 1775-1820* (2 Vols.) (MSV), p. 43; Misc. *Records 1682-1690* (MSV), p. 337 (Steere); *Proprietary Grants No. 1 Vol. 38* (MSV), pp. 417, 482; *Abstracts of Grants & Commissions* . . . (MSV), pp. 179, 244; *Grant Book* C (MSV), p. 152 (Williams). Williams may have died in 1725, which would have made him 76 years old if he had been 20 when he arrived. It is equally possible, however, that the James Williams who died in that year was his son, and I have, therefore, not included Williams in my calculation of average life spans.

CHAPTER FIVE

From Servitude to Freedom II: Servants into Planters

I. The Spectrum of Wealth Acquisition in Carolina, 1670-1690

Because few former servants left wills and even fewer had their estates inventoried and appraised, a complete discussion of what the group as a whole ultimately achieved in Carolina is not possible. That is, we cannot establish the number of pots and pans, cedar tables, hand tools, blankets and sheets, or suits of clothing possessed by enough former servants to sketch a picture of the "average" level of wealth attained by members of the group. However, the most valuable assets settlers in early Carolina might acquire were not such items for personal use (except for gold or silver jewelry or plate, of course), but rather land, the buildings and livestock which existed upon it, and laborers bound for a period of years or, in the case of slaves, for life. Land acquisition can be measured both for individuals and for the entire group and, hence, in considering upward mobility among former servants, the discussion must focus on land.

Between the arrival of the first fleet and 1690, 22 deceased Carolinians' estates were inventoried.[1] These itemize holdings which

[1] I am indebted to Mrs. Agnes L. Baldwin of Summerville, South Carolina, for providing me with a manuscript in which she has categorized the items listed in estate inventories between 1678 and 1690. Mrs. Baldwin was able to locate inventories of the estates of 20 settlers: George Sturman (December, 1678) *Records of the Secretary 1675-1695* (MSV), p. 64; William Brett (February, 1679), *ibid.*, p. 67; Richard Fowell (February, 1679), *ibid.*, p. 58; Margaret Jackson (February, 1679), *ibid.*, p. 56; Teige Cantey (May, 1679), *ibid.*, pp. 61-62; Hugh Bidwell (March, 1680), *ibid.*, p. 74; Richard Banks (July, 1681), *ibid.*, pp. 84-85; Thomas Newe (February, 1683), *ibid.*, p. 131; Samuel Osbone (December, 1682), *ibid.*, p. 135; John Horton (September, 1682), *ibid.*,

ranged in value from a little over £18 controlled by the tailor Henry Huse, to the more than £663 accumulated by the "marriner" John Williamson, and the £861 controlled by the merchant John Van Aerssen.[2] Of these 22 persons, only one, John Horton, had come to the colony as a servant. The others occupied a wide range of positions in Carolina's society and filled a variety of roles in its economy. There were three "gentlemen," three "Esquires," five merchants, three tradesmen, one widow of a tradesman, one "Spinster," and one "Lord." The rest were probably "planters."[3] Thus, although heavily biased in favor of the upper levels of wealth and status, these estate inventories do represent a cross section of the kinds of settlers living in the colony during the first two decades of settlement. Their property accumulation can therefore be examined in an effort to define both what Carolinians actually did achieve and, equally important, what new arrivals in the colony might have expected to achieve for themselves. For it is reasonable to assume that immigrants, including servants, based their goals on what they perceived to be the levels of success displayed by those who lived and died in the colony before 1690.

The average value of these estates is a little over £150. However, when the two wealthiest and two poorest settlers' estates are excluded, the average computes to slightly under £100. It is also instructive to note that of the 22 estates, eight were appraised at under £50 in value, while two others totalled between £50 and £54. Since virtually half the men and women in this small sample managed to accumulate property worth less

---

p. 110; John Hill (August, 1682), *ibid.*, p. 111; John Smith (February, 1683), *ibid.*, p. 21; James Collins (February, 1683), *ibid.*, p. 137; Margaret Sympson (January, 1684), *ibid.*, p. 192; John Van Aersen (January, 1684), *ibid.*, p. 291; John Williamson (March, 1679), *ibid.*, p. 301; Henry Huse (November, 1688), *ibid.*, p. 325; Richard Codnar (December, 1688), *ibid.*, p. 340; Edward Paty (1689), *ibid.*, p. 472; and Alexander Pepin (March, 1689), *ibid.*, p. 342. I have been able to locate two additional estate inventories, those of Peter Simpson (March, 1690), *ibid.*, p. 404, and Joseph Dalton (January, 1683), *ibid.*, p. 125. I have excluded lists of goods possessed or transported by merchants which clearly were not estate inventories.

[2] See footnote above for references. The £861 estate of John Van Aersen consisted mostly of his stock of trade goods, and thus does not reflect the worth of property he used personally. While he had £200 "In money," "2 Negros" worth £40, "one silver sword" worth £2, and "his owne wearing apparell" valued at £30, he probably had little personal use for "120,000 of severall sorte of Nails" worth £22, "250 pound of sope" worth £5, "100 pound of candles" worth £1 15s., "36 hats" worth £7, or "4 Dozen of lookeing Glasses" worth 5 shillings.

[3] One gentleman, one Esquire, and Lord Van Wernhaut were also merchants.

than half the adjusted[4] average of all inventoried estates, and since the median of the entire series is Teige Cantey's estate valued at just over £68, it is likely that when gauging their opportunities in Carolina and formulating their expectations, those starting at the very bottom of white society considered the acquisition of property worth £50 to £60 as a measure of success.

As noted earlier, land values varied widely in early Carolina. These 22 inventories reflect that inconsistency, with one house and town lot being assessed at £17, while two were valued at £25, and a fourth at £30.[5] Although these values appear fairly stable, they conceal the fact that one house valued at £25 sat on only one-quarter of a lot, or that the property valued at £17 contained a full "halfe an acre in towne."[6] Even more difficult to use in establishing a measure for comparing the values of property accumulated by former servants with that acquired by those who came to Carolina as free persons, is acreage which was not situated in towns. Six of the estate inventories include appraisals of such property, ranging in size from the "sixty-eight acres of land with the houses benches stools and the crop thereon" owned by John Hill and valued at £50,[7] to the "600 acres of land" held by Margrett Sympson worth £60.[8] The 293 acres held by Joseph Dalton, situated nicely at the junction of two rivers, and containing an unspecified number of buildings, was appraised at £70.[9] William Brett's "1 house and plantation," with no specific acreage cited, added £20 to his estate, but a guess at its size based on what seem to have been similar properties which received equivalent values is extremely difficult. For James Collins' "plantation containing one hundred twenty seaven acres . . . wth a house upon it neare . . . Charles Towne" was valued

---

[4] The average after the top and bottom two estates were discarded.

[5] See Pepin inventory (1689), Sympson inventory (1684), Hill inventory (1682), and Horton inventory (1682). *Records of the Secretary 1675-1695* (MSV), pp. 343, 192, 111, 110.

[6] *Ibid.*, pp. 110, 111.

[7] *Ibid.*, p. 111. The other land he held was a town lot and house valued at £17.

[8] *Ibid.*, p. 192.

[9] *Ibid.*, p. 125.

at £40,[10] while "1 house and plantation containing 200 acres" owned by Margrett Sympson was worth only £35.[11] The situation becomes still less clear when one considers that John Williamson's "130 ackers of land" with "twenty head of cattle in the woods" brought an appraisal of £50.[12] Cattle appeared frequently in these inventories and their values are listed. The problem is that the values attributed to them fluctuate wildly, ranging from a little less to a little more than £1 per head in several cases[13] to over £4 per head in others.[14]

Given the great variation in land values established by these inventories of estates, can they be of use in a discussion of mobility among former servants? They are useful, of course, because although the inventories fail to define specific prices which were attributed consistently to certain species of property, it is clear that land was by a wide margin the most valuable asset settlers might acquire. A survey of the six inventories which include farm or pasturage land owned by the deceased reveals that in five cases that single item contributed more to the total value of the estate than did any other possession, composing well over one-half the total value of the estate in four instances.[15] These 22 inventories also confirm that the price at which the proprietors sold land, 12 pence or one shilling per acre[16], was substantially lower than the value of land which had been held for a number of years and, presumably, improved.

---

[10] Mrs. Baldwin's list enters £10 as the value set for Collins' plantation. However, my reading of the manuscript inventory indicates that the value had to be £40, given the total estate value of over £100. If the land had been worth only £10, the estate would have totalled only a little over £70. *Ibid.*, p. 137.

[11] *Ibid.*, p. 192.

[12] *Ibid.*, p. 301.

[13] *Ibid.*, pp. 16, 21, 137.

[14] *Ibid.*, pp. 21, 192. The Smith inventory alone displays a wide variation in the value attributed to cattle: "4 cowes" are valued at "4 pounds each," "foure heffers" are listed at 11 pounds, yet "three bull calves" are valued at three pounds. "a yearling bull" is worth two pounds, and "cattle 23 viz. four oxen" are listed at 16 pounds.

[15] See inventories of Brett, Hill, Sympson, Collins, Dalton, and Williamson. Only John Williamson whose "silver and gold in cash & plate" contributed nearly a third to the value of his estate of over £663, fails to conform to this pattern. *Ibid.*, p. 30.

[16] The value I have used in assessing what servants were "worth" to their masters.

For example, the 293 acres owned by Joseph Dalton were appraised at £70 (89.7% of the total value of his estate), or 4.8 shillings per acre[17]. Margrett Sympson's 600 acres, which contained neither buildings nor crops, were valued at £60, or two shillings per acre. Her 200 acre plantation, which included a house, was appraised at £35, or 3.5 shillings per acre.[18] Since such properties, owned by persons who died during the second decade of settlement, had been acquired at about the time Carolina's first servants were completing their terms of service and therefore claiming their own land concessions, we can assume that land held by those former servants in all probability was similarly worth more than the one shilling per acre at which the government offered to sell land. Of course, because land secured during the first decade of settlement was situated in the most heavily populated area of the colony near Charles Town, and on the choicest sites, it is only logical that such property would be valued more highly than land which could be purchased from the proprietors after 1685. These inventories also tell us that persons who lived in Carolina during the first two decades of settlement commonly failed to accumulate property worth more than about £50, even if they had begun life in the colony as free persons or had practiced a trade.[19]

Finally, the estate records make abundantly clear that it was not essential for a settler to own or to work land in order to enjoy wealth and high status, much less to exist in moderate comfort, in seventeenth century South Carolina. The largest estates inventoried were controlled by men who engaged in trade and whom the records identify as merchants. Needless to say, such Carolinians surely came to the colony with large amounts of capital. They did not, therefore, begin at the bottom of the economic order and slowly work their way to economic and social prominence. However, even those who, while failing to accumulate vast estates, did come to possess sufficient property to be considered more

---

[17] *Ibid.*, p. 125.

[18] *Ibid.*, p. 192.

[19] Henry Huse, a tailor, held property valued at £18, 13 s., 6.5 d. at his death in 1688. Edward Paty, a cooper, controlled approximately £30 at his death in 1689. *Ibid.*, pp. 325, 472.

Those whose estates were valued at under £60 were: George Sturman, William Brett, Margaret Jackson, Hugh Bidwell, Thomas Newe, Samuel Osbone, John Horton, Peter Simpson, Henry Huse, and Edward Paty.

prosperous than most other early settlers, frequently did not control or use land. That is to say, land for planting or grazing was not included in the list of possessions owned by these settlers when they died. Of the 14 persons whose estates were valued at £50 or more, only five seem to have held such acreage. It is, of course, quite possible that a number of these settlers had sold off or given away to their children all of their land some time before they died. Or, the majority of estate inventories may fail to show land simply because settlers relied on warrants to secure possession of property, and refused to expend the time and money required to obtain a formal land grant which would have guaranteed ownership but necessitated the payment of rents. They thus might have controlled and used parcels of land which they never actually "owned," and which, therefore, could not be included in inventories of their estates. Thus, for example, John Smith's estate was valued at more than £283 in February 1683, and included three white servants, three black male slaves, one black female slave, one mulatto, four black children, four Indian children, and at least 76 head of cattle. Such possessions clearly imply that Smith engaged in extensive farming and grazing operations. Moreover, Smith had received warrants for 1800 acres in 1675.[20] But his estate inventory includes no land on which his livestock could have grazed or his servants and slaves labored.

In fact, some Carolinians held rather extensive numbers of cattle, yet never secured the use of land through warrants, much less legal title to it by completing the process required to obtain a grant. Promotional literature asserted that the colony was so well endowed by nature that owners of stock might merely let their herds roam in the woods where sufficient food and water abounded, and where the climate was mild. Thus, in such a bountiful setting a settler's herd could be left with little

---

[20] *Ibid.*, pp. 21-2; *Warrants, 1672-1679*, pp. 105-06, 110. Like Smith, Richard Codnar owned a large number of cattle ("eight cowes . . . seaventeene heifers and steeres, one Bull . . . thirteene Yearling heifers and steeres"), but no land. *Records of the Secretary 1675-1695*(MSV), p. 340.

Carole Shammas, "The Determinants of Personal Wealth in Seventeenth Century England and America," *Journal of Economic History*, XXXVII (Sept., 1977), 685, notes that among groups she has studied, "wealth increased steadily until the over 60 age group, when it declined rather sharply." One explanation for this, she suggests, is "generational transfer before death . . . whereby families put the bulk of their resources at the disposal of . . . their more vigorous offspring." It may well be that the failure of Carolina estates to display farming acreage was due to such transfer of assets to younger family members who would be able to utilize them fully prior to the time when the original owner had his or her estate inventoried.

concern or attention, and not only sustain itself, but increase in size as well. As one settler wrote in the fall of 1683,

> The cattle only feed in the woods, on the plains and on the savanna, the bulls, the cows and the rest of the cattle feed themselves perfectly well at no cost whatever; one has only to keep the calves to the house to bring all the cows back every evening—the only trouble they are is to milk them and they give you a calf every year; which is a good profit costing no more to feed a lot than a few; you feed them by their thousands in the woods.[21]

John Smyth's inventory noted "thirty head of cattle of severale sorts run wild in the woods"; John Williamson's included "twenty head of cattle in the woods . . .;" and Henry Huse's referred to "One heifer and Calfe but her and her increase are all in ye Wild Grange and has not beene seene since."[22] Clearly there were risks involved in letting stock feed in the woods. But the point is that apparently one did not need to own vast acreage in order to maintain a sizeable herd of cattle.[23]

If a settler did want to raise a small herd on his or her own property and engage in farming as a major source of income, how much land was required? Thomas Nairne asserted that in Carolina "as little will serve to put a Person into a Way of living comfortably as in any Place whatever, and perhaps less." He specified that "to live comfortably, after a Man's own and Family's Passage is paid, and cloaths bought for the first Year or two," in addition to the labor of two slaves, a few head of cattle and hogs, and a small house, a settler required 200 acres of land. These things "are of Necessity to one who would settle with any tolerable Decency. And from this small Beginning, by moderate Industry, accompanied with the Blessing of Heaven, a Man may get a competent

---

[21] Letter of Louis Thibou, September 20, 1683. The original (in French) and a typed translation are in the South Caroliniana Library, Columbia, South Carolina. Thomas Nairne, writing almost twenty years later, confirmed that the practice persisted well into the eighteenth century. "Our Cows," he wrote, "graze in the forests, and the Calves being separated from them, and kept in pastures, fenced in, they return home at Night to suckle them. . . ." Nairne, *Letter*, p. 46.

[22] *Records of the Secretary 1675-1695* (MSV), pp. 22, 301, 326.

[23] There was another alternative available to those who wanted to raise cattle but who did not possess land—to use the land of neighbors or friends. Thus, Henry Huse's estate inventory refers to "the amount of Cattle at Richard Wakefields," "the am^{t} of Cattle wch wee had from the report of John Wattkins and his Wife," and "An account of what Cattle we doe heare there was seene uppon Capt. Daniells Island about four or five yeares agoe. . . ." *Ibid.*, pp. 325-26.

Estate, and live very handsomly." He even noted that "there are many who settle without any Slaves at all, but labour themselves."[24] Evidently Nairne was aiming his "report" at potential settlers who presumably had the capital and the inclination to avoid harsh toil themselves, for he devotes two pages to a discussion of the initial outlay of capital needed to amass a vast estate which would yield £300 profit per year to the investor-settler.[25] Nairne thus has left us a guide for assessing property accumulation in early Carolina. Assuming that a settler acquired 200 acres (almost exactly what a newly-freed servant would control if his and his wife's freedom dues were secured), and that he proved willing to work, according to this testimony he could live comfortably from the outset, and with perseverance, in time "live very handsomly." A settler who was able to secure 1000 acres could be considered truly wealthy (if he also enjoyed the labor of others). Thus, if Nairne's assessment of the property needed to "succeed" in Carolina is reasonable—and there is no basis for doubting it—the proprietors' land concessions virtually guaranteed that any servant who survived to claim a headright, who multiplied the number of acres he or she controlled through marriage, and who was willing and able to work, would attain at least a status and level of wealth sufficiently high to insure independence and comfort.

In describing the colony's inhabitants, Nairne classified whites in three categories according to how they made their livings. He wrote:

> All People are either Planters, Traders, or Artisans . . . A Planter is a Common Denomination for those who live by their own and their Servants Industry, improve their Estates, follow Tillage or Grasing, and make those Commodities which are transported from hence to *Great Britain*, and other Places.

Nairne estimated "traders," or merchants, to compose a little less than 13% of the white population. About 7% of the whites were "Artisans." The remaining 70% of the free white inhabitants were, he stressed,

---

[24] Nairne, *Letter*, pp. 46-48.

[25] Nairne specified 15 male and 15 female slaves, 20 head of cattle, and 1000 acres as the necessary ingredients for establishing such a plantation in Carolina. *Ibid.*, pp. 48-49. He also included the wages tradesmen were able to secure in the province, noting that "those who have no Substance to bring with them, they are either Labourers or Tradesmen." The highest paid were blacksmiths who, according to Nairne, received seven shillings six pence per day. Bricklayers earned six shillings a day, while tailors netted five shillings for a day's work. Shoemakers were the poorest paid—they were able to command but two shillings six pence a day. *Ibid.*, p. 50.

"Planters."[26] Thus, any servant who immigrated during the first decade of settlement could, by this definition, pursue an occupation which was shared by the vast majority of whites. While the term "planter" embraced persons whose estates ranged in size (and value) from tiny to huge, it was not merely applied to identify the way a settler supported himself. "Planter" was also a title, a status, and connoted that a person was free, independent, self-sufficient, and capable of moving upward in Carolina's social and economic order. It signified that a person owned and used land. It represented a real step upward, even if small in most cases, from the status of servant.

II. Routes to Property Acquisition

In theory all who began life in Carolina in servitude could, if they survived, readily achieve significant upward mobility—both socially and economically. For if a servant survived his or her term, claimed the land concession offered by the proprietors, and married someone who had similarly acquired the *minimum* acreage to which he or she was entitled, the amount of land thus controlled would approach the limit specified by reliable sources as necessary to live decently, and to define oneself as a "planter."

According to the instructions issued by the proprietors in 1669 to Carolina's first governor, male or female servants who arrived prior to March 1671, would receive 100 acres when their terms of service expired. Those servants (again, no distinction was made between males and females) who reached the colony after March 1671, would be eligible to receive 70 acres when set free.[27] Thus, any former servant who married would have the use of 140 acres, at minimum. If a former servant married someone who had entered Carolina as a free person, the acreage due them through proprietary concession would have been even greater, since free immigrants received somewhat larger headrights than did those who came to the colony unfree. The point is not to calculate the sizes of parcels of land which might have been obtained by settlers of different backgrounds who decided to marry and thereby combine their headrights; it is rather to

---

[26] *Ibid.*, pp. 39-40.

[27] *Shaftsbury Papers*, p. 121; Ackerman, "South Carolina Colonial Land Policies," p. 36.

emphasize that the colony offered to even its lowliest white immigrants a real chance—a genuine opportunity to become full participants in an emerging society and economy. Virtually any servant who survived and married would have at his or her disposal (if he or she adhered to the scheme the proprietors intended when they established their land distribution system) sufficient acres of land to survive in comfort. If they were industrious and enterprising and remained healthy, men and women provided with such property at the outset of their free lives in Carolina might some day amass significant wealth. At least these must have been the expectations servants brought to the colony.

But did the reality of life in Carolina conform to the hopes of its first settlers when they embarked for the colony? Did men and women who started at the very lowest social and economic level occupied by whites, and who survived their terms of servitude, actually fulfill their dreams? Did they conform to the outlines of property accumulation the proprietary land distribution system dictated they should? Did they amass more property than the "minimum" as defined in that policy? Or did they acquire less than they must have anticipated they would when they agreed to engage themselves as servants?

Since land records from the earliest period of settlement are ample—and in the case of warrants seem to be complete—it is possible to formulate answers to these questions which probably reflect at least a close approximation of the reality experienced by Carolina's first group of freed servants. It is, nevertheless, essential to bear in mind that given the previously discussed difficulties encountered by scholars working in the early colonial records of the colony, it would be foolhardy to assume that this work presents absolute answers. Specifically, the inability to ascertain with certainty that data on any person are accurate or complete, much less that they apply to a specific individual as opposed to someone else with the same name (or a child named after the parent), precludes any claim to total accuracy. Moreover, that early settlers seem to have used warrants to establish possession of land, but refrained from completing the process which would have given them formal title to it, means that the amount of land legally and permanently owned by a settler frequently seems to have been much less than that which he or she actually controlled and used. At the same time, one must bear in mind that colonists commonly chose to renew warrants in the public record to ensure their "right" to a piece of property. Therefore, it is impossible to know with absolute certainty whether any warrant (especially one for a large amount of land to a settler who had received land warrants in the past) represents land allocated for the first time, previously distributed land combined by the "owner" into one "package" which could conveniently be secured by one warrant, or a combination of both newly and previously warranted property. While scrupulous examination of the records combined with careful analysis lessens the likelihood of error, one must remain aware that complete accuracy is impossible to ensure.

I have employed a number of procedures to minimize the risks involved in attempting to calculate the amount of property accumulated by former servants. As noted earlier, my estimates will tend to be low for two reasons. First, I have only counted land which clearly belonged to the settler under consideration. Second, I have always assumed that for any grant there was an earlier and corresponding warrant for the same parcel, and have therefore never *added* property identified by grant to the total attributed to an individual by totaling his or her warrants. However, since grants clearly represented a more authoritative transfer of land from the proprietors to settlers than did warrants, I have always given precedence to grants over warrants when gauging any colonist's holdings. That is, in the few cases where the number of acres conveyed to an individual by grant exceeds the number he or she acquired by virtue of warrants, I have counted the number indicated in the grant or grants. Thus, for example, William Cason, upon gaining his freedom, received a warrant for 100 acres in May 1674. But in November of the following year Cason shared a grant with John Hooper, another former servant, for 240 acres. Cason's share of 120 acres exceeded the size of his warrant, and may, in fact, have been *in addition* to land he held and was using on the basis of that warrant. Or the grant of 120 acres may have simply included the 100 acres for which he had already received a warrant, and given him (and Hooper) an additional 20 acres for which no earlier warrant had existed. In any case, it is clear that Cason controlled *at least* 120 acres. While he may actually have held an additional 100 acres by virtue of his 1674 warrant, I have credited him only with 120, which, it is clear, represents the minimum he enjoyed as a free settler.[28]

Since Carolina's first settlers bought and sold land freely, it is not surprising to discover quite a few former servants adding to their holdings by purchasing real property from other colonists, or once the proprietors

---

[28] On the Cason-Hooper grant, see: *Records of the Register and the Secretary 1675-1696, 1703-1709* (MSV), p. 71; *Calendar of State Papers, Colonial Series Vol. IX, 1675-76*, p. 717; *Proprietary Grants No. 1, Vol. 38* (MSV), p. 10. Cason's warrant is in *Warrants, 1672-79*, p. 75. Hooper held warrants for 290 acres.

agreed to sell land directly to Carolina's settlers, from the proprietors' agents. I have, of course, added land acquired in this way to the total attributed to any individual after working through his or her grants and warrants. In some cases, land purchased represented only a small fraction of a former servant's holdings. For example, James and Martha Williams, a servant couple, ultimately held warrants for 2580 acres and grants for 2230 acres (they were obviously scrupulous about converting warrants into grants, possibly because they were sufficiently wealthy to be able to pay the required fees and subsequent quitrents on their large holdings). In June 1676, James purchased 25 acres from Samuell West, the only property he or Martha obtained by purchase from a private party in 37 years of land accumulation in the colony. Thus, of the 2605 acres they controlled, only 25 were bought from a fellow settler; the remainder came from the government.[29]

Other former servants such as James Green gained a sizeable portion of their land through purchase. In 1676 Green secured his only warrant, for 100 acres, as "one of ye settlers of this Province," not quite three years after arriving as a servant. He probably farmed that land, for in October 1674, when he bought 100 acres from Peter and Mary DuMoulin, he labelled himself a "planter." The following spring he purchased a small lot in Charles Town "scituate and beinge in a back street." Green was dead by 1686, when his widow Lydea sold part of her inheritance. Green had privately bought as much farming land as he had received from the proprietors, as well as having purchased his town lot.[30]

There were other ways in which settlers, no matter what their origins, might acquire land or come to enjoy the use of land. One obvious method of doing so was to inherit property. By far the most common circumstances surrounding the acquisition of land through inheritance involved widows or

---

[29] Williams was one of only three former servants to acquire the title "Esquire." He became coroner of Colleton County, and almost from the outset had practiced medicine, being referred to as a "chirugian" as early as 1683. For his land acquisitions, see: *Warrants, 1672-79*, pp. 91, 99; *Warrants, 1680-92*, pp. 37, 94, 185; *Warrants, 1692-1711*, pp. 71-72, 83, 95-96, 175, 241; P.R.O., CO 5/398, pp. 13, 20; *Proprietary Grants No. 1 Vol. 38* (MSV), pp. 164, 334, 378-79, 417, 482; *Proprietary Grants No. 2, Vol. 39* (MSV), p. 19 (son); *Records of the Register and the Secretary 1675-96, 1703-09* (MSV), pp. 186 (purchase of 25 acres from West), 427; *Grant Book C 1694-1707, 1722-1740* (MSV), pp. 104, 106, 170; *Memorial Book Vol. 1* (MSV), p. 244; *Memorial Book Vol. 3* (MSV), p. 45.

[30] See *Warrants, 1672-79*, p. 121; Misc. *Records 1682-1690* (MSV), pp. 181-82, 386A, 387A, 388A, 312-13; *Memorial Book Vol. 1* (MSV), p. 79.

widowers receiving all the property formerly enjoyed by them and their deceased spouse. However, alternative sources of property obtained through inheritance did exist. John Hopkins, for example, received 35 acres, one heifer, one bull calf, and an unspecified number of hogs when, late in the summer of 1683, his friend William Jackson succumbed to illness and bequeathed the property to him. Both had started life in the colony as servants.[31] While they had not shared a common master, perhaps their similar beginnings in the colony had contributed to their relationship. For Jackson left property not only to former servant Hopkins, but also to former servant Miliscent Jackson (How), to former servant Patrick Steward, to Steward's wife, and to his own white servants who were simultaneously set free. In addition, Jackson instructed his overseers to insure that his two godsons, William Jones and William Rubery, both children of former servants, "be brought up to some convenient Learning Suitable to them." Clearly, shared origins served as the basis for friendships in the colony, at least for those who started at the bottom of the white social and economic order.[32]

---

[31] Hopkins' total land accumulation was 305 acres. See *Records of the Secretary 1675-95* (MSV), pp. 174-76, 188-89. The bequest was not without conditions, however, as Hopkins was instructed to "deliver unto my overseers . . . one halfe of all & singular he hath gained & purchased since his departure. . . ." Where Hopkins had gone or why Jackson imposed the restriction are not discussed.

[32] *Ibid.*, pp. 188-89. Jackson did not immediately free his two Indian "servants."

It would be misleading, I suspect, to read too much into the seemingly extensive dealings between former servants which appear in the records. Needless to say, there are numerous examples of former servants trading, selling land, buying land, witnessing legal documents, sharing property, loaning money, borrowing money, etc., among themselves. It might even be possible to make a case for a "community of former servants" supporting one another and rising on the social and economic scale as a group. I have concluded, however, that such was not the reality of life in the settlement. Rather, I think the limited size, both geographically and numerically, of Carolina brought former servants together repeatedly in social as well as business contexts. No doubt common origins as servants and occasionally deep friendships originating in service to a common master did work to create relationships which were evidenced by preferential treatment of some by other settlers (for example, in making loans or in selling parcels of land), but I think the incidence of such was not so frequent that it signifies a situation which merits much more than these passing remarks. Former servants who seem to have been predisposed to such "preferential" relationships with others who shared their social origin were: Samuel Boswood, Philip Braidy, William Cason, William Chambers, William Cockfield, Christopher Edwards, Christopher Field, John Hooper, John Hopkins, Thomas Hunt, William Jackson,

A more intriguing instance of property acquisition through inheritance involves Jane Lawson and her master Joseph Dalton, who came to the colony aboard the *Carolina* with the first fleet.[33] She must have wholly endeared herself to Dalton, for when he set off to sea in August 1676, he drafted a will which conveyed his entire estate to her. Dalton survived the perils of that voyage, but in the six years which passed between the writing of his will and his death, his feelings for his servant remained constant. The document which disposed of Dalton's entire estate valued at more than £77, and containing 293 acres, was the same will he had composed in 1676 in which he named Jane Lawson "spinster" as his sole heir. Lawson apparently never married. Throughout her life in Carolina, which can be traced to 1701, she appears in the public records as "Jane Lawson, spinster." We can only speculate as to the reasons why an eligible and propertied woman living in a province where the sex ratio was overwhelmingly unbalanced, remained without a husband for more than 30 years. But it is not unreasonable to suspect that the emotions which bound Dalton to his servant may well have endured long after Dalton died. The property he left to her was sufficient to provide for her sustenance, and she never hesitated to use it for profit. Jane Lawson as a seller of property is not an uncommon character in Carolina's surviving records of land transactions. In any case, for this servant the relationship which developed between her and her master served as the source of her property and of her rise upward in society.[34]

I have discovered only one example of a servant marrying her master (and no cases in which a servant married his mistress), and thereby gaining both property and status. I suspect the reason has much to do with

---

William Jones, Thomas Mackanellor, Dennis Mahone, Philip Orill, James Powell, George Rubry, Abraham Smith, Patrick Steward, and Henry Sumpton.

[33] *Shaftsbury Papers*, p. 134.

[34] Lawson first sold land she inherited from Dalton the same year he died, parting with six acres for twenty shillings. A year and a half later she sold virtually the entire estate for £300, but a year after that reacquired the property, which she then proceeded to sell off in smaller pieces at intervals until 1701, her final appearance in the records, when she went to court to regain the last 54 acres of Dalton's estate which she had sold two years earlier. See *Records of the Register and the Secretary 1675-96, 1703-09* (MSV), pp. 523-25; *Records of the Secretary 1675-94* (MSV), pp. 124-25; Misc. *Records 1682-90* (MSV), pp. 47, 61-62, 172-73, 275; *Records of the Secretary 1694-1705* (MSV), pp. 361-64 (W.P.A., pp. 409-13); *Records of the Register 1696-1703* (MSV), pp. 155-56.

the very limited numbers of "candidates" for such marriages. There were few female servants, and even fewer female masters who were unmarried. Furthermore, it is reasonable to assume that of the male masters who did acquire female servants, many or most were already married. Finally, any female servant who did marry her master would have thereby altered her surname, thus adding yet another barrier to those which impede precise identification of individual settlers. I have, on the other hand, identified a servant who did gain entrance into his master's family by marriage. John Hooper came to Carolina a servant to Thomas Lane. Lane held a warrant for 740 acres due to him for having paid the passage to the colony of "himselfe, Mathew Harris and Robert Leeds arriveing in July, 1672. and Trisimus Morrison, John Hooper, David Derling, Hester Lane and Judith Lane arriveing in May 1673."[35] Needless to say, Hester and Judith were Lane's daughters.[36] Within a year of their arrival, John and Hester were married, John was free, and they held a warrant for the 140 acres due them as their proprietary land concession for having immigrated.[37] A little over a year later, Hooper, now identified as a "planter," was appointed a "viewer of tobacco," an office created to ensure "that all the tobaccoes to be brought in may be m^r^chantable and good."[38] And two years later the advantages of having a prosperous father-in-law emerged in material form when Hooper "and Hester his wife" received a warrant for 150 acres "in ye right of" Thomas Ingram and Thomas Lane. Ingram had sold Lane a parcel of land four years earlier, and this may well have been that piece of property, traced through its two previous owners to avoid any doubt as to its location and true owners. Or the land may merely have been a gift from Lane and one of his friends. In either case, it is clear that Hooper had benefitted materially from his marriage to his master's daughter.[39]

---

[35] The servant who married her master Hugh Carteret is unnamed in the records. See *Warrants, 1680-92*, p. 81; *Warrants, 1672-79*, p. 64.

[36] In a land sale by Hooper recorded in *Records of the Register and the Secretary 1675-96, 1703-09* (MSV), pp. 29-31, Hester is identified as the "Daughter of Thomas Lane late of ye Province."

[37] *Warrants, 1672-79*, p. 74.

[38] *Council Journal, 1671-80*, p. 79.

[39] See *Warrants, 1672-79*, p. 135; *Records of the Register and the Secretary 1675-96, 1703-09* (MSV), p. 24, for the sale of land by Ingram to Lane. Hooper served

If Hooper gained property through a fortunate marriage, so did a number of other former servants—women who enjoyed the use of property either wholly or in large measure acquired in the right of their husbands, as opposed to the amount they received independently as immigrants. Sarah Pope, for example, came to the colony in April 1678. We do not know who her master was. We do know, however, that she married the planter and mariner William Brockus, who added the 70 acres due her as her own land concession to those he acquired on his own. His property—and hers—totalled 1940 acres.[40]

Sarah Pope's marriage allowed her to join the economic elite in Carolina. More typical were the fates of Elinor Stevenson and Jone Jones, each of whom contributed the same 70 acres to her married estate as did Sarah Pope. The difference, of course, was that Elinor Stevenson married William Wilkinson, who was able to add only his own 70 acres to hers, yielding a total property accumulation of 140 acres; and that Jone Jones was married to Evan Jones, whose two warrants in his own right which totalled 100 acres combined with her one warrant to produce an estate of 170 acres.[41] In each of these cases I have attributed the property accumulated by the former servant and her husband to the servant, since she not only benefitted from but also had access to, use of, a degree of control over, and inheritance rights to the entire estate.

I have followed a comparable procedure when considering property accumulated by the several married couples who immigrated together as servants. Since both husband and wife were included as *individuals* in my count of the total number of servants in the colony prior to 1680, and since each had full rights to every acre they acquired together, it would be misleading when assessing the *average* amount of land accumulated by former servants to count only one member of such couples, or to divide the

---

as the witness to the sale. *Memorial Book Vol. 1* (MSV), p. 188, records a land sale of 140 acres in 1703 which notes that the property involved was part of 390 acres originally granted by the proprietors to "Thomas Lane and John Whooper late of the said province planters deceas[d.]" This is the only reference to such a grant I have found. Therefore, I have not added any of this acreage to the total I credit Hooper with having amassed on the basis of his warrants and his one formally recorded grant (shared with William Cason). I cite the reference only because it suggests that Hooper and his father-in-law had business dealings which extended beyond the gift of 150 acres discussed in the text.

[40] *Warrants, 1680-92*, p. 82.

[41] *Warrants, 1672-79*, pp. 114-15; *Warrants, 1680-92*, p. 154.

estate into a husband's and a wife's individual shares. For in every acquisition, aside from their initial headrights which allocated acreage to each as individuals, land was acquired by the couple jointly. All the servants who immigrated as individuals, whether men or women, have been credited with the *total* property to which they had legal claim, including that which they acquired after marrying. For example, when a male former servant married and added a number of acres to his (and his wife's) estate through proprietary concession for *her* immigration, those acres obviously ought to be counted as part of his total land accumulation. Therefore, when computing the amount of land secured by former servant couples, I have specified the total acres possessed by the couple as also being held by each as an individual former servant. Thus, the servant couple John and Mary Thomas, for example, acquired 140 acres during their lives in Carolina. In figuring the average amount of land servants in the colony actually succeeded in obtaining, I have counted them as two servants and assumed that each was able to acquire control over 140 acres.[42]

Needless to say, in my calculations of land acquired by former servants, I have included only land obtained through their direct participation. Thus I have not included property secured by a spouse after the death or probable death of a former servant, even if the land was conveyed in the former servant's name. The case of Mathew Smallwood is instructive. In March 1692, Governor Seth Sothell ordered that the estate of Mathew Smallwood "deceased" be inventoried and appraised.[43] However, Mathew Smallwood had a formal grant for 400 acres dated January 11, 1700. In addition, Mathew Smallwood held warrants for another 1000 acres dated June and October 1704. His son was named Richard. Yet in my computations Mathew Smallwood has been credited with having accumulated only the 250 acres conveyed to him prior to the date on which his estate was ordered appraised.[44] Similarly, former servant Abraham Smith has been credited with only the 450 acres he and his wife secured during his lifetime. After his death, as noted earlier, his

---

[42] The Thomases arrived in 1671, servants to Thomas Clutterbooke, who remained in Barbados. Their only land warrant, for 140 acres, is dated July 1675. *Warrants, 1672-79*, pp. 15, 100.

[43] *Records of the Secretary 1675-95* (MSV), pp. 457, 461.

[44] It is, of course, possible that he had a second son named Mathew to whom the 400 acre grant and the 1000 acres in warrants actually belonged. See *Proprietary Grants No. 1, Vol. 38* (MSV), pp. 389-90; *Warrants, 1692-1711*, pp. 188, 193.

wife Hannah continued to acquire land.[45] So did Hannah English, after the death of her former servant husband Matthew. During his lifetime, the Englishes were able to secure only 100 acres and two town lots in Charles Town. As a widow, and later after having remarried, Hannah embarked on a spectacular career of land acquisition (in her own name, as opposed to her second husband's), land selling, and even money lending.[46]

It is thus clear from the colonial records of Carolina that men and women who began their lives in the colony as servants were able not only to survive their terms of servitude, but also to acquire real property. They did so through the proprietary concession of land to all immigrants based on age, sex, and date of arrival, and by purchase, inheritance, and marriage.

The estate inventories from this early period of settlement, in detailing the possessions of a cross-section of the colony's population, give us some sense of the kinds of property early Carolinians owned and of the values of their estates. In addition, the inventories allow us to gain some sense as to how common it was for early Carolinians to own land at time of death. They also provide us with a means to gauge the proportion of a total estate value which such property composed. Moreover, the inventories, especially when supplemented by testimony from observers such as Thomas Nairne, give us an idea of the amount of real property a settler needed in order to live decently in the colony.

Yet how common was real property acquisition by former servants? And even if the typical freed servant did receive land, how much property might he or she acquire? In other words, did the careers of former servants, as measured by property acquisition, compare favorably with the levels of success displayed by a sample of early Carolinians (whose estates were inventoried) or with what reports from the colony said settlers might expect to achieve?

---

[45] See *Proprietary Grants No. 1, Vol. 38* (MSV), p. 152.

[46] As Hannah English "widdow" and as "Hannah English alias Williams," Mathew's wife received actual grants for 1000 acres and for two town lots. See *Proprietary Grants No. 1, Vol. 38* (MSV), pp. 188, 243, 285-86; P.R.O., CO 5/398, p. 9; *Records of the Secretary 1692-170* (WPA), p. 543; *Grant Book C* (MSV), p. 76. In September 1712, she loaned £400 to Arthur Langhorne with 500 acres of his land as security for the loan. *Records of the Register and the Secretary 1711-15* (MSV), pp. 238-40. The same month she sold a town lot to what seems to have been her and Mathew's son, Henroydah English, for £200. Within a month, Henroydah resold it at a 300 percent profit for £600. *Records of the Register and the Secretary 1712-13* (MSV), pp. 121-29.

CHAPTER SIX

From Servitude to Freedom III: Land Acquisition and Status Mobility

I. Pitfalls and Anomalies

It can be quite misleading to focus a discussion of economic mobility in colonial Carolina on land acquisition. Regrettably, given the virtually compete absence of alternative data, land is the only species of property which can be employed in such an endeavor. Land was widely held, and all immigrants were entitled to receive it from the proprietors. Most settlers, no matter what their pursuits, acquired land. And the records for land acquisition, at least the warrants, seem rather complete. Nevertheless, it would be wrongheaded to assume that by measuring real property accumulation for a group of individuals and analyzing the results, one was gaining more than only the most general impression of the reality of mobility upward by those who began their lives in the colony as indentured servants.

Consider, for example, the careers of two former servants, Michael Lovell and Joseph Pendarvis. Lovell arrived in August 1671, a servant to John Coming. After becoming free he never recorded a warrant for farming land, even though he certainly could have done so. Instead, since he chose to practice a trade—he was a sawyer—he must have sensed that his fortune would benefit from an urban existence. He acquired one town lot, the only real property which appears as his in the public records.[1]

[1] *Warrants, 1672-79*, p. 45; *Proprietary Grants No. 1, Vol. 38* (MSV), p. 60; *Records of the Register and the Secretary 1675-79, 1703-09* (MSV), p. 174; Misc. *Records 1682-90* (MSV), pp. 170-71 (for his sale of the lot); *Records of the Register 1705-09* (MSV), p. 250 (for evidence confirming that Lovell's lot was the site of the French Church in Charles Town, but that Lovell did not donate it to the church as

Lovell's career did not involve or depend on the accumulation of land. It would be misleading, therefore, to assess his mobility by measuring the number of acres he acquired. In my calculation of property accumulation by former servants, I have assumed only that Lovell owned land. I have not included his small parcel in the total acreage amassed by former servants, nor have I included him in the group whose size serves as the number by which that total acreage is divided in order to arrive at an average for the former servant population.

Joseph Pendarvis presents a somewhat different problem from that posed by Lovell. While Lovell's "success" cannot be assessed through a consideration of the number of acres he accumulated because his work had nothing to do with control of land, Pendarvis did employ real property in seeking his fortune, and he did acquire a significant amount of land. In one early land grant (1675) he is referred to as Joseph Pendarvis "planter," and his estate, inventoried in the spring of 1695, included ten slaves, 16 "sheepe," six lambs, three "Yew Goates," seven "Cowes," seven "Steares," five "Young Yearlings," one bull, and eight horses. Obviously Pendarvis engaged in some farming on the 320 acres which the records show he controlled. However, to judge his "success" solely on the basis of the

---

suggested in the *Shaftsbury Papers*, pp. 394-95). Lovell is referred to in the records also as Loveing and as Lovering.

It is interesting that another former servant, James Powell, pursued a similar course, perhaps even serving as a prototype for Lovell. Powell arrived in the colony in the summer of 1671 and was free by late winter 1674, when he secured a warrant for the 70 acres to which his immigration as a servant entitled him. Even before his warrant was recorded, Powell had sold the acreage to John Barton. Barton and Powell proceeded to arrange for a formal grant to be issued, probably because they wished to ensure that the sale would never be jeopardized in the future. Thus we find Powell and Barton receiving a grant in August 1676, for land Powell had sold to Barton in November 1674. In any case, Powell was a "Taylor," and clearly preferred the £10 sterling Barton gave him for the property to holding it or using it himself. Powell may have acquired other real property at a later date, for a land sale recorded in November 1684, notes that the property being sold butts land owned by Powell. See *Warrants, 1672-79*, p. 93; *Calendar of State Papers, Vol. 9, 1675-76*, p. 1224, hereafter cited as *C.S.P.*; *Proprietary Grants No. 1, Vol. 38* (MSV), pp. 12-13; *Records of the Register and the Secretary 1675-96, 1703-09* (MSV), pp. 42, 82, 53, 85; Misc. *Records 1682-90* (MSV), p. 123.

It is also important to recall that there is evidence which suggests that some servants achieved freedom and apparently simply failed to claim their land warrants. For example, the case of Samuel Morris, discussed earlier (he engaged himself as a seaman and left no record of having taken up land or having secured a warrant for land), is instructive. See Chapter Two, footnote 4, *supra*.

amount of land he acquired would be to underestimate dramatically what he achieved in the colony. That seven of his ten slaves were women and not field hands gives some hint as to the focus of his existence. He did, of course, engage in planting, but that activity represented only a portion of his interests. Most of the parcels of land which he owned, for example, were located in town, and were small in size. At the time of his death he held seven houses, at least five of which were on lots in town. In addition, he owned two town lots upon which he had not built. He had sold off other town lots during his lifetime. He was of sufficient stature in the society to be labelled "Esquire" by the proprietors' land agents. His estate was valued at more than £754. Obviously, Joseph Pendarvis' career was exceptionally successful. Most of his wealth did not reside in farming land. Although his 320 acres of such property have been included in the total acreage acquired by former servants, his example serves to remind us that quantities of land do not necessarily correlate with levels of success, much less measure wealth with precision.[2]

Joseph Pendarvis' 320 acres have been included in the total for former servants. Michael Lovell's one town lot, however, has served only to add his name to the group of former servants who I can identify as having acquired real property. Three other former servants similarly have been

---

[2] The records of the colony are literally full of references to Joseph Pendarvis and his family. His warrants for farming land are in *Warrants, 1672-79*, pp. 26, 111. His warrants for town lots are in *Warrants, 1680-92*, p. 31, and *Warrants, 1692-1711*, p. 5. His grants are in *C.S.P. Vol. 9, 1675-76*, p. 717; Public Record Office, London CO5/398, pp. 1, 3, 5 (hereafter cited as P.R.O.); *Proprietary Grants No. 1, Vol.* 38 (MSV), pp. 3, 49-50, 94-100, 256; *Records of the Register and the Secretary 1675-96, 1703-09* (MSV), pp. 14, 163, 236-38, 238-41; *Grant Book C* (MSV), p. 11. His will is in *Records of the Secretary 1692-1700* (MSV), pp. 183-87. The inventory of his estate is in *ibid.*, pp. 222-23. His land sales are recorded in *Records of the Register and the Secretary 1675-96, 1703-09* (MSV), pp. 258-62. He sold liquor and lent money or engaged in trade also. See Misc. *Records 1682-90* (MSV), pp. 347, 359. His son John continued his father's upward rise. John's estate at his death in 1724 totalled more than £3377 and included 25 slaves, 14 horses, 32 cows, eight oxen, and three steers. He left his three sons 2109 acres of land. See *Records of the Secretary B 1722-16* (WPA), pp. 373-75; *Records of the Secretary D 1724-25* (WPA), pp. 130-32; P.R.O., CO5/398, p. 15; *Proprietary Grants No. 1, Vol.* 38 (MSV), pp. 181, 182, 364; *Proprietary Grants No. 2, Vol.* 39 (MSV), pp. 43, 44, 171; *Records of the Register and the Secretary 1675-96, 1703-09* (MSV), p. 495; *Grant Book C* (MSV), pp. 251-52; *Records of the Register 1696-1703* (MSV), pp. 190, 281-82; *Records of the Register 1709-12* (MSV), pp. 13-17; *Records of the Register 1705-09* (MSV), pp. 202-07, 209-13; *Records of the Secretary Vol. D, 1704-09* (MSV), pp. 102-04; *Memorial Book I* (MSV), pp. 243, 245-46, 248-49, 250, 251, 252, 255-58, 258-60, 261-63.

counted only as landowners, without the size of their holdings being added to the figure for the entire group. Jonathan Barker, for example, who arrived with the first fleet, surely came to own some property prior to the summer of 1672. For in July of that year another settler appeared before the Council and requested a warrant for "land belonging to . . . Barker." Whether Barker had died or moved on, we do not know. Nor does any surviving record indicate the size of the property he had acquired.[3]

We also know that runaway Bryan Fitzpatrick had acquired property in Carolina prior to his defection to the Spanish in St. Augustine. For in May 1673, when John Gardner secured a warrant for land, it was specified that the property would be bounded on the "westward" by that owned by Fitzpatrick. Again, the size of Fitzpatrick's holdings is unknown, and cannot therefore be included in the total acquired by former servants.[4] Neither can the property of Edward Howard, who reached Carolina in 1671. Here the problem is simply that the first warrant under his name, for 70 acres, identifies him as "one of the free persons of this province" and probably dates from 1679, while the second warrant attributed to him, dated March 1683, allocates 140 acres as a concession "for the transportation into this province of himselfe & wife."[5] Since servants whose immigration had allowed their masters to claim headrights could not, by definition, have paid their own passage and therefore claimed their own land concession for having done so, it is impossible to ascertain just how much property Howard had amassed. As with Lovell, Barker, and Fitzpatrick, I have merely added Howard's name to the list of those who survived servitude and secured land, but have not included data on him in my calculations involving the average amount of land controlled by former servants.

Data on other former servants who *may well* have owned land have been discarded from both computations. In two cases, those of John Willson and Thomas King, there is ample evidence that property was acquired. The difficulty centers on proper attribution, since there were at least two settlers with each of those names. All four came to the colony as

---

[3] *Council Journal, 1671-80*, p. 43; *Shaftsbury Papers*, p. 410.

[4] *Warrants, 1672-79*, p. 63.

[5] *Ibid.*, pp. 113, 203; *Warrants 1680-92*, p. 102. He also had a 100 acre grant in September 1705. See *Proprietary Grants No. 1, Vol. 38* (MSV), p. 501; *Abstracts of Grants & Commissions of Lords Proprietors 1692-1718, 1733-1736, 1775-1820* (2 Parts), (MSV), p. 195.

servants. It is unclear, however, which land acquired under either name applies to which settler, and there is no way to determine if *both* or if only one King or Willson acquired land. The data on land acquisition by these settlers have been ignored in my calculations, even though it is clear that at least two of the four certainly did hold property in Carolina as free persons who had begun their lives in the province as servants.[6]

Data on eight other settlers have also been excluded because of my inability to ascertain with a reasonable degree of certainty that land cited in the records as belonging to them was, in fact, owned by former servants. Consider the case of Robert Smith who arrived in the autumn of 1675 as a servant to John Smith. While Robert's only grant (he held no warrants) dates from 1682—indicating a reasonable time span of seven years between arrival in servitude and freedom—the size of the grant leads one to doubt that it conveyed land to the Robert Smith who had been a servant. For it is not likely that the first land transferred from the proprietors to a newly freed servant would fail to produce a warrant, and it is still less likely that the number of acres conferred would total 600. Needless to say, both reasons for skepticism apply to the case of Robert Smith, and he therefore fails to contribute either his name or his acres to my discussion of land acquired by former servants.[7]

---

[6] One Thomas King arrived as a servant to Oliver Spencer in August 1672. Another Thomas King appeared on the passenger list of the Carolina in the first fleet as a servant to Florence O'Sullivan. One of these men became a "joyner." One of them married a woman named Mary and had died by early March 1707. See *Warrants, 1672-79*, p. 84; *Shaftsbury Papers*, pp. 134, 136; *Records of the Secretary 1694-1705* (MSV), p. 196 (as joyner); *Records of the Secretary 1700-10* (MSV), pp. 119, 184. The picture becomes still more cloudy when one considers that in January 1678, "Leah King, Thomas King & Leah King ffree persons of this province" held a warrant for 300 acres, and that Thomas King had another warrant for 500 acres in March 1703. See *Warrants, 1672-79*, p. 201; *Warrants, 1692-1711*, p. 178.

One John Willson came to the colony a servant to Jacob Wayte in September 1675. A second John Willson indentured himself to John Strode & Co. of Barbados in January 1672. In the spring of 1685 one of them was captured while on an exploring expedition. Land was acquired under the name John Willson in 1707 and in 1710. See *Warrants, 1672-79*, p. 104; *Warrants, 1692-1711* p. 227; Records of the Secretary and the Register 1671-75, p. 63; B.P.R.O.-S.C. *Vol. 2*, pp. 61-2, 67, 68; *Proprietary Grants No. 2, Vol. 39* (MSV), pp. 26-27.

[7] See *Warrants, 1672-79*, p. 106; *Proprietary Grants No. 1, Vol. 38* (MSV), p. 225. A survey of Jamaica dated September 1670, shows two Robert Smiths, one in Clarendon Parish with 180 acres, and another in St. David's Parish with 374 acres. Either of these free residents of Jamaica may well have emigrated to Carolina and had

The problem with employing data from the other seven servants is not the size of their first warrant or grant, but rather that an inordinately long period of time elapsed between their arrival in the colony as servants and their acquisition of real property. While there is a possibility that land allotted 20 to 40 years after a servant's immigration to someone with that servant's name might actually have been acquired by that servant, it is far more likely that the property was conveyed to the servant's child or to a settler who shared a name but no genes with the servant. Thus the John Cooke who had been involved in Dennis Mahone's runaway scheme but had avoided punishment (which probably means he had informed the authorities of the plan or had testified against Mahone) *may* ultimately have become a prosperous planter with vast estates. For John Cooke had actual land grants for 900 acres in the colony. The earliest of these, however, dates from 1705, 34 years after the arrival in Carolina of John Cooke the servant.[8] It is unreasonable to attribute that land to the former servant, or to argue that he had acquired land in the colony. I have, of course, done neither. Similarly, Randolph Evans had at least 500, and perhaps 1000 acres in Carolina by proprietary grants, the earliest of which dates from January 1710. Randall Evans, a servant, arrived in Carolina in August 1671, fully 39 years earlier. No land has been attributed to him in this study.[9] This is no need to cite the details of the remaining five cases in which the interval was so long between arrival as a servant and the acquisition of land by someone with the servant's name, that one is compelled to doubt that the property was obtained by that servant. It is sufficient to note that if Edward Perry the servant actually acquired land, it had taken him 21 years to do so; for Daniel Sullivan the period between

---

the capital necessary to acquire the 600 acres granted in 1682. See *C.S.P. Vol. 8, 1669-74*, pp. 100, 103, 409 (for document relating to the endowment of a church by Robert Smith in 1671).

[8] See *Warrants, 1672-79*, p. 55; *Council Journal, 1671-80*, p. 14; *Proprietary Grants No. 1, Vol. 38 (MSV), p. 535*; Proprietary Grants No. 2, Vol. 39 (MSV), pp. 155, 171; *Abstracts of Grants 1692-1718, 1733-36, 1775-1820* (MSV), pp. 334, 361, 375.

[9] Evans, the servant, married the daughter of John Norton, a prominent settler, and the grants made may have been for a child of that marriage. See *Warrants, 1672-79*, p. 113; *Warrants, 1692-1711*, p. 232; *Shaftsbury Papers*, p. 341; *Proprietary Grants No. 2, Vol.* 39 (MSV), pp. 140-41, 434-35; *Abstracts of Grants 1692-1718, 1733-36, 1775-1820* (MSV), p. 346; *Records of the Register and the Secretary 1711-15* (MSV), p. 195; *Memorial Book Vol.* 3 (MSV), pp. 23-24.

arrival and land ownership computes to 30 years; for William Westbury it is 36 years; for George White 28 years; and for Benjamin Wood 35 years.[10] In this study none of these servants has been credited with having acquired land in Carolina.

II. Levels of Land Acquisition Reached by Former Servants

Two hundred forty-one indentured servants arrived in Carolina prior to 1680. Of these, 102 or slightly over 42% survived to appear as free persons in the colonial records. Of the 102 free settlers who had begun as servants, 87, or just over 85%, acquired real property and therefore can be said to have "succeeded" in the colony. For even if their parcel were tiny and their existence meager, they had moved upward out of the class of propertyless and unfree whites. While there is no doubt that such a "success" rate is significant, we must retain the perspective provided by looking at one last number—the total servant population in the first

---

[10] On Perry, see *Warrants, 1672-79*, p. 112; *Warrants, 1692-1711*, pp. 105, 202; *Records of the Register 1705-09* (MSV), pp. 87-8, 96-7; P.R.O. CO5/398, p. 11; *Proprietary Grants No. 1, Vol.* 38 (MSV), pp. 185, 313, 481, 516-17; *Records of the Register and the Secretary 1675-96, 1703-09* (MSV), p. 515; *Grant Book C* (MSV), p. 203; *Abstracts of Grants and Commissions 1692-1718, 1733-36* (MSV), p. 162 (land mentioned in grant to John Cattle, 1704). It is worth noting that while all the above date from after 1696, and that the Perry involved, as well as another settler named John "Perriey" whose land butted Edward's, were both cited as "Esquire," an Edward Perry bought 100 acres privately from James Humphreys in the fall of 1689, only 14 years after the arrival of Edward Perry the servant. Nevertheless, there is no warrant or grant for any Edward Perry prior to 1696, and it is likely that the 100 acres were purchased by a different Perry (or a son) as well. See Misc. *Records 1682-1690* (MSV), pp. 337-38.

On Sullivan, see *Warrants, 1672-79*, pp. 37, 104; *Warrants, 1692-1711*, p. 163.

On Westbury, see *Warrants, 1672-79*, p. 106; *Warrants, 1692-1711*, pp. 206 (for land identified as being "att Wm Westburys savana"), 236; *Proprietary Grants No. 2, Vol.* 39 (MSV), pp. 151, 196; *Memorial Book Vol. I* (MSV), pp. 415-16; *Memorial Book Vol. III* (MSV), pp. 127-28; *Memorial Book Vol. IV* (MSV), pp. 226-29 (for reference to daughter of "William Welsby deceased").

On White, see *Warrants, 1672-79*, pp. 37, 104; *Warrants, 1692-1711*, p. 180; *Proprietary Grants No. 1, Vol.* 38 (MSV), p. 483; *Proprietary Grants No. 2, Vol.* 39 (MSV), p. 172; *Abstracts of Grants and Commissions 1692-1718, 1733-36, 1775-1820* (MSV), pp. 180, 375.

On Wood, see *Warrants, 1672-79*, p. 63; *Warrants, 1692-1711*, p. 203.

decade of settlement. When one recalls that 241 persons ventured their futures in Carolina, the number who "succeeded," as defined by having acquired a piece of land, dwindles to only 36%. In other words, fewer than four of ten white servant immigrants survived and acquired land—"succeeded"—in the colony, even when "success" is defined in the most generous possible terms.

Four of the 87 former servant landowners held an unspecified number of acres, or property which was limited exclusively to town lots. Their holdings cannot be used to calculate the size of the average amount of land held by such settlers. Thus the data on land acquisition by 83 former servants seem sufficiently accurate and extensive to permit some generalizations about property accumulation in the seventeenth-century American South. These 83 immigrants acquired a total of 30,624 acres of Carolina land. Therefore, the *average* size of the estate secured by the average former servant in the colony works out to have been 369 acres. That is surely an unrealistic figure, representing a huge upward bias caused by the unusual success of a few individuals such as Cattell, Raven, or Rowser. A number probably more typical of the amount of land secured by most freed servants can be determined by excluding the most and the least successful 10% of land accumulators—by focusing on property acquisition by the middle 80% of the sample. When the 16 most atypical former servant landowners are excluded, the remaining 67 colonists acquired 13,422 acres, or 200.33 acres each. That is the exact number of acres which observers such as Thomas Nairne had asserted was required to live decently in the colony, and the possession of which entitled one justly to be labelled a "planter." Equally important, that figure also means that the "average" servant who survived and acquired land moved upward beyond the level to which a headright alone would have placed him or her. It means that a typical history of mobility involved acquiring one's headright concession and, at some later date, acquiring some additional acres. It suggests that the promise of upward mobility meant not merely that a servant might expect to become a free person with a small piece of land, but that continued mobility beyond that point was to be anticipated. It implies that the promise made to prospective immigrants to the colony was in large measure fulfilled—at least for a vast majority (85%) of those who survived servitude and achieved their freedom.

In fact, of the 83 former servants whose land acquisition can be quantified, only 29, or just under 35%, came to own fewer than 101 acres. It is this group which managed to complete only one step upward beyond attaining freedom itself—the acquisition of a total number of acres which probably represented no more than their actual headright. Another 11 came to hold between 101 and 150 acres, which means they probably acquired at least two different parcels of land. Even so, their total land accumulation was small, and when these two groups are combined, the result indicates that 40 of the 83 landowners, or fully 48%, amassed estates of fewer than 151 acres.

Eighteen, or 22% of the group, acquired between 151 and 250 acres. It is fair to say that this group, about one-fifth of those who survived servitude and took up land, achieved significant upward mobility. They surely had completed the transformation from servant to planter. They certainly possessed sufficient assets to live in security and maintain their economic independence. All this means, of course, that the remaining 25 servants, or 30% of the entire group, achieved really substantial upward mobility. Ten of them, or 12% of the group, came to hold from 251 to 400 acres. Another ten amassed estates which ranged in size from 401 to 1000 acres. Five, or 6% of former servant landowners, acquired properties totalling in excess of 1000 acres. The servants whose careers are referred to here, with dates of arrival, literacy information, and estate sizes are listed on pages 134–135.

III. The Impact of Literacy, Skills, and Date of Arrival on Property Accumulation by Former Servants

From our vantage point the 241 servants, with only a few exceptions, seem to have initiated their careers in Carolina from virtually identical starting points, and to have confronted an economic and social environment which gave all of them a fair chance to succeed. All were white. All would, if they lived, have ample opportunity to acquire at least one piece of land. No legal, social, or religious barriers were interposed between them and a prosperous future. A few, of course, did arrive with special advantages such as the genuine or claimed background which permitted James Williams to practice medicine, or skills acquired prior to arriving in the colony such as Samuel Boswood's ability to set himself up as a tailor.

Name	Date of Arrival	Literate	Estate Size (Acres)
Archcraft, Thomas	1670	No	280
Baker, Elizabeth	1671	?	100
Barker, Jonathan	1670	?	?
Barnard, George	1675	?	330
Bevin, William	1670	?	100
Boswood, Samuel	1671	No	750
Braidy, Philip	1671	Yes	170
Bryan, James	1671	No	156
Cason, William	1673	?	120
Cattell, John	1672	No	4082
Chambers, John	1671	No	375
Chambers, William	1670	No	150
Chaplin, John	1678	No	240
Churne, Elizabeth	1670	?	200
Cockfield, William	1670	No	100
Cole, John	1670	?	70
Cooke, William	1672	Yes	70
Dale, Edward	1671	Yes	40
Darkenwell, Nathanyell	1670	?	100
Edwards, Christopher	1670	No	370
English, Mathew	1671	No	100
Farrington, John	1671	Yes	70
Field, Christopher	1671	?	420
Fitzpatrick, Bryan	1670	Yes	?
Fraiser, John	1670	?	100
Gantlett, George	1671	Yes	378
Green, James	1674	No	200
Grey, William	1671	?	30
Hartley, John	1671	?	70
Hooper, John	1673	No	290
Hopkins, John	1672-1674	Yes	305
Horton, John	1674	?	170
How, Millicent	1670	No	100
Howard, Edward	1671	No	?
Huddlestone, John	1670	?	100
Hunt, Robert	1670-1671	?	150
Hunt, Thomas	1673	Yes	210
Hutton, James	1671	No	70
Jackson, William	1673	No	90
Jones, Henry	1670	?	100
Jones, Jone	1672	?	170
Jones, Phillip	1671	?	10
Jones, William	1673	No	210
Jones, Ann	1673	?	210

Name	Date of Arrival	Literate	Estate Size (Acres)
Jones, William (Jr.)	1673	?	400
Kinder, Susanna	1670	?	10
Lawson, Jane	1670	No	293
Layton, Robert	1671	No	110
Lewis, Hugh	1671	Yes	70
Long, William	1672	?	70
Lovell, Michael	1671	Yes	?
Mackanellor, Thomas	1672	?	70
Mahone, Dennis	1670	No	490
McLaughlin, Thomas	1679	?	70
McLaughlin, William	1679	?	70
May, John	1670	Yes	150
Mills, John	1671	?	70
Morgan, Richard	1674	No	500
Orill, Philip	1671	No	110
Pendarvis, Joseph	1671	Yes	320
Poore, Richard	1671	?	100
Pope, Sarah	1678	?	1940
Powell, James	1671	No	70
Raven, John	1672	Yes	3350
Reede, Thomas	1675	?	70
Rowser, Richard	1671	?	630
Rubry, George	1671	?	300
Smallwood, Mathew	1670	Yes	250
Smith, Abraham	1670	No	450
Steere, Thomas	1671	No	120
Stevenson, Elinor	1679	?	140
Steward, Patrick	1673	Yes/No	860
Sumpton, Henry	1671	Yes	170
Swaine, Christopher	1670	?	200
Thomas, Robert	1671	?	140
Thomas, Mary	1671	?	140
Thomas, John	1677	?	640
Thomas, Mrs. John	1677	?	640
Wheelwright, Stephen	1670	Yes	100
Wigglesworth, Hugh	1670	No	200
Wigmore, Nathaniel	1672	No	140
Williams, James	1670	Yes	2605
Williams, Martha	1670	?	2605
Williams, John	1670	?	200
Wilson, Edward	1671	?	170
Wintrop, Henry	1671	?	70
Worme, Thomas	1670	No	185

Yet one characteristic did separate servants into two distinct groups—literacy. Scholars understandably have been intrigued by the impact of the degree of literacy on the lives of settlers in early America. It is possible to employ the data we have on land acquisition and literacy among Carolina's servants to venture a few broad generalizations about the ways literacy related to "success" in the early colonial South.

Of the 87 former servants who acquired land, and whose mobility can therefore be measured, it is possible to ascertain the ability or inability to sign one's name in 45 cases, or for almost 52% of the sample.[11] In this group of 45 former servants who acquired land, 28, or more than 62%, could not sign their names and are presumed to have been illiterate. The significance of the fact that only 17, or just under 38%, were literate can only be determined when the average sizes of the estates accumulated by them are compared with those amassed by illiterate former servants. For, given the availability of land through headright concession to all early immigrants, a discussion of the relation of literacy to success in Carolina must focus on quantities of land rather than on the quantity of former servants who acquired land. In other words, one might argue that illiterates took up land more frequently than their better educated counterparts precisely because they enjoyed no options other than hard work in the fields, or were unaware of better opportunities elsewhere.

When the average amount of land secured by the 17 literate former servants is computed, the result works out to 551 acres.[12] However, when the two most and the two least successful examples are excluded from the computation, the average for literate former servants is transformed sharply, to 199.4 acres. This is almost exactly the size of the adjusted average estate of 200.3 acres secured by the entire group of servants, the literate, the illiterate, and those whose literacy cannot be ascertained. The mobility displayed by illiterate servants is equally unsettling to those who would argue that education has historically been a valuable tool to employ in raising one's status. The average size estate gained by the 28 illiterate servants who acquired land was 379 acres.[13] When this figure is

---

[11] I have eliminated Patrick Steward from this discussion, for it is not clear whether he was literate or illiterate.

[12] Only 15 cases can be used in this computation, since two of the literate servants, Fitzpatrick and Lovell, acquired estates of unspecified size.

[13] Here 27 examples were used, since the acreage acquired by the illiterate servant Edward Howard is unknown.

adjusted by excluding the three most and the three least successful cases, the average for servants who could not write their names works out to have been 222.3 acres—larger than the size of the estate built by the typical former servant who could read and write. Among the literate servant population, of 15 estates whose size can be measured, five, or one-third, were less than 101 acres, and eight, or 53%, were smaller than the 199.4 acre adjusted average for the group. Among the 27 servants who were illiterate and whose property can be measured, only six, or 22.2%, acquired fewer than 100 acres, while 16, or 59.3%, were unable to acquire at least the 222.3 acres which typified their group.

It appears that in the early colonial South, for those starting out at the bottom of white society and thus presumably most subject to the positive impact on their fortunes of *any* advantage, the one factor commonly believed to have had such an impact and to be associated with success—education—had, in fact, virtually no effect on the success (as measured by land accumulation) of settlers. For literate servants on average achieved no more than their less educated fellows.

It is crucial to recall here that most scholars accept the notion that those for whom literacy can be gauged—those men and women who were called upon to participate in activities which required or allowed them to sign their names or make their marks—probably represent a more successful segment of the entire population than do those whose literacy cannot be ascertained because they failed to do so. For the kinds of documents which commonly were signed involved property—land or goods being bought, sold, appraised, granted, inherited, or bequeathed. The poorest classes, the dispossessed, of course, would not be expected to have been principal participants in such transactions, and seldom would be called upon to witness them for others. Forty of the servants whose property accumulation can be measured failed to leave any record of their literacy. And, in fact, these former servants did accumulate less land than those who did sign or mark documents. The average amount of land acquired by those whose literacy we cannot gauge works out to have been 282 acres, or almost 100 acres less than the average for servants who clearly were illiterate. When the most atypical 20% are excluded from the computation, the adjusted average for former servants whose ability to read and write cannot be measured works out to a little over 167 acres. The 43 former servants who secured land and also had the opportunity to sign or mark documents acquired an average of 450 acres of land in the course of their lives in Carolina. When only the middle 80% are included in the tabulation, the average works out to be 234 acres.

Two considerations deserve mention here, if only to avoid being ahistorical. First, in early Carolina one did not need any education in order to acquire real property, or to "succeed" in pursuits commonly linked to the use of land, such as farming or grazing. In fact, knowledge gained through experience was probably more effective and useful in successfully pursuing such careers than that available in written sources. A logical corollary to this is the fact that Carolina was, in the years being considered here, a rather primitive place. The economy and society were simple and rural, even in Charles Town. There was little specialization among workers, and an absence of advanced technology. Education, then, in such a place at such a time, would have less value, especially in terms of its influence on economic success, than it would in other societies which were contemporaneous yet more complex, and certainly less value in influencing success than it would in the twentieth century.

If education, defined as an ability to read and write, was of little consequence in the quest by freed servants for property in early Carolina, did other factors have a bearing on the level of measurable wealth such settlers ultimately reached? As we have seen earlier when examining the careers of Michael Lovell and James Powell, knowledge of a skilled trade might lead a craftsman away from acquisition of the kind of property employed here to measure success. For such settlers may have sensed that they did not need land and hence would have sold off rather quickly any real property usable for farming, or any rights to such land, and avoided seeking to amass large landed estates as their lives progressed. Conversely, Sam Boswood, also a skilled craftsman, seems eagerly to have striven to acquire land. In other words, possession of a skill, commonly perceived as having a positive influence on economic success in frontier communities, would not *necessarily* stimulate land acquisition, though it might of course amplify the *ability* to acquire land by providing money or goods which could be exchanged for land.

As we have already noted, servants who arrived earliest in Carolina, that is, prior to 1672, "survived" at a somewhat lower rate than did servants who came to the colony between 1672 and 1680. Did those who arrived later also display a pattern of land accumulation which differed from that of the earlier servant immigrants? That is, was time of arrival a factor in the "success" achieved by former servants? Did, as one of the standard American dicta states, those who reached the frontier quickest secure for themselves a disproportionate share of the available resources?[14]

When considering those servants immigrating to Carolina during the first decade of settlement, the answer seems to deny the dictum. Seventy-one percent, or 170, of the 239 servants whose arrival in the colony can be dated, came prior to 1672. Sixty-nine, or 29%, arrived between 1672 and 1680. Of the 87 former servants who survived and acquired land, 59, or 68%, immigrated prior to 1672, while 28, or 32%, came later. Thus, date of arrival seems to have had neither a positive nor a negative influence on the fact of land acquisition. Seventy-one percent of the servants and 68% of the property acquirers came before 1672. Twenty-nine percent of the servants and 32% of the property acquirers came between 1672 and 1680. In fact, therefore, those who came earliest acquired property at a slightly *lower* rate than did those who arrived later. Again, since proprietary land policy dictated that every immigrant coming in this period was entitled to receive a land concession, the fact that date of arrival was of no great significance in the securing by former servants of a piece of land is hardly surprising.

However, the "common wisdom" on the process by which Americans secured wealth on the frontier goes beyond the solitary consideration of property acquisition. It acknowledges that the frontier was bountiful and the wilderness vast, so that virtually everyone might be expected to *acquire* land. But the essence of the argument is that those who arrive earliest get not only land, but the *best* or the *most* land. For even in a lush wilderness, some areas are surely richer or better situated or more desirable than others, and it is only logical to assume that the earlier a settler started to amass property, the better off he or she ultimately would be. It is, of course, impossible for us to assess the relative quality of various parcels of land owned by former servants in seventeenth-century Carolina. It is worth noting, however, that prior to the eighteenth century, the population of the colony was small enough and the wilderness vast enough for virtually everyone to locate land of the sort he or she desired. For warrants and grants issued well after the years discussed here consistently refer to such highly regarded assets as water frontage or proximity to centers of population. Doubtless those who came at the outset did find that their land appreciated in value at a higher rate than did property acquired by later immigrants, especially if the early arrivals had secured land in Charles Town or along the Ashley or Cooper Rivers near the town.

---

[14]This theme is brilliantly discussed by Daniel J. Boorstin in *The Americans: The National Experience* (New York), 1967), pp. 97-107.

However, in terms of its "quality" for planting, grazing, or as a source of timber, it is safe to assume that those who came later located and came to own land just as good as that acquired by the very first immigrants. In fact, since the site of Charles Town was moved from its original location to "Oyster Point" at the junction of the Ashley and Cooper Rivers in 1680, some later arrivals who had failed to secure prime locations in the center of the urban settlement as initially situated, may well have benefitted if the relocation of the town moved its focus in the direction of land which initially had seemed less than ideally located.

Thus, once again we are left with a less than ideal tool to use in resolving questions about the levels of success displayed by earlier as opposed to later arrivals. We must focus our discussion not on the relative "quality" of land owned, but rather on the quantity acquired by former servants. In other words, since we cannot ascertain the richness of the soil, timber, or grass on property acquired by former servants and thereby measure its quality, comparison of the wealth amassed by early as opposed to later arrivals must be based on a consideration of the numbers of acres they acquired.

Did servants who came at the outset acquire more real property than those who arrived later? Did those who commenced their careers as free settlers while others were just starting out as bound servants ultimately achieve more because of their head start? Or, conversely, did later arriving servants not only endure and acquire land at a higher rate than the first arrivals, but secure larger estates as well?

The data clearly show that servants reaching Carolina after the first wave of settlement—those who came between 1672 and 1680—enjoyed markedly greater success (as defined by total acres acquired) than did those who immigrated during the first years of colonization. It appears that not only was early arrival *not* an economic advantage, but in fact it may have somehow worked *against* later success. The average property accumulation of the 59 servants reaching Carolina by 1671 works out to have been 273 acres. The adjusted average for this group—the number yielded when the six most and the six least successful are excluded from the calculation—is only 168 acres, or below the average for the entire servant population. The 28 later arrivals, however, averaged 559 acres each during their careers in the colony. When the three largest and smallest estates are discarded, the adjusted average works out to 276 acres, or a little above the average for all former servants who acquired land.

It may be that later arrivals built larger estates for reasons similar to those postulated in an attempt to explain their higher rates of survival.

Those early immigrants who helped to establish a colony might have been more likely to become disenchanted with what they found than those who came to a place already partially built and about which they had some foreknowledge. Thus early arrivals may have taken up their first land concession only in order to have something to sell or trade, and thereby gain sufficient funds to allow them to depart the colony and seek their fortunes elsewhere. They would thus appear in the records both as having gained freedom and having acquired property, but never more than their very first (and solitary) small parcel of land. They may, in other words, have failed to continue to acquire property in Carolina because they were not living in the colony. Those who stayed longer because they knew before they immigrated what life was likely to be in the American South, would naturally display higher levels of real property accumulation precisely because they did remain in the colony.

The striking differences in property acquisition by the two groups may be related to the kinds of men and women involved. It is reasonable to suggest that the lower levels of "success" achieved by the first servants resulted from a situation in which landowners desperately wanted to import large numbers of servants because only by doing so could they acquire sizeable estates, and only by settling acres thus acquired could they retain possession of them. Thus those who aspired to create large estates in the colony would have been impelled to induce virtually anyone to contract himself or herself for a term of service, with little regard for the dedication, intellect, education, background, or personality of the candidate. What was important was numbers of servants, and not necessarily the "quality" of the people secured to occupy that status. In this context, it is well to recall observations of Carolina's first servants which noted that those from Barbados were "addicted to Rum," and that others were simply "bad."[15] This is not to say that these first servants were uniformly undesirable—I have previously pointed out that they were not criminals or derelicts. It is to say that at the outset of settlement, the central concerns of both the free settlers and the proprietors involved the allocation of land and the securing of a permanent foothold in the American wilderness. To accomplish either aim required that people be brought to the colony, and it is readily understandable that any servant's potential for becoming a solid citizen who would strive to succeed, once free, might be glanced over in the search for people who were willing to accept servant status in a frontier settlement.

---

[15] See Chapter 3, note 9, and *Shaftsbury Papers*, p. 387.

Needless to say, later arrivals might have been more calculating in assessing their likely fates in the colony. And those who sought to import them into Carolina might have given priority to the character of any they were about to engage. That terms for servants seem to have lengthened after 1672 tends to bolster this line of reasoning. Masters wanted labor and commitment from their servants, not merely their bodies to serve as the basis for land warrants and as a deterrent to potentially hostile neighbors. And servants, confronted with longer terms, must have been people who were resolved to work to improve themselves. The period of high adventure, risk, and uncertainty in a wilderness outpost may have attracted some at first who were not firmly wedded to the notion of staying in a settled colony as farmers or tradesmen. That period had largely passed by 1672. In all likelihood, those who arrived after that date came prepared for unglamorous work, and probably harbored few illusions about what would be required of them. It is, therefore, not unlikely that a different sort of person became a Carolina servant after 1672 than had done so earlier, and that the later arrivals may have been predisposed both to stay in the colony even if faced with hardships, and to strive to succeed once freed, because they had come to the colony determined to do both. And they may have known, in a way the first arrivals never could, that both perseverance and hard work would be required of them if they were to succeed. They also would have known what form success was likely to take in the colony—that, for example, there would be no precious stones lying about merely to be snatched up, or streams filled with gold nuggets waiting to be gathered up—and to have decided even before they immigrated that what the colony did in fact offer was what they wished to attain.[16]

---

[16] For purposes of discussing the relationship between time of arrival and later success, it is possible that the entire group of servants who reached Carolina prior to 1680 ought to be defined as the first arrivals—those who reached the resources of the frontier first. Later arriving servants, then, would be considered as having missed the wide opportunities and the great bounty of the first decade as opposed to the first couple of years of settlement. Menard has pursued this approach in Maryland and demonstrated that, in fact, opportunities did dwindle for those arriving during the second decade of colonization. However, it is well to recall that Bernard Bailyn's early work on Virginia counters this view, for that colony's future leaders and most economically successful settlers, as a group, appeared not at the outset but rather in a second and later wave of immigration. In Carolina, land—the focus of our discussion—remained plentiful throughout the seventeenth century, so there is no reason to think servants coming to the colony after 1680 had less access to real property than had the colony's first servants. In any case, the point of my discussion

IV. Symbols of Mobility: Titles and Offices

We have at our disposal two other indicators of status which merit consideration—offices or positions of responsibility to which settlers were either elected or appointed, and formal or informal titles[17] which occasionally accompany settlers' names in surviving documents. Some titles combined information about both occupation and status. *Planter*, for example, conveyed the image of an independent free person who engaged in farming, as did *yeoman*. Only one former servant, John Cattell, earned citation in a public document as a yeoman.[18] However, fully 20 former servants (Cattell was not among them) were identified at some time as

has been to consider the relative advantages of coming at the very beginning, when the colony was least developed, as opposed to arriving a little later when more was known about the colony and the kinds of people who would be able to live in the environment it provided. See Menard, "Servant to Freeholder," pp. 61-62; Bernard Bailyn, "Politics and Social Structure in Virginia," in Paul Goodman, ed., *Essays in American Colonial History* (New York, 1967).

Richard Waterhouse, in "England, the Caribbean, and the Settlement of Carolina," *American Studies* 9 (December 1975), has argued that in Carolina there was no displacement of an earlier by a later-arriving elite. "In South Carolina," he writes, "a relatively large proportion of those who, in the middle of the eighteenth century, were among the wealthier inhabitants, were descended from those families who arrived in the colony during the first twenty years of its settlement." Carolina's "eighteenth-century elite did not," he stresses, "arrive to take advantage of the labours of previous inhabitants but were themselves, from the earliest years of settlement, engaged in . . . the development of the colony" (pp. 280-81). See also Waterhouse, "South Carolina's Colonial Elite: A Study in the Social Structure and Political Culture of a Southern Colony, 1670-1671," Ph.D. dissertation, The Johns Hopkins University, 1973, pp. 316-17. Here Waterhouse writes, "the pattern established in seventeenth-century Virginia and Barbados of the displacement of one elite by another was not repeated in South Carolina" (p. 316).

[17] In the following discussion I shall use the word *title* to signify not an inherited status linked to nobility (such as Duke, Lord, Cassique, Landgrave, etc.), but rather as a way of referring to terms which denoted status, respect, or distinction, such as *Mister*, *Gentleman*, or *Esquire*.

[18] In January 1704, Oliver Spencer sold part of his town lot for £183 current money to John Cattell, "The Elder . . . Yeoman." *Records of the Register 1709-12* (MSV), pp. 161-64. Cattell purchased the rest of that town lot from Nathaniel and Hannah Law in May, 1705 for £160 current money. That sale also identified Cattell as a yeoman. *Ibid.*, pp. 157-60.

planters.[19] Six former servants, including three who had also been referred to as planters, were called *freeman* in public documents.[20] William Chambers not only managed to be labelled a freeman and a planter, but he also found his way into the records as a *Captain.* However, this title seems to have denoted occupation rather than military rank, for Chambers repeatedly appears in the records as a mariner. In all likelihood he exercised some authority on one of Carolina's trading vessels, which generated the "Capt." before his name.[21]

A very small number of servants ultimately came to enjoy titles which conveyed not merely information about their freedom, the way they maintained themselves, or both, but rather which implied high social rank. Only eight men who began their lives in Carolina as servants enjoyed as free men the prestige associated with being referred to as "Mr.," "Esquir.," or "Gent." In the case of Edward Perry "Esq$^{r.}$" the title may

---

[19] The "planters" (with one citation for each) were: William Cason—*Proprietary Grants No. 1, Vol. 38* (MSV), p. 10; William Chambers—*Records of the Register and the Secretary 1675-96, 1703-09* (MSV), p. 101; William Cooke—*Warrants, 1680-92*, p. 161; Edward Dale—*Records of the Register and the Secretary 1675-96, 1703-09* (MSV), p. 59; Christopher Edwards—*Ibid.*, p. 81; John Fraiser—*Ibid.*, p. 55; James Green—*Misc. Records 1680-1691* (MSV), pp. 181-82; John Hooper—*Shaftsbury Papers*, p. 473; James Hutton—*Records of the Register and the Secretary 1675-96, 1703-09* (MSV), p. 122; William Jackson—*Records of the Secretary 1675-95* (MSV), pp. 188-89; William Jones—*Ibid.*, p. 10; Robert Layton—*Misc. Records 1682-90* (MSV), pp. 254-55; Dennis Mahone—*Records of the Secretary 1675-95* (MSV), pp. 186-87; Philip Orill—*Misc. Records 1682-90* (MSV), pp. 127-28; Joseph Pendarvis—*Proprietary Grants No. 1, Vol. 38* (MSV), p. 3; Richard Rowser—*Records of the Secretary 1675-95* (MSV), p. 196; George Rubry—*Records of the Register and the Secretary 1711-15* (MSV), pp. 332-33; Mathew Smallwood—*Records of the Secretary 1675-95* (MSV), p. 54; Patrick Steward—*Misc. Records 1682-90* (MSV), p. 25A; and Nathaniell Wigmore—*Ibid.*, pp. 129A-130A. One servant, John Cole, who did become free and acquire land, was referred to as a planter while he was still a servant. This "title" denoted his status and occupation prior to engaging himself as a servant. He is not, therefore, included in the group discussed above. See *Shaftsbury Papers*, p. 253.

[20] The six were: John Chambers—*Warrants, 1672-79*, p. 197; William Chambers—*ibid.*, p. 126; William Cooke—*ibid.*, p. 135; John Huddlestone—*ibid.*, p. 127; William Jackson—*ibid.*, p. 133; and Christopher Swaine—*ibid.*, pp. 168-69.

[21] For references to him as "Capt.", see: *Warrants, 1680-92*, p. 44; as "marriner," see *Proprietary Grants No. 1, Vol. 38* (MSV), pp. 44-45; *Records of the Register & the Secretary 1675-96, 1703-09* (MSV), p. 159; *Records of the Secretary 1675-95* (MSV), p. 114. This surely is the same William Chambers called a "planter", for in *ibid.*, p. 112, his widow is referred to as ". . . Mary the relict of William Chambers late of this province planter deceased. . . ."

well have been added to the name of a son, or may have referred to an Edward Perry who immigrated as a free person, for the first land transferred from the proprietors to any Edward Perry was conveyed 21 years after the arrival of Edward Perry the servant.[22]

"Mister" appeared along with the name of three former servants in Carolina's public records—John Cattell, George Gantlett, and Hugh Wigglesworth. It is clear, therefore, that "Mr." denoted respect and perhaps social status rather than vast property holdings, for while Cattell came to possess over 4000 acres of land, Gantlett held fewer than 400, and Wigglesworth only 200 acres in Carolina. Needless to say, they may have enjoyed other assets which fail to appear in records we can study, but I suspect that the title in these cases more than anything else represents recognition by their fellow colonists that they were solid, respectable, admirable settlers.[23]

Aside from Edward Perry, four former servants acquired the titles of *Gentleman* or *Esquire*. That John Raven, who came to own 3350 acres, also came to merit being labelled a gentleman is hardly surprising.[24] That William Cooke, on the other hand, whose recorded holdings totalled 70 acres, similarly was referred to as a gentleman defies explanation. There is no evidence that more than one William Cooke immigrated to Carolina prior to 1680, although that may have been the case. However, one would expect that had a man of such status entered the colony, he would have appeared in the records with a land warrant based on his immigration as a "free person," or as "Mr." William Cooke, or as William Cooke, "Gent." No such entires can be found in the land warrants. It is intriguing to speculate on the reasons why a former servant whose real property holdings totalled only 70 acres and whose "loveing Brothers" and executors were mere tradesmen (a "carpenter" and a "Bricklayer"), came to be called a gentleman. But at this distance we can do no more than

---

[22] Perry has been excluded from my discussion of land acquisition by former servants because of the exceedingly long span of years between arrival and property holding. See footnote 10, *supra*. For Perry, or "Perrie," or "Perriey" as Esquire, see *Warrants, 1692-1711* , p. 202; *Records of the Register 1705-09*(MSV), pp. 87-88; *Proprietary Grants No. 1, Vol. 38* (MSV), p. 517 (for "John Pierriey Esq[r.]").

[23] For their property holdings, see pages 134–135 above. For references to them as "Mister," see *Records of the Secretary 1675-95* (MSV), p. 392 (Cattell); *ibid.*, p. 401 (Gantlett); *Council Journal, 1692*, p. 60 (Wigglesworth).

[24] For Raven, see pages 39-41 above.

speculate.[25] In addition to Edward Perry, the former servants who achieved the designation *Esquire* were Joseph Pendarvis and James Williams. Both were wealthy, prominent settlers with vast holdings in the colony—men who quite logically would have commanded the respect and enjoyed the prestige that such a title conveyed.[26]

Former servants thus acquired titles only rarely. Equally unusual was a former servant who came to hold either an appointive or an elected office in the colony. Former servants John Hooper and Thomas Hunt were appointed Viewers of Tobacco late in 1675.[27] Richard Morgan appears never to have secured a public office, but he merited one. A letter of September 1685 to Governor Joseph Moreton from the proprietors noted that Morgan was "well qualified for ye Publick Service of Carolina," and ordered the colonial officials to provide him with at least 500 acres of land.[28] Three former servants, Mathew Smallwood, Hugh Wigglesworth, and Thomas Worme were selected to serve on juries.[29] James Williams, both wealthier and socially more prominent than they, was a member of the colony's Grand Jury.[30] He also was the coroner of Colleton County, and won election to the Commons House from Colleton County for the first assembly in 1692-1694, the third assembly in 1696-1697, and the eighth assembly in 1706-1707.[31] Three other prominent settlers who had started out in Carolina as indentured servants—John Cattell, Joseph

---

[25] Cooke's solitary land acquisition is in *Warrants, 1672-79*, p. 135. He did control, but not legally own, additional acres, for *Warrants, 1680-92*, p. 161, contains a petition from Edward Patey for a special warrant for lands formerly owned by Daniel Lacey, "now in the posession of Wm. Cooke of this Province Planter." His brothers Thomas and William Elliot were named by him to be his executors, and both his will and the document by which they were legally invested with that power refer to Cooke as a gentleman. *Records of the Secretary 1675-95* (MSV), pp. 384-85.

[26] On Pendarvis, see pp. 126-27 above. On Williams, see p. 118 above.

[27] *Council Journal, 1671-80*, p. 79; *Shaftsbury Papers*, p. 473.

[28] "Proprietors to Jos Moreton," September 10, 1685, *B.P.R.O.-S.C., Vol. 2*, p. 90.

[29] For Smallwood, see *Records of the Register 1696-1703* (MSV), p. 254; for Wigglesworth, see *Council Journal, 1692*, p. 60; for Worme, see *ibid.*, p. 60.

[30] *Ibid.*, p. 59.

[31] He became coroner on April 21, 1692. *Ibid.*, p. 12. For his service in the Commons House, see *Biographical Directory of the South Carolina House of Representatives Vol. I, Session Lists 1692-1673* (Columbia, 1974), pp. 21, 23, 28-29.

Pendarvis, and John Raven—also were elected to sit in the assembly.[32] Needless to say, the four former servants who did come to hold elective office represent the most upwardly mobile segment of the servant population. The *average* land accumulation of these four computes to 2589 acres, even when Joseph Pendarvis' relatively meager 320 acre estate is included in the calculation.

Only two other former servants held offices in the colony. Mathew English was named the Provost Marshall of Carolina some time prior to the autumn of 1684,[33] and Stephen Wheelwright was appointed Surveyor General in July 1673, a post he held until September 1677.[34]

In sum, then, it is clear that those who began life in Carolina in servitude generally failed to achieve recognition in the records by titles of distinction, and even less frequently were chosen to exercise power in an office to which they were elected or appointed. Access to seats in the assembly by former servants was limited exclusively to those who had attained a level of wealth which insured economic and perhaps social prominence in the colony. On the other hand, that four former servants did in fact come to sit in the assembly does establish that the path to the highest levels in colonial Carolina's society was open, and that having started at the very bottom of the white social order did not entirely close off the possibility of future ascendancy. Clearly, Carolinians were content

---

[32] Cattell was elected to the fifth assembly from Berkeley and Craven Counties for the years 1700-1702. Pendarvis served in the first assembly from 1692-1694 for Berkeley County. Raven represented an unspecified constituency in the second assembly which met in 1695, in the ninth assembly which met in 1707, and in the 11th assembly which met in 1708-1709. He represented Colleton County in the sixth assembly from 1702-1703, the seventh assembly from 1703-1705, the tenth assembly from 1707-1708, the 13th assembly from 1711-1712, the 14th assembly from 1713-1715, and the 15th assembly from 1716-1717. He was elected but declined to serve in the 12th assembly which met in 1710-1711. See *Session Lists*, pp. 21-40. See also *ibid.*, p. 43, for election of Capt. John Raven to the 17th assembly in 1720-1721. Raven also served as one of the trustees for his church, along with his son John Raven, Jr. See *Records of the Register and the Secretary 1712-13* (MSV), pp. 60-62.

[33] In September 1684, English was ordered by the colonial officials to make an arrest. He was still serving the following summer, but exactly how long he held the office is not known. See Misc. *Records 1682-90* (MSV), pp. 153-54; B.P.R.O.-S.C. *Vol.* 2, pp. 65, 69, 75-76.

[34] That is the date of the last entry in *Warrants* which directs him, as Surveyor General, to lay out property. See *Council Journal, 1671-80*, p. 61; *Warrants, 1672-79*, pp. 65-145.

to place in office men who had arrived in servitude, but only those who had demonstrated by their economic success that they were worthy of such consideration.

CHAPTER SEVEN

Servant Mobility in a Comparative Context

It is obvious that Carolina's servants comprised only a fraction of the colony's white population. And even as the first decade of settled life in the province progressed, the proportion of servants, or of those who had started out as servants, dwindled in relation to the percentage of settlers who had arrived as free persons. Thus any discussion of mobility in early Carolina really must consider, at least in passing, those settlers who entered the colony with control over their own labor. Equally important, virtually all of the questions scholars have about the achievements of former servants cannot be answered adequately solely by accumulating and reporting data which relate exclusively to those servants. For servant mobility can be understood fully only when it is considered in a comparative framework. We must know what nonservants achieved if we are to make sense out of servant accomplishments in the colony. Similarly, only by examining what men and women, servant and free, achieved in other colonies can many of our questions about Carolina itself be resolved. Thus we are impelled to seek information about nonservants, and about non Carolinians, if we are to comprehend fully the significance of what has been learned about Carolinians who arrived as indentured servants.

Data on settlers in other English mainland colonies have been published, and making comparisons between early Carolina society and some other roughly contemporaneous English settlements is not difficult. However, virtually no work has been done on free white immigrants to Carolina at any point prior to the American Revolution, much less during the first decade of settlement. Largely this is a result of the lack of systematic records, especially of church records, commonly considered essential to such endeavors. I have earlier discussed the problems encountered by historians seeking the kinds of data necessary for any discussion of social or economic mobility in colonial Carolina, and identified some of the questions which cannot be answered given the data that were recorded, and the volumes that have survived. These caveats, needless to say, apply with equal force to research on free immigrants as they did to investigation of servant immigrants. It is possible to accumulate exactly the same kinds of data on persons who began life in Carolina as free settlers as were retrievable for those who began as servants. Therefore, while neither as precise nor complete as would be possible were a different settlement being considered (or Carolina at a later time), examination of the relative accomplishments of free as opposed to servant immigrants can take place.

I have made no effort to acquire data on every white settler who entered Carolina prior to 1680. Nor have I attempted to draw a sample from the colony's entire white population during each of the first ten years of settled life in the colony. For data on any individual are so haphazardly available that selecting a few names from each year's arrivals during Carolina's first decade might open the resulting study to severe biases caused not by the process employed to select settlers for study, but rather by the disproportionate way in which facts about specific colonists are distributed and have survived. There are many strategies for acquiring from the total list of settlers in Carolina between 1670 and 1680 a "representative" group which would serve as the starting point for research on free immigrants. But there is no way to ensure that the names selected by any method would identify colonists about whom substantial and useful information can be found. It would also be risky to examine the careers of free immigrants chosen specifically because we knew beforehand that data on them were available. The biases inherent in such a procedure are obvious. I have, therefore, chosen to study not a sampling of individuals who settled in Carolina during each of its first ten years as an English colony, but rather to look at surviving data on *every* settler who immigrated as a free person during the year 1671.

By focusing on those who arrived in 1671, I have attempted to avoid the potential biases inherent in selecting either the very earliest free settlers in the colony, or those who arrived after the heaviest waves of immigration. Men and women who reached Carolina in 1671 were likely to have had sufficient foreknowledge about what the place actually was to minimize early departure, inefficient work, discontent, disenchantment, or disappointment generated by surprise. At the same time, 1671 was close enough to the actual establishment of the colony that men and women who arrived then would have encountered a largely unspoiled wilderness environment with plenty of prime land and choice sites available for acquisition and use. These settlers would probably have been predisposed to hard work in a setting that largely fulfilled their pre-arrival expectations as to what it would be. And they would have encountered an environment uncluttered with settlers who had reached the wilderness before them and had already secured much of what was most desirable. They would, in other words, have been psychologically prepared to take advantage of the bounty that was available.

I. Numbers and Gender

I have succeeded in identifying 52 Carolinians who arrived as free persons in the year 1671. If we accept as reasonably accurate Joseph Dalton's report of the colony's population in January 1672, there were 238 free settlers who had arrived during the first two years of settlement. Thus, slightly more than one-fifth of those living in Carolina in 1672 had arrived in 1671. According to Dalton, of the January 1672 population, 190 were free men and 48 were free women.[1] The 52 free immigrants of 1671, however, included 48 males and only four females—a staggering sex ratio of 12 male immigrants for every female immigrant! Of Carolina's 1672 population, only 8% of the free women (4 of 48), and 25% of its free men (48 of 190) had immigrated in 1671.

This strikingly imbalanced male-female ratio among 1671's free arrivals may reflect a perception on the part of potential settlers that Carolina in 1671 was not quite "ready" for settled family life—that its society was too undeveloped to permit stable husband-wife-child relationships to flourish. The sex ratio exhibited by those immigrating in 1671 seems therefore to support my speculation that later arrivals "survived" at a higher rate than did earlier immigrants, precisely because they arrived with more foreknowledge about the place. Perhaps many of the 1671 male immigrants were married, but elected to postpone the immigration of their wives because they had reason to believe that the settlement was not yet sufficiently developed to be conducive to the kind of family life they wanted. Or perhaps they held property in their place of departure which they left in the care of their wives. In any case, it seems that one can explain the fact that in 1671, 12 free men immigrated for every free woman, because settlers knew something about the colony that

---

[1] See page 59, *supra*.

was not known a full year earlier when 185 free persons came, of whom 141 were men and 44, or nearly 24%, were women.

Of course it is also possible that only a few of 1671's free male immigrants were married prior to their arrival in the colony. Even so, one cannot escape the conclusion that once Englishmen had lived in Carolina for a full year—once something substantive about settled life in the colony was known—free males perceived their *immediate* chances of survival and success as being far greater than did females. For in 1671 free men chose to come to Carolina in overwhelmingly greater numbers than did free women.

It is important to recognize that this imbalanced sex ratio does not seem to have been caused by what can be called a "get-rich-quick-in-the-colonies-and-return-home" syndrome that tends to explain the behavior of many Spanish conquistadors, most of those who became buccaneers, and a majority of the early English settlers in Jamestown. Many in these groups seem to have come to America not to erect stable settled communities, but rather to seize readily available wealth, to exploit it, to export it, and then to enjoy it in older more developed societies.[2] In the era of discovery,

---

[2] See, for example, A.O. Exquemelin, *The Buccaneers of America* (Baltimore, 1969), for an account of all-male, mobile (unsettled) societies in the New World established to secure wealth. The most stirring account of the goals of the conquistadors (whose exploits surely influenced early Englishmen in America) is Miguel Leon-Portilla, *The Broken Spears: The Aztec Account of the Conquest of Mexico* (Boston, 1966). Work by Edmund S. Morgan on Virginia, especially "The Labor Problem at Jamestown, 1607-1618," *American Historical Review*, 76 (1971), pages 595-611, makes a strong case for this interpretation. On the other hand, the view that early English settlers in Virginia failed to work hard because their pre-arrival expectations involved not work in the fields, but rather gold-gathering, or supervision of the labor of others (Indians), or military exploits of conquest (all part of a scenario that could have been derived from prior Spanish experience in Mexico and Peru), has been challenged by Karen Ordahl Kupperman in "Apathy and Death in Early Jamestown," *Journal of American History*, 66 (June, 1979), pages 24-40. Kupperman suggests that the appropriate model to use in analyzing English labor problems in Virginia is not mistaken preconceptions as to what awaited them in the colony on the part of early settlers, but rather the experiences of American prisoners-of-war in Korea. She argues that disease combined with confinement and a sense of isolation to produce in both Virginia's first settlers and in American prisoners-of-war, symptoms and behavior patterns which appear to the unenlightened observer to be nothing but mere laziness. Prior to actual settlement in Carolina, it is clear that some at least *hoped* to locate easily-seized wealth of the sort the Spanish had found in Mexico and Peru. The "Barbados Concessions" of 1664, for example, in ensuring prospective settlers that they would have full enjoyment of lands granted to them by the proprietors, still

exploration, and colonization, the Americas did serve as a magnet for men, acting singly or in groups, who sought to locate riches, secure them, and then to return to a place they considered "home." The free men who entered Carolina in 1671 do not fit this model. While a few departed the colony sometime after settling there, I have located no evidence that any of these early settlers came to Carolina intending to make a quick or easy fortune and then to leave.

Many of the 48 males stayed in Carolina long enough to acquire property over time—to secure land from the proprietors in addition to that which they received initially. They held offices. They practiced trades. They planted crops. These men were (and they perceived themselves as) settlers, not conquerors or overseers. It is not likely that they would have come to the colony seeking a quick fortune, and then have been transformed into the kinds of men who sought to establish themselves as farmers, merchants, or craftsmen. If some who came at the very start of colonization fantasized that immigration would lead to quick wealth, by 1671 it was generally recognized that Carolina (at least the area in the process of being settled) would not provide easily secured gold, silver, precious stones, or entire nations of Indians willing to submit to European domination. Englishmen who came would have to work, or hire other Englishmen to work, or to amass sufficient capital to buy slaves. Thus Carolina's 1671 male immigrants seem to have intended from the outset to stay. And since they came to stay they must have planned, at some future time when either they or the colony had changed, to add women to their society. Therefore, that the overwhelming majority of those who came in 1671 were males, tells us that the colony must have seemed to prospective immigrants to be suited to men *at that time*.

By the end of the century the male-female ratio for all adult whites approached 1.5:1. Evidently the gender imbalance of the early years related to frontier conditions—to the need for laborers, to fears about the colony's security, and to uncertainties over what enterprises, if any, would prove successful. Once concerns about such matters were resolved, the male-female ratio would begin to approach parity. That far more women, both in terms of a true number and as a fraction of the total population, came during the first year of colonization than during 1671 suggests only that the very uncertainty about what Carolina was and would be, along with pre-colonization propaganda by the proprietors and their agents,

---

reserved for the proprietors "ye half part of Mynes of Gold & Silvo[r]"which might be developed. *Shaftsbury Papers*, p. 48.

combined to induce a larger number of women to immigrate during 1670 than would have done so had Englishmen actually lived in the province before.[3]

II. Origins

Among indentured servants who arrived in Carolina between 1670 and 1680, 65% came directly from England.[4] Still, a significant number of servants came to Carolina from the West Indies. Free settlers who arrived in 1671, however, displayed a pattern in their geographical origins that was almost entirely uniform—nearly everyone came from Barbados. Of the 52 free colonists who arrived in 1671, a likely point of departure can be identified for 27. Fully 21 of them, or 78%, left Barbados for Carolina. Another came from Jamaica. Three emigrated from Virginia. One began in New York. And only one free immigrant came from England to settle in Carolina in 1671.

---

[3] On early efforts to recruit colonists, see Hope Frances Kane, "Colonial Promotion and Promotion Literature of Carolina, 1660-1670," Ph.D. dissertation, Brown University, 1930, pp. 21-60. One should recall that the proprietors had expressed a measure of concern over the "quality" of immigrants, and had instructed colonial agents to induce settlers to immigrate who would support themselves, and not become a burden on the government. If Carolina agents acted on these instructions, they may have sought male as opposed to female colonists in 1671. But given the real shortage of single free women in Carolina at this time, it is difficult to imagine that the proprietors or their agents would have feared that single female settlers were likely to prove incapable of finding a place in the community, or to become a burden on the government. Any woman's chances of marrying a settled colonist must have been great, and I doubt that proprietary agents refrained from recruiting single women because of concerns over their ability to sustain themselves in a labor-intensive economy in a frontier setting, even though male immigrants were "better suited" to such a place, both as laborers and as fighters. See *Shaftsbury Papers*, p. 364, for Ashley's letter to Captain Halsted urging him to "forbeare to invite the poorer sort yet a while, for wee finde ourselves mightily mistaken in endeavouring to gett a great Number of poore People there . . . who relye and eate upon us." Ashley did, in the very same sentence, urge Halsted to induce "substantiall men and theire Familyes" to come. This would, of course, include women. *Ibid.*, page 389, is a memorandum of a letter from Halsted to Ashley early in 1672 saying he had told ships' masters to bring to Carolina only those who had provisions to last eight months. Thus while he was responsive to proprietary concerns over a seemingly large number of poor colonists who required maintenance by the government, he had not acted to limit immigrants to males who could work and fight.

[4] See page 57, *supra.*

This overwhelming preponderance of Barbadians among 1671's arrivals cannot have been caused by mere chance. We are compelled to inquire why, one year after the colony began, immigration which at the outset had included substantial numbers from England and the West Indies, now came to be composed almost wholly of settlers from Barbados. The explanation, I think, must come from a consideration of timing and economics. Since the first fleet had departed from England only a year earlier, and had been preceded by adequate public notice, it is reasonable to assume that most Englishmen who were inclined to settle in Carolina as free persons would have taken advantage of that opportunity to make the long voyage. That first fleet did, of course, stop in the West Indies prior to heading for the mainland colony, and many Barbadians joined those from England to initiate settlement in Carolina. But it is crucial to understand that it cost far less to travel from Barbados to Carolina than it did to go from England to Carolina, and that there were obviously far more opportunities to make the short rather than the long voyage—there was more traffic between Carolina and the Indies than between the colony and Britain. Since free persons were likely to be paying their own passage, the cost of the voyage to passengers did, in all probability, play a key role in determining the points of departure for free settlers entering Carolina in 1671. It was, in short, easier and cheaper for a settler in Barbados to come to Carolina than for a resident of England. In any case, among 1671's free arrivals, West Indians outnumbered Englishmen 22 to one.

III. Literacy

Slightly over half of Carolina's early indentured servants whose literacy can be assessed demonstrated the ability to sign their names, and therefore are assumed to have been literate.[5] However, this figure is derived from a sample that includes only 60 servants—only one in four participated in an activity that required a signature or a mark on a public document. It has seemed probable that only the more successful former servants would have had opportunities to do so. The free immigrants of 1671 provide us with a bit of evidence suggesting that such a line of reasoning is correct. For, when we study a group whose members began in the colony in freedom, we can measure literacy for nearly two-thirds of

---

[5] See page 70, *supra*.

the subjects. Specifically, 34 of the 52, or 65%, of the free immigrants in 1671 had occasion to sign their names or make their marks on documents that have survived. Thus, those who began as free persons were far more likely to engage in activities which involved signatures than were those who immigrated as servants.

Not only were free immigrants far more likely than servants to appear in the public record as participants in activities which required signatures, but they also were far more likely to have been literate. None of the four free female immigrants arriving in 1671 has left evidence of her literacy. However, of the 48 males in this group, only 14 failed to sign or to mark an extant document. And of the 34 whose literacy can be gauged, 26 or over three-fourths (76%) were literate. The group of 14 male and four female free arrivals whose literacy cannot be measured precisely because they never had occasion to sign a public document, may have included a smaller percentage of literate members than those who did so. Therefore, one ought not to assume that three of four free immigrants to Carolina in the seventeenth century could read and write. On the other hand, it is clear that, at least during 1671, those who entered Carolina as free settlers were likely to have been literate. For even if we assume that *all* of those whose literacy cannot be measured were actually illiterate,[6] still, 26 of 52 settlers, or 50%, would be literate. Data on literacy among Carolina's early free settlers tend to confirm impressionistic suspicions about the kinds of people who settled in colonial America as servants or as free persons. Those who came as free settlers were, in fact, as a group both better educated (more literate), and more likely to engage in activities such as property transfers which required public documentation than were those who came to the colony as servants.[7]

---

[6] Several who failed to sign a Carolina document surely must have been literate.

[7] None of this, of course, necessarily means that literacy rates can be used to gauge property accumulation. Pages 136-138, *supra*, argue that for servants, the ability to read and write had little effect on property acquisition. And those servants whose literacy could be determined (both the literate and the illiterate) averaged only 34 acres more than the entire servant group, and 67 acres more than those whose ability to read and write cannot be ascertained.

IV. Titles

Among those who began in Carolina as servants, only a small fraction came to be identified in the public records as skilled craftsmen or as planters, and only a few acquired titles of distinction such as "Mr." or "Gent." When one looks at those who entered the colony free, however, quite a different pattern emerges. Of the 52 free settlers who came to Carolina in 1671, only 20 failed to appear at some time in the colonial records with a label or title which indicated either their trade, occupation, or status.[8]

Thus, 32 of the free immigrants, or over 60%, can be identified with some precision in terms of their occupation, their social rank, or both. Seven appear as practitioners of some skill which served as a source of economic independence.[9] Seven were identified as planters.[10] And six derived their income from trade—they appeared in the records or engaged in activities which identify them as merchants.[11] Moreover, a

[8] Here it is useful to recall that of the 102 former servants who appear as free persons, only 21 achieved the distinction of being labelled "planters," only six were referred to as "freeman," only three earned the label "Mr.," three others were identified as "Esqr.," and only two were cited as "Gent." Moreover, as discussed above, there is reason to doubt that all who achieved such distinctions actually were the settlers with that name who had immigrated as servants. See pages 144-146, *supra.*

[9] They were: David Abercromby, "seaman"—*Council Journal, 1671-80*, p. 4; Nicholas Bushell, "clothworker"—*Records of the Secretary and the Register 1671-75*, pp. 30-31; Thomas Holton, "carpenter"—*Proprietary Grants No. 1, Vol. 38* (MSV), p. 279; Morgan Morris, "caulker"—Misc. *Records 1682-90* (MSV), pp. 218-19; John Norton, "carpenter" and "turner"—*Records of the Secretary 1675-96* (MSV), p. 172 (carpenter) and *Records of the Register and the Secretary 1675-96, 1702-09* (MSV), pp. 69, 89 (turner); John Pinke, "cooper"—*Council Journal, 1671-80*, p. 17; and John Simpson, "carpenter"—*ibid.*, p. 76.

[10] They were: John Barton—Misc. *Records 1682-90* (MSV), pp. 70-72; George Cantey—*Proprietary Grants No. 1, Vol. 38* (MSV), p. 14; Philip Comerton—*Records of the Secretary and the Register, 1671-75*, pp. 59-60; James Donahue—*Council Journal, 1671-80*, p. 71; Thomas Hurt—*Records of the Register and the Secretary 1675-96, 1703-09* (MSV), pp. 57-58, 78; John Morgan—*Records of the Secretary 1675-95* (MSV), p. 459; and John Norton—*Warrants, 1672-79*, p. 185.

[11] They were: Richard Banks—*Records of the Secretary 1675-95* (MSV), p. 81; Richard Berry—*Records of the Secretary and the Register 1671-75* , p. 64; Timothy Biggs—*Records of the Secretary 1675-95* (MSV), p. 73; Joseph Dowden —*Records of the Secretary and the Register 1671-75*, pp. 11, 34-35; John Maverick—*ibid.*, pp. 42-43.

large number—18 of the 48 males who immigrated as freemen in 1671—were honored either by being referred to as "Mr." or "Gent.," by election to an assembly, or by both.[12]

V. Mobility

A key motivation for studying mobility by those who began as servants in Carolina is that they started, by definition, at the very bottom of the white economic, and in all probability, social hierarchy. In looking at former servants we discover the most absolute boundaries of mobility in early America. We are allowed to measure opportunity in the widest possible frame. There is, however, one crucial liability involved in focusing a discussion of mobility on those who began at the bottom—it becomes impossible to demonstrate zero status mobility (unless, of course, a subject remained a servant for his or her entire career). Moreover, the data on former servants are not sufficiently abundant to display examples of downward mobility, involving the loss of property previously acquired. To gain a clearer sense of mobility in the early American south, therefore, we must look at the careers of those who began at least with their freedom, and with some real property.

---

[12] Those who were cited as "Mr." or "Gent." were: Richard Banks—*Warrants, 1680-92*, p. 37; Richard Berry—*Council Journal, 1671-80*, p. 62; Joseph Dowden—*Records of the Secretary and the Register 1671-75*, pp. 34-35; George Cantey—*Proprietary Grants No. 1, Vol. 38* (MSV), p. 291; John Culpeper—*Records of the Secretary and the Register 1671-75*, pp. 32-33; Thomas Fluellin—*Records of the Secretary 1675-95* (MSV), p. 173; Gyles Hall—*Records of the Secretary and the Register 1671-75*, pp. 18-19; Edward Mathews—*Proprietary Grants No. 1, Vol. 38* (MSV), p. 7; Joseph Oldys—*Council Journal, 1692*, p. 50; John Pinkard—*Records of the Secretary and the Register 1671-75*, pp. 49-50; Christopher Portman—*Records of the Register and the Secretary 1675-96, 1703-09* (MSV), p. 107; Thomas Sceman—*Council Journal, 1671-80*, pp. 13-14; and, of course, Sir John Yeamans who was named governor of the colony in 1671—*ibid.*, p. 29.

Those who were elected to serve in an assembly were: Timothy Biggs—*Council Journal, 1671-80*, p. 30; John Culpeper—*ibid.*; Amos Jefford—ibid.; John Maverick—*ibid.*; John Pinkard—*ibid.*; and George Cantey—*Session Lists*, p. 27. Those selected for the Council were: Thomas Grey—*Warrants, 1672-79*, p. 3; Christopher Portman—*Council Journal, 1671-80*, p. 30 (Portman had previously been elected to the assembly which, in turn, chose him to serve on the Council); and John Robinson—*ibid.* (Robinson, like Portman, first won election to the assembly.) Sir John Yeamans served on the Council as a proprietary appointee prior to being named governor. *Ibid.*, pp. 3, 29.

Of the 52 free immigrants arriving in 1671, 43 acquired land which can be measured in acres, as opposed to town lots or to property whose size never was recorded. These free settlers must have entered the colony anticipating that, over time, they would improve their economic status. While a gain in social prominence probably could have been wished for, few were likely to have expected to become gentlemen or esquires, or to have harbored resentment or felt ill-used by the colony's promoters had they failed to achieve such a status. On the other hand, it is reasonable to assume that most hoped that their property accumulation would not cease with their very first warrant or grant. Although real property acquisition is not an entirely suitable tool to employ to measure wealth accumulated over time in Carolina—especially by, for example, men who were "merchants"—it still is the only device available to historians that can be used to do so.

While 43 of the free settlers acquired measurable real property, 20 or nearly one-half, failed in the course of their careers in the colony to add to the amount of land they obtained from the proprietors upon their arrival in the colony. These settlers, therefore, demonstrated no economic mobility. It is important to understand, however, that included among these 20 settlers are individuals who clearly did not center their economic existence on land, or on real property acquisition. For example, Morgan Morris was a "caulker," and may have chosen to use his skill to survive. He might, therefore, have remained content with his initial parcel of 70 acres, since he never acquired additional land.[13] John Robinson, a sailor and military officer, may have had little interest in, or need for acres he personally could not use while aboard ship. His first property measured 200 acres, which is all he ever acquired in Carolina.[14] Or consider Richard

---

[13] Morris' career in Carolina was unusual. He never held more than 70 acres in Carolina, but he did not keep the land originally conveyed to him by the proprietors. He had a warrant for 70 acres in 1677 for which he did secure a formal grant two years later. However, in 1684 he exchanged that property for a parcel the same size owned by Robert Leverick. Leverick also handed Morris 40 s. Morris' origin in Carolina is confusing, for in the spring of 1684 one Richard Simpson secured 700 acres, partly in his own right, and partly in his father's right. A number of his father's acres apparently were allocated for the arrival of Morris, but Morris never appears in any document as a servant. See *Warrants, 1672-79*, p. 128; *Warrants, 1680-92*, p. 149; Misc. *Records 1682-90* (MSV), pp. 187, 218-19, 346; *Proprietary Grants No. 1, Vol. 38* (MSV), p. 222; *Memorial Book Vol. 5* (MSV), p. 95.

[14] *Warrants, 1672-79*, p. 54. Robinson seems to have had ample time to acquire more land than his 200 acre first warrant. He appears in a 1699 deposition by the

Banks, gentleman and merchant. Banks secured 540 acres at the outset of his career in Carolina. He never added to them. But he may have derived substantial wealth from his mercantile endeavors, and not measured his success by the number of acres he owned in the colony.[15]

Banks is a good model for several of the free immigrants who obtained only one piece of property in the colony during their careers. His first land acquisition was so very large that it, in itself, may have been all he ever wanted or could use, regardless of other income-producing activities in which he engaged. John Simpson's first, and only, property measured 550 acres, and he was also a skilled craftsman.[16] Thomas Grey, a council member and a proprietary deputy, secured 700 acres as his first parcel of land, and never added to it.[17] Such settlers hardly can be said to have failed to succeed, or to have proved incapable of realizing economic ambitions they brought to the colony. To do so would be to misrepresent the nature and extent of opportunity in the colony.

However, 17 of the 1671 free immigrants acquired fewer than 211 acres when they began their lives in Carolina, and never were able to increase the size of their holdings. Only one of these colonists, Morgan Morris, had a skill; and only two, David Abercromby and John Robinson were aboard ship, and therefore may not have assessed their own success in terms of land accumulation. Two other settlers who held small parcels at the outset of their careers in Carolina and failed to add to them may not have needed or wanted to do so. Richard Berry started out with 100 acres in Carolina, which was all he ever acquired. But he was a merchant, and of sufficient stature to appear in the public records as "Mr." Richard

---

seamen of the ship *Civilian* which had been captured by pirates. His will is dated October 13, 1715. See *Records of the Secretary 1694-1704* (W.P.A.), p. 193; *Charleston Wills Vol. 1 (1711-1718)*, p. 76; *Records of the Secretary 1711-18* (W.P.A.), p. 78. David Abercromby also was a sailor. He began and concluded his career in Carolina with 100 acres of land. *Warrants, 1672-79*, p. 7; *Council Journal, 1671-80*, p. 4.

[15] *Warrants, 1680-92*, p. 37. Banks had ten full years to accumulate additional real estate in the colony, for he died in July 1681. *Records of the Secretary 1675-95* (MSV), pp. 81, 84-85.

[16] *Warrants, 1672-79*, p. 128. He died some time prior to November 1683, when his widow died. Her estate was inventoried at a little over £222. *Records of the Secretary 1675-95* (MSV), pp. 191-92.

[17] *Warrants, 1672-79*, p. 28.

Berry.[18] Thomas Sceman attained the same level of property accumulation in Carolina as Berry, but he was labelled "Gent." in public documents, and owned really substantial property, including at least two houses in England which were rented to tenants. These holdings provided him with a source of income unrelated to his acres of land in the colony.[19]

The remaining 12 settlers' failure to add property to their initial acquisition of 210 acres or less cannot be explained by noting sources of income other than use of their land for farming or grazing. Thus, 12 of 43, or almost 28%, of free settlers arriving in 1671 who acquired measurable acres made no progress upward economically when progress is defined as continued acquisition of real property over time. One must conclude from all this that for the free immigrants of 1671 Carolina provided noticeable opportunity. For about 70% of those who arrived that year either acquired a substantial estate at the outset, had a source of income which did not involve or require the use of land, or actually did add to the property they received initially in the province—did, in other words, continue to move upwards economically in Carolina.

There was, of course, another scenario which could be played out by immigrants who started with more than their freedom. It was, after all, possible for someone neither to move upward, nor to stay in one economic status over time in the colony. It was possible to fail—to lose property—to demonstrate downward economic mobility. And, in fact, Carolina did serve as the setting for such careers. Seventeenth-century America was not a place where everyone who lived succeeded, where all immigrants fulfilled their dreams.

In June 1673, four prominent Carolinians, all of whom had arrived in 1671 and held offices in the colony, were involved in "acts of [d]elinquincy and rebellion" and were identified by the Council as

---

[18] *Ibid.*, p. 79; *Council Journal, 1671-80* , p. 62; *Records of the Secretary and the Register 1671-75*, p. 64.

[19] Early in 1672 Sceman was owed £12 by one renter of a house he owned, £24 by another, £5 annuity from the Wardens of Clothworkers Hall, and £24 interest plus £100 principal on a loan to his brother. *Records of the Secretary and the Register 1671-75*, pp. 14-16. He sold his 100 acres immediately upon his arrival in Carolina, for although publicly recorded in 1672, the actual land sale was dated January 25, 1671. Sceman thus may never actually have taken possession of his land concession, but instead, may have sold it when he received it. *Ibid.*, pp. 30-31. Being a gentleman did not ensure a tranquil life in Carolina. In November 1671, he was found guilty of having stolen "one Turkey Cock" a month earlier. He received, as punishment, nine lashes on his naked back. *Council Journal, 1671-80*, pp. 13-14.

"fugitives" and "Delinquents."[20] The details of the situation are not clear, but it seems that John Culpeper, Thomas Grey, John Pinkard, and John Robinson had built a sloop, had become indebted to the proprietors for £70 sterling, had failed to repay the debt, had violated a governmental order to cease "fitting & rigging their sloop" until the debt was settled, and had resisted the efforts of colonial officials to execute the government's instructions. Ultimately the government seized the sloop and the goods on it. Culpeper, Grey, Pinkard, and Robinson fled the settlement. The following March the estates of the four were appraised by agents of the government, and public notice was given that any who were owed money or goods by these men should appear before the Council to make their claims.[21]

It is not known what distress the flight of Robinson and Culpeper caused their families. However, Jane Grey—wife of a merchant, Council Member, Major, and proprietor's Deputy—was reduced by her husband's departure to plead before the Council for relief of "her great necessity." The Council allowed her to remove from the sloop "the greater Kettle her necessary weareing Apparell, her childrens clothes, 3 pewter Dishes, 6 Plates, and all her provisions. . . ." Later she would reappear, to request and receive "two sheets and a halfe and some leather. . . ." Apparently the Greys had loaded the ship with many of their possessions, and had planned to flee the colony, without repaying the debt to the proprietors.[22]

John Pinkard returned to Carolina in March 1674, although it is not clear whether he did so voluntarily or had been seized by governmental officials. In any case, when the Council learned of his arrival in Charles Town, Pinkard was ordered to be "taken into secret custody . . . and be kept in irons. . . ." He soon was released, and actually received a favorable ruling from the Council in a claim he made to collect £17 sterling from another colonist. But at the same time he was ordered to appear before the next general court "to answere to such matters. as shall be objected against him."[23] Pinkard did not prosper. In fact, in the winter of 1674 the Council "considered the poor condition of John: Pinkerd," formerly a member of the colony's Parliament, literate, and a "Gent.,"

---

20 *Ibid.*, pp. 59-60.

21 *Ibid.*, p. 67.

22 *Ibid.*, pp. 60-61.

23 *Ibid.*, pp. 68-69.

and "thought fit to order that one Crosscut saw, one Muskett, and one fowling peece, . . . and one frying pann . . . be forthwith delivered to him requireing the same, for the p^r^sent releife of himselfe and his family."[24] Pinkard had not proved able to survive without governmental assistance.

VI. Survival

Recorded cases of downward mobility among 1671's free immigrants are thus rare, and relate directly to difficulties with the colonial government. If the precipitating factor in the decline in fortune of Culpeper, Grey, Pinkard, and Robinson was a debt to the proprietors, it may have been precisely their "favored" position in the colony as office holders and prominent citizens which allowed them to become indebted in the first place. Less "substantial" colonists may have been denied access to proprietary largesse, and thus not have been as likely to encounter financial and legal difficulties. This is not to say that only those who were the most wealthy and powerful could experience reverses. Surely other free immigrants, both those who arrived in Carolina with wealth and social status as well as those who began only with their own headright concession, must have failed in the colony. But we have no information on such cases.

The rather large number of free immigrants who acquired real property in addition to that which they received at the outset of their careers in the colony suggests that many were able to endure in the environment—to live long enough to realize dreams or ambitions they carried to Carolina. It is helpful to recall that an overwhelming majority of these settlers came to Carolina from the West Indies. They therefore were, in a sense, already well "seasoned" prior to their arrival. While life on the mainland must have differed from life in the Indies, these men and women had encountered American diseases, American heat, and American storms before 1671. They thus might be *expected* to demonstrate a higher rate of survival than those who came from England, as did a majority of the servants who arrived between 1670 and 1680. It is also important to remember that although the colony was economically unsophisticated, and that although many masters probably worked, ate, and lived alongside their servants, the free immigrants of 1671 included a substantial number of settlers who were sufficiently wealthy that they never participated in activities commonly associated with farm life on the frontier. Those who were merchants, for example, were not likely to have

---

[24] *Ibid.*, p. 73.

spent their days toiling in the fields. These colonists, then, aside from immunities to disease gained from prior experience in the Indies, might be expected to survive longer than servants because they lived less strenuously, less debilitatingly.

Having noted the principal factors which might bias the outcome of an investigation into the life expectancy of 1671's free immigrants, just how long did these colonists tend to live? Was a life which began in freedom in Carolina likely to be longer than one which began in servitude?

The data are scanty. We can ascertain death dates for only 13 of the 52 colonists. And ages at some point in their lives are specified for three others. Therefore, as with the servants, we have no precise data on age at death which might serve as the basis for definitive answers to our questions about longevity in the colony.

We do know that George Cantey was 27 in 1677, which means he was 21 upon his arrival in Carolina in 1671.[25] James Donahue was 30 in 1674, which means he was 27 when he came to the colony.[26] And Thomas Hurt was 25 in 1676, making him 20 in 1671.[27] We know when none of these men died. And it would be wrong to assume that the average age of the three on arrival in Carolina—22.6 years—by itself serves as more than a most general guide to the average age on arrival of the group as a whole.

While it would be reckless to use 22.6 years as an average age at arrival for the 1671 group without additional evidence to support that number, it does seem reasonable to assume that free immigrants may well have been somewhat older at time of arrival than those who came as servants. The reason is that free immigrants generally can be assumed to have paid their own passage, unless, of course, they were being brought to Carolina by a parent or spouse already in the colony, or were being sent by parents to the colony to make their own way as independent adults. I suspect that most of the 1671 group did, in fact, bring themselves to Carolina.[28] And to have been able to do so would have required some

---

[25] Cantey witnessed the will of William Snipes on February 10, 1677. His age was "27 Yeares or thereabouts." *Records of the Secretary 1675-95* (MSV), p. 65.

[26] Donahue testified before the Council in 1674, and was identified then as a "planter aged 30." *Council Journal, 1671-80*, p. 71.

[27] Hurt witnessed the will of Richard Rich in 1676, giving his age as 25. *Records of the Secretary 1675-95* (MSV), p. 62.

[28] There is no evidence that any were children of parents already resident in the colony. Only one, Joanna West, may have been a wife or a close relative of a colonist.

money to pay for passage, and for provisions to begin life in a new location—resources that would more likely be exhibited by older rather than younger immigrants. In fact, the data we have on death dates for 1671's free immigrants make a compelling case for assuming that those who came to Carolina as free settlers were older on arrival than those who came in servitude. For the number of years enjoyed in the colony by 1671's free immigrants averages to have been 17.8 years, or almost exactly three years less than the average for those who came to the colony as servants.[29] Of course, the death dates for the free immigrants of 1671 include those of three colonists who survived only four years or fewer after their arrival. Any servants who died so soon after their immigration might have failed to achieve freedom and therefore would not have been included in my calculation of life spans for the servant group. I have failed to find even a single report of the death of a servant, although many who entered Carolina in that status surely died prior to achieving freedom. Nevertheless, that the free immigrants of 1671 lived on average only a little more than 17 years and ten months in the colony suggests that they may have begun their lives in Carolina at a more advanced age than did servant immigrants.

Of the 13 free immigrants for whom death dates are known, three, or 23%, lived 33 years or longer after their arrival.[30] Three lived four years or less,[31] and another three lived from 21 to 25 years in the colony.[32]

---

[29] See pages 105-106, *supra*. The data on servants show that they averaged 20.7 years in Carolina after their arrival.

[30] These were: John Norton, d. 1705 (his will was dated September 30, 1705)—*Shaftsbury Papers*, p. 341; Thomas Holton, d. 1704—*Records of the Secretary 1700-1710* (W.P.A.), p. 102; and John Robinson, d. 1715—*Charleston Wills Vol. I (1711-1718)*, p. 76.

[31] These were: James Needham, Council member and explorer, who was killed by Indians early in 1675—*Shaftsbury Papers*, pp. 452-53; Edward Roberts who reached Carolina in February 1671, and was dead by December. In his will, dated October 14, 1671, he noted that he was "much weakened and impaired in body by a disease w[ch] dayly hangeth upon me. . . ."—*Records of the Secretary and the Register 1671-75*, pp. 21-22; and Sir John Yeamans. Yeaman's death is confirmed in *Records of the Register and the Secretary 1675-96, 1703-09* (MSV), p. 11, which is a grant to Lady Margaret Yeamans, his widow, of 1070 acres. Since we know that Yeamans was aged when he came to Carolina in 1671, it would be absurd to use his date of death (1674) as evidence that free immigrants were able to survive only a few years in the colony. Clearly Yeamans was not representative of the free immigrants arriving in 1671 in terms either of age on arrival or of years spent in Carolina as a productive citizen.

The remaining four, or almost 31%, lived between ten and 13 years after immigrating.[33]

Given such limited data on age at arrival, as well as dates of death for those who came as free immigrants to Carolina in 1671, no estimate of the age to which such settlers lived can be made with great confidence. However, if Carolina servants probably lived to age 40-41, we can assume that free immigrants lived about as long. For servants who survived the "seasoning" period and the rigors of servitude itself might be expected to display lifespans as long as those of other colonists. Perhaps, of course, they lived even longer than free immigrants because merely by surviving to appear as free persons they evidenced a hardiness that predisposed them to long life. In any case, if 1671's free arrivals lived on average to age 40-41, then they would have averaged about 23 years of age on arrival (40.7 minus 17.8), or almost exactly the average age at arrival of the three whose actual age upon immigrating can be ascertained.

What all this means is that we know very little about survival in the seventeenth-century south. There can be no definitive answers to even the most fundamental questions historians raise about longevity. The extant data from Carolina simply do not permit such basic questions to be resolved. However, by employing a comparative approach we can, in what admittedly is still a most speculative way, begin to define the problem. That is, numbers tentatively postulated here as indicative of age at death for Carolinians can be placed alongside numbers from other seventeenth-century English American settlements. This procedure can be highly instructive.

It has become apparent as demographers have worked through various New World communities, that life expectancy increased as one moved further north. One suspects that this pattern derived from the greater healthfulness of cooler as opposed to hotter climates. As two historians have written, "radically different mortality schedules seem to have obtained in New England and the Chesapeake region. Men and

---

[32] These were: Joseph Oldys, d. 1692—*Council Journal, 1692*, p. 50; John Barton, d. 1694—"Abstracts from the Records of the Court of Ordinary of the Province of South Carolina, 1692-1700," S.C.H.G.M., 10 (January, 1909), 10; and John Morgan, d. 1696—*Records of the Secretary 1692-1700* (W.P.A.), p. 461.

[33] These were: Richard Banks, d. 1681—*Records of the Secretary 1675-95* (MSV), p. 81; Thomas Finden, d. 1682—*Ibid.*, pp. 5-6; John Simpson, d. 1683—*Ibid.*, pp. 191-92; and Thomas Turpin, d. 1681—*Ibid.*, p. 5.

women in the northern colonies tended to live considerably longer lives than did their counterparts to the south."[34] The chart on page 168 shows expected years to live for males who reached age 20 in a number of English communities in seventeenth-century America.[35]

The progression displayed in the chart shows that life expectancy for adult white males in English America increased in direct relation to how far north one's home was located. Indeed, even within Massachusetts itself, those who lived farthest north seem to have lived longest.[36] The point, however, is less to bolster the thesis that Englishmen lived longer the further north they settled by adding limited and speculative data on Carolina to numbers based on far more complete and reliable data from other colonies, than it is to gain insight into life expectancy in Carolina itself by accepting the thesis, and thus using it to establish more firmly a life expectancy for seventeenth-century Carolinians. For if Carolina settlers could be expected to live fewer years than colonists who settled further north, and if, as one moved south from Massachusetts to Virginia and Maryland life expectancy dropped from about 65 to about 45 years, then it is reasonable to assume that 40.7 might well be a fairly accurate lifespan for a Carolinian, especially if there are some data upon which

---

[34] Darrett B. and Anita H. Rutman, "Of Agues and Fevers: Malaria in the Early Chesapeake,"*William and Mary Quarterly*, 3rd Series, XXXIII (January, 1976), 49.

[35] I have compiled these figures from similar tables presented in *Ibid.*, p. 48, and Lorena S. Walsh and Russell R. Menard, "Death in the Chesapeake: Two Life Tables for Men in Early Colonial Maryland," *Maryland Historical Magazine* 69 (Summer, 1974), 224. Richard Dunn, in *Sugar and Slaves: The Rise of the Planter Class in the English West Indies, 1624-1713* (New York, 1973), p. 330, reports that a count of tombstones in Jamaica and Barbados for 354 persons who died between 1660 and 1750 yields an average age at death for males of 45. However, his time frame does not mesh with mine, and tombstone counting is of dubious value. Dunn himself remarks that his own efforts yield results which lead "one to question the validity of graveyard research for demographic purposes" (p. 330). Walsh and Menard maintain that Dunn's work "presents some qualitative evidence that adult males in the islands usually died in their mid-thirties." "Death in the Chesapeake," 224.

[36] Within individual colonies such as Massachusetts, death rates could vary with coastal vs. interior location, rather than with northern vs. southern location.

Comparative Life Expectancies
for Twenty-Year-Old Males

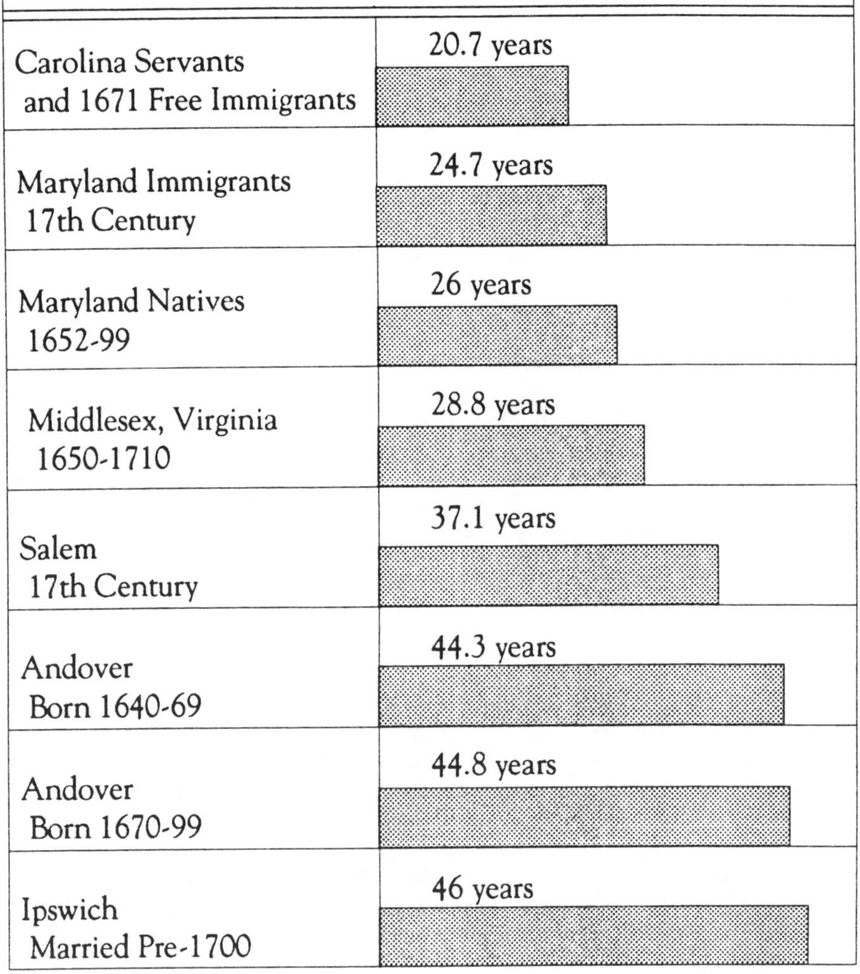

such an estimate can be based. Thus, the comparative framework allows us to accept with fewer reservations what actual, though very limited, data from Carolina seem to show. At the same time such an approach tends to confirm the notion that free immigrants probably lived about as long as did servants who survived to become free settlers. For if free immigrants lived substantially longer than did servants, then the life expectancy of Carolinians would fail to fit into the pattern displayed in the table above. This approach also supports the suggestion that those who came to Carolina in freedom were somewhat older on arrival than those who entered the colony as servants.

VII. Land

Students of early Carolina's free immigrant population have too few data on age and death dates to formulate definitive answers to questions about longevity among members of that group. We can be more comfortable dealing with questions about real property accumulation, because we have adequate reliable information to employ in framing our answers. Moreover, the property accumulated by those entering Carolina as free settlers in 1671 can be compared with that secured by the 1670 to 1680 servant immigrants, as well as with land cited in estate inventories recorded in the years just after Carolina's establishment. In addition, work on property acquisition in seventeenth-century Maryland has been published, and serves as a yardstick with which to evaluate the magnitude of achievements by Carolina's early settlers.

Of the 52 free immigrants arriving in Carolina in 1671, we can measure real property acquisition for 43. There are no extant data on the specific acreage secured by Miles Man, James Needham, Joseph Dowden, or Mathias Halstead. Joanna West acquired no land in her own name, although she probably was related to future governor Joseph West, who received land on the basis of her arrival.[37] Similarly, it is not clear how

[37] Her exact status is not clear. Neither is her relationship to Joseph West. If she was, in fact, his wife, then she could be credited with his holdings. However, I cannot establish that such was the case, and since West was a substantial property-owner with at least 1720 acres, to credit Joanna West with this land might introduce a serious bias into the averages reported for the group. I have, therefore, simply excluded her from the discussion of land acquisition by 1671's free immigrants. It is possible, of course, to view the warrant to Joseph West in which Joanna's arrival is documented as demonstrating that she was not a free person, but rather a servant. For Joseph West

much land Sr. John Yeamans held prior to his death in 1674, although his widow acquired 1070 acres in her own name shortly after he died.[38] Other 1671 free arrivals, Joseph Oldys, Gyles Hall, and Mitchael Smith, secured only town lots in Carolina.[39] Their land acquisition, therefore, cannot be counted in an effort to ascertain the average number of farming, grazing, or timber-producing acres held by members of the group.

The 43 settlers whose land can be measured, acquired in the course of their lives in Carolina 22,884 acres of land, or an average of 532 acres for each free 1671 immigrant. When this number is adjusted by excluding the eight most atypical landholders, the remaining 35 colonists' holdings averaged 332.9 acres. The immediate, and obvious, conclusion is that the "typical" free immigrant of 1671 was substantially more successful than the "typical" servant immigrant, when success is defined by measuring the number of acres acquired. The chart on page 173 demonstrates this clearly.

The average 1671 free immigrant acquired an estate in Carolina fully 163 acres larger than that built by the average servant immigrant. And when the numbers are adjusted so that only the middle 80% of each group is considered, free arrivals still achieved a significantly higher level of "success" than did servants. They averaged 132.6 acres more land during their lives than those who arrived in servitude.

We are compelled to inquire why those who started as free settlers in Carolina acquired, over time, more land than those who started as servants. There seems to have been no overt bias against former servants in the colony. A few ultimately became wealthy, socially prominent, and politically powerful. And many achieved substantial economic success, securing more land than the average 1671 free immigrant. But were opportunities, in fact, limited, or in some cases, denied to those who began unfree in the colony? Were, on average, free immigrants favored by the government? Did, in general, arrival as a servant "mark" a settler as somehow inferior, or unworthy, even if expression of such sentiments or

---

secured land for her arrival, meaning she did not pay for her own passage. However, she is listed in the warrant as "M$^{rs:}$ Joanna West" while those who clearly were servants appear as "Elizabeth Baker" and as "Millicent How," without Mrs. before their names. *Warrants, 1672-79*, p. 63, and pp. 23, 55 for land initially held by Richard Cole which Joseph West secured in 1681.

38 *Records of the Register and the Secretary 1675-96, 1703-09* (MSV), p. 11.

39 See for Oldys, *Ibid.*, p. 168; for Hall, *Records of the Secretary and Register 1671-75*, pp. 18-19; and for Smith, *Ibid.*, pp. 13-14.

examples of favoritism toward free immigrants at the expense of former servants fail to appear in the public record? Were those who chose indentured servitude as a means of reaching America somehow less capable, less intelligent, less resourceful than those who were able to arrange for their own passage and thereby start out as free and independent settlers? Did, in other words, the fact of choosing to submit to another's control for a period of time—of choosing to give up one's independence, even if for a good reason—signify that a person was less fit to succeed than another who came to the New World in control of his or her own immediate future?

Such ideas relate directly to popular and impressionistic images of servants as poor, idle, depressed, disadvantaged, and dishonest—as men and women who had committed crimes and were sentenced into that role, or chose it only to avoid prison. One wonders if the single statement by a prominent Carolinian that servants had been "bad," or the occasional cases of servant disobedience or idleness actually represented patterns of behavior that typified the servants, which were rare public manifestations of traits shared by most in the servant group, and which, once servants became free colonists, doomed them to achieve less than they could have achieved had they been "better."

Some servants may, in fact, have risen socially and economically less than was possible because of defects in character which initially caused them to become servants. Yet it is possible to view the servant group's failure to accumulate as much property as did 1671's free arrivals from a different perspective—from a vantage point based not on the total acreage secured in Carolina from arrival to death, but instead by focusing only on the amount of land acquired subsequent to the initial parcel secured. In other words, if we disregard what early Carolinians started with, and look instead only at what they achieved later, the careers of former servants might more closely approximate those of the free immigrants who arrived in 1671. Such a line of inquiry is grounded on the assumption that free arrivals would ultimately hold more property than former servants, *even if both groups were equally successful in acquiring land during their actual careers in the colony, because free immigrants began with more property than newly-freed servants*. We know that a servant's initial real property acquisition would most likely have been his or her headright concession, and would have totalled from 70 to 100 acres, but for occasional exceptions such as servant couples whose combined headrights would have netted them nearly twice as much land at the outset.

And we might guess that a free immigrant would have started with substantially more than that number of acres.

When the very first land acquisitions of the free immigrants of 1671 are combined, the resulting property totals 11,580 acres, or 269.3 acres per settler. When this number is adjusted by excluding the four largest and four smallest initial parcels conveyed to members of the 1671 group, the average works out to 186 acres. It thus seems likely that free immigrants did start out in the colony with more land than did newly-freed servants. Therefore, if both groups were equally upwardly mobile in terms of land acquisition, those who started out as free persons would appear in retrospect to have been more successful than those who came as servants.

It is possible to identify the size of the first parcel of real property acquired by 79 of the 83 servants who came to Carolina before 1680, and who later secured land whose size can be measured. The amount of land acquired at the outset of their careers by newly-freed servants totalled 8112 acres, or an average of 102.8 acres each. This is almost exactly the size of the headright concession a single servant reaching the colony prior to 1671 would have received. When this number is adjusted by removing the eight largest and eight smallest first land acquisitions by members of this group, the remaining 63 recently-freed servants started with 6000 acres, which averages to 95.2 acres for each person. Thus, servants clearly began their free careers in Carolina with fewer acres than did men and women who had arrived as free settlers. Starting with more, those who came in freedom would, if all Carolinians were able to add similar amounts of land to their initial holdings, end with more. The chart on page 175 demonstrates this point.

When land acquisition by every individual is considered, the chart shows that servants and free immigrants over time in Carolina were able to secure almost exactly the same number of acres. The average servant, in the course of his or her free career, added 266 acres to the parcel with which he or she had started. The average free settler arriving in 1671 was able to add 263 acres to his or her initial estate. For both groups, upward mobility was a reality. And servants moved upward as far and as rapidly as settlers who arrived in freedom. The adjusted averages, of course, indicate that those who started as free settlers not only began with more land, but also proved able to acquire a greater number of additional acres over time in the colony—about 42 acres more than freed servants. While 42 acres represents a sizeable piece of land, the difference is not overwhelming, and alone probably would not have served to distinguish one colonist from another socially or economically. However, when added

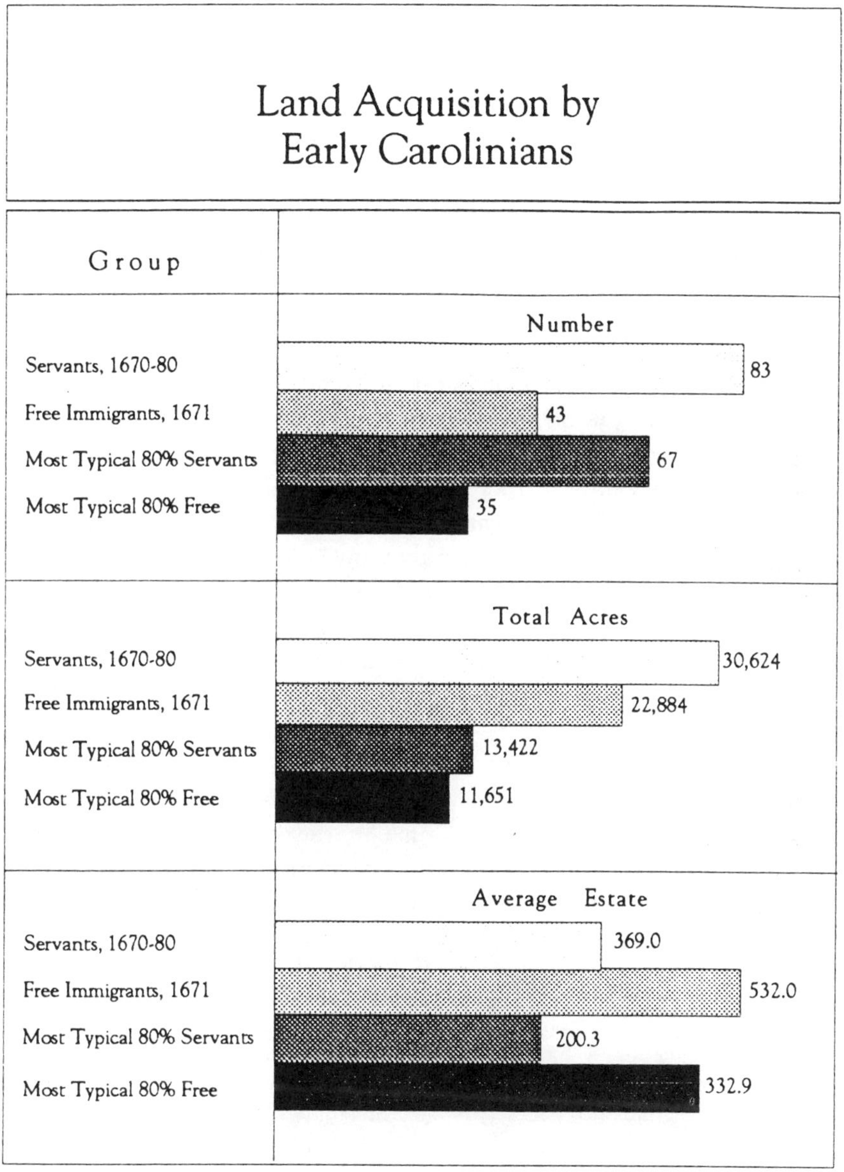
Land Acquisition by
Early Carolinians
Group
Number
Servants, 1670-80
83
Free Immigrants, 1671
43
Most Typical 80% Servants
67
Most Typical 80% Free
35
Total Acres
Servants, 1670-80
30,624
Free Immigrants, 1671
22,884
Most Typical 80% Servants
13,422
Most Typical 80% Free
11,651
Average Estate
Servants, 1670-80
369.0
Free Immigrants, 1671
532.0
Most Typical 80% Servants
200.3
Most Typical 80% Free
332.9

to an initial tract which was significantly larger, the combined acres surely meant that free immigrants were, and were perceived as being, "above" former servants on a social and economic scale.

The numbers above establish that upward mobility and continued advancement were open to those who came to Carolina as servants, and that such immigrants not only did move ahead economically (and, obviously, socially), but also moved about as far as those who came in freedom. At the same time, it is clear that servants were not, as a group, able to accumulate total estates nearly as large as colonists who began as free settlers. For the difference between the 369 acre estate of the typical servant and the 532 acre estate of the average 1671 free settler (or the adjusted estates of 200.3 as opposed to 333 acres) represented the difference between independent and relatively secure planters on the one hand, and substantial if not wealthy colonists on the other hand.

It may be, of course, that free immigrants secured fewer additional acres than they might or could have, simply because they began with estates which they considered wholly satisfactory in terms of location and size. Many thus may have neither needed nor wanted much more land than the amount with which they began in Carolina. Such suggestions are purely speculative, for we have no evidence that any colonist actually acted upon such sentiments. Of the 44 1671 free immigrants whose land acquisitions can be measured, 23, or 52%, acquired real property in addition to the parcel with which they began. At the same time, it is clear that 45 of 81 servant immigrants, or 55.6%, secured at least one parcel of land at some point after their initial land acquisition.[40] While we cannot assess seventeenth-century Carolinians' personal goals or feelings, that over half of the settlers studied here continued to advance—increased the size of their real property holdings—over time in the colony does imply that opportunities were relatively great, and that men and women could fulfill dreams that must have been among the significant forces leading them to emigrate.

---

[40] Here I am able to consider 81 servants because two of them, John Raven and Christopher Field, clearly had more than a solitary initial property acquisition, although I have not been able to measure the size of their first pieces of property. Hence, 79 servants provided data for the preceding discussion, to which group Raven and Field are added here.

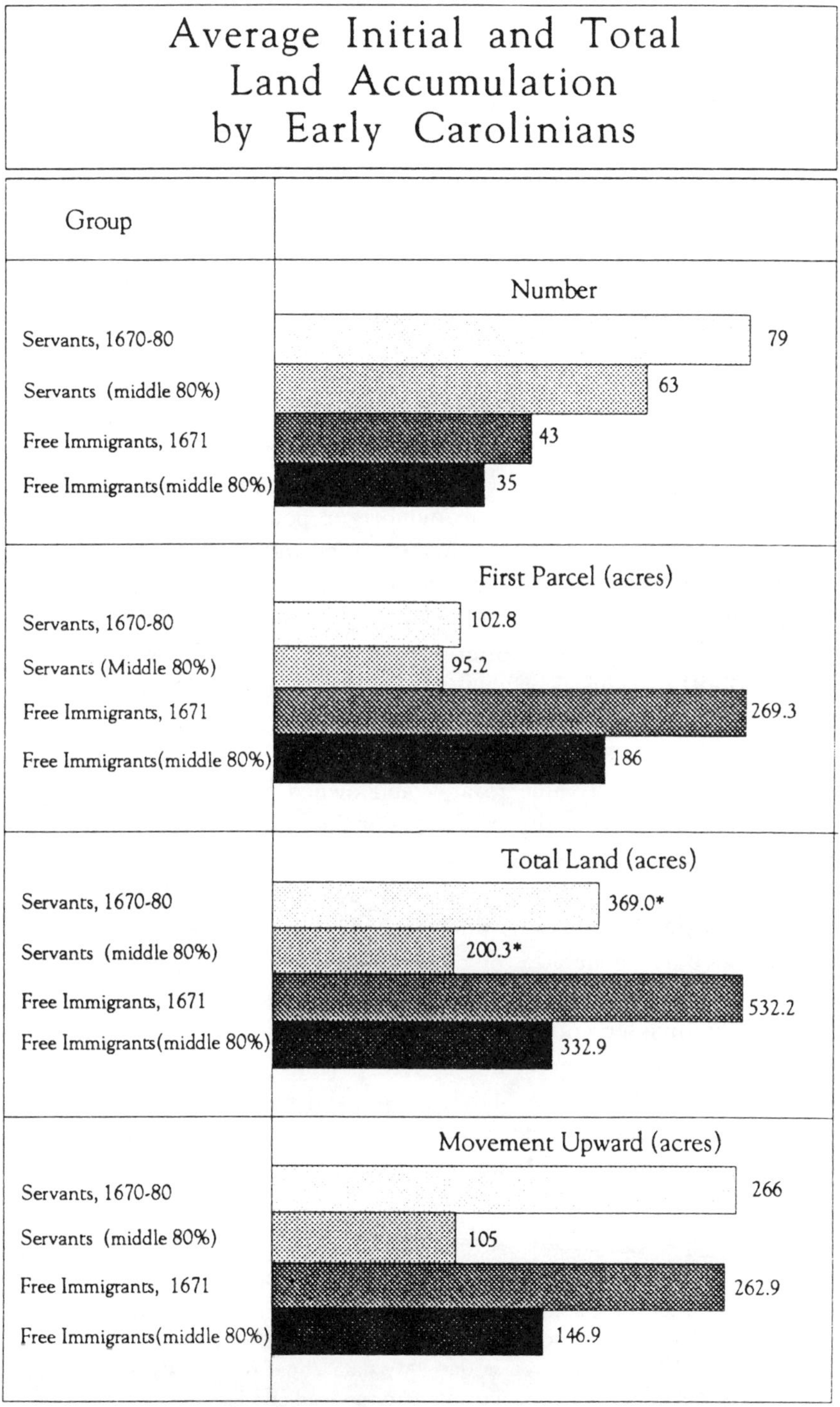

*Based on data from 83 former servants.

**Based on data from 67 former servants.

We can gain a clearer sense of these early Carolinians' likely feelings about their own property accumulation by looking at what other groups accomplished. For it is reasonable to assume that the men and women upon whose careers this discussion has focused, formulated their own views of what they had achieved at least partly in response to what Englishmen had done elsewhere in America, and surely in response to the levels of wealth other settlers in Carolina had attained.

Historians have completed much work on early Maryland, including analysis of estate inventories from the seventeenth century. As with the Carolina estate inventories discussed earlier, these documents yield numbers which specify the values of entire estates. They therefore fail to submit to direct comparison with my figures, which measure only real property. However, by accepting a monetary value for Carolina land of one shilling per acre—the price at which the proprietors sold land—we can convert numbers of acres into numbers of pounds. That figure can be used to determine if early Carolina servants and 1671 free immigrants achieved levels of "success" comparable to those attained by other Carolinians, and by settlers in Maryland.

The 22 estate inventories recorded in Carolina prior to 1690 averaged £150 in value. This adjusts to a little under £100 when the four most atypical inventories are excluded. The median estate was valued at £68. Ten of the 22 were valued at under £54. All these Carolina inventories assigned a value to any land owned by the deceased settler, and included it as part of the total value of the estate.

Work done on Maryland's very first servants has little specific to say about real property accumulation by individuals. Among those entering Maryland as servants prior to 1642—roughly the first decade of settlement—only about 50% of those whose freedom can be established "eventually acquired land" at all. It is important to recall here that over 85% of Carolina servants arriving during the first decade of settlement who later appear in the records as free persons acquired real property. Of those former servants in Maryland who did secure real property, 60% accumulated estates valued at less than £100. Livestock provided, on average, more than half of that total.[41] Regrettably, the value of the estate

[41] Menard, "Servant to Freeholder," pp. 40-41. Menard bases his discussion of property acquisition by servants entirely on estate inventories. My discussion of property acquisition by Carolina servants is based on actual land records. Menard, thus, generalizes on the basis of only 31 former servants in Maryland, out of 158 who actually survived to become free settlers. My data come from analysis of property secured by 87 out of 102 Carolina servants who survived and became free. It would, of

accumulated by the "typical" Maryland servant who arrived at the outset of settlement is not reported.

Other work on Maryland indicates that those who came to that colony as servants did not fare particularly well. Certainly they did not secure property as frequently as did those who began in servitude in Carolina. For of the 137 servants who entered Maryland in the five years from 1648 to 1652, 72, or a little over half, survived to appear in the records as free settlers, and of these, "41 to 43 . . . became landowners."[42] Thus, at best, 43 of 72, or 60% of those whose survival to freedom can be established acquired real property in Maryland.

When the entire population of Maryland—both those who began as servants as well as those who started in freedom—is considered, the

---

course, be useful if we knew how many acres individuals actually acquired in Maryland, as opposed to total estate values. Focusing on Charles County at a slightly later period (1658-1705), Walsh has discovered that in 1659 the mean acreage of former servants was 366 acres. In 1705 the mean was 245 acres. The mean for all property holders in Charles County was 546 acres in 1659 and 468 acres in 1705. "Servitude and Opportunity," p. 126. Recall that numbers for Carolina are virtually identical—369 acres for former servants, and 532 acres for 1671's free immigrants. See p. 173, *supra*.

[42] Russell R. Menard, P.M.G. Harris, and Lois Green Carr, "Opportunity and Inequality: The Distribution of Wealth on the Lower Western Shore of Maryland, 1638-1705," *Maryland Historical Magazine*, 69 (Summer, 1974), 181-82. The authors argue that since, of the 72 who survived, "five died soon after completing their terms and eleven others quickly vanished," 41 to 43 of 56 should be labelled land acquirers, or fully 75%. I tend to be less optimistic than they, and think that since death or disappearance (due to death?) were real possibilities for immigrants, the fact of death soon after achieving freedom should not cause a subject to be dismissed from a survey of land acquisition by former servants. Nor should disappearance sometime after becoming free necessarily remove a settler from consideration, unless the historian wishes (and is able) to establish an arbitrary "grace period" during which failure to acquire property "will not count." In Maryland, as in Carolina, custom and statute dictated that servants "out of their time" would receive "freedom dues." In Maryland a 1640 statute fixed the amount of land freed servants were to receive at 50 acres, and land was given as part of one's freedom dues until 1683. See Smith, *Colonists in Bondage*, pp. 239-40. Lois Green Carr and Russell R. Menard, "Immigration and Opportunity: The Freedman in Early Colonial Maryland," in Thad W. Tate and David L. Ammerman, eds., *The Chesapeake in the Seventeenth Century: Essays on Anglo-American Society* (Chapel Hill, 1979), p. 207, note that the 50 acres were not offered after 1681. Walsh, "Servitude and Opportunity" tells us that of 216 Charles County freedmen, only about one-third of those whose status could be ascertained acquired land. Of that group, 19.2% came to own about 200 acres, 16.8% acquired between 250 and 600 acres, and 3% amassed estates of more than 1300 acres (p. 118).

numbers provided by historians are derived from probate records which excluded land and improvements on it since such types of property "could not be hidden or removed and [therefore] . . . escaped the inventory."[43] Thus we have images of wealth in early Maryland which do not include what must have been major components of any settler's total property.[44] What can be said about levels of wealth in early Maryland is that after 1670 the median of estate inventories hovered "at just over £50 into the early eighteenth century." The mean of these inventoried estates was about £115 from 1658 to 1680, and about £126 from 1681 to 1699.[45] These estate values correlate nicely with the 22 Carolina inventories surveyed earlier, if one can assume that the Carolina median of £68 is higher than the Maryland median of £50, and the Carolina mean of £150 is higher than the Maryland mean of £115 to £126 because in Carolina, land and buildings *were* included in estate appraisals.

Such data on total estate values obviously do not readily compare with measurements of wealth based exclusively on the number of acres a settler accumulated. In order to examine the relative economic success of these various groups of early American settlers, real property acquisition by Carolina's 1670 to 1680 servant immigrants and the free immigrants of 1671 cannot simply be placed alongside total estate values for Maryland servants, for Maryland colonists (servant and free), or for Carolina settlers whose estates were inventoried before 1690. If data on real property accumulation in Carolina were converted into estimates of total estate values, however, such comparisons could be made. And it is possible to accomplish that conversion. For we can ascertain the exact number of acres owned by six of those Carolinians whose estates were inventoried and appraised prior to 1690. These settlers also, of course, have left us a record of their total wealth. It is therefore a simple matter

---

[43] Menard et al., "Opportunity and Inequality," pp. 169-70.

[44] The authors note that "for historians, this omission is unfortunate, since real property was a major portion of many estates." They do not attempt, however, to tell us how large a portion. They do say that "wills, deeds, patents, and quit-rent rolls make it possible to determine in many cases whether or not a decedent owned land and often precisely how much he owned." *Ibid.*, 170.

[45] *Ibid.*, pp. 172-73. Carr and Menard show that freed servant craftsmen and agricultural laborers who failed to establish their own homes, but lived instead as "inmates" in the households of others, accumulated estates valued at £17.58 and £19.52 between 1658 and 1680, and at £21.18 and £13.56 between 1681 and 1705. "Immigration and Opportunity," p. 216.

to gauge the average percentage of total wealth contributed by real property holdings for this tiny group of Carolinians. Then, by assigning a standard value to land, any colonist's accumulated acreage can be multiplied by that amount, and the resulting value can be assumed to represent a specified fraction of that settler's total estate.

Needless to say, such speculative history fails to provide the kinds of answers based on extant hard data that scholars seek. However, it is worth engaging in such activities if the several pitfalls inherent in the endeavor are kept in mind. First, comparisons with numbers from Maryland still will not be precise, because land was not included in Maryland inventories. Second, we cannot determine the extent to which data derived from the six Carolina inventories that included real property are representative of those we would encounter were additional inventories available. Nor do we know if the six colonists are representative of the colony's population as a whole. In any case, even given the drawbacks of such an approach, it is important to attempt to put the "success" achieved by the men and women whose lives have been examined here in perspective. And that can be accomplished only by looking at comparable numbers from other contemporaneous groups in Carolina and Maryland.

Of the six Carolina estate inventories recorded prior to 1690 which specify farming land among the property appraised, three also include town lots with houses. This means that these three decedents' estates were increased in value by a kind of real property which many of the servants who arrived before 1680, as well as many of the 1671 free immigrants had acquired, but which does not appear in my tabulations of their property acquisition. For I have been able to quantify only real property that was measured in acres, as opposed to town lots whose size traditionally was reported as "a full lot in town" or "one half lot," and whose value per acre, obviously, was far greater than that of similar amounts of land used for grazing or planting. Since many of the early Carolinians in both the servant and the 1671 free group did hold property in town in addition to the acres whose size represents the only measurable wealth visible to us, I have included data on town lot values in my computations based on the six inventories. That is, assuming that it was not unusual for an early settler in Carolina to acquire real property to farm as well as a lot and house in town, values assigned to such species of urban property ought to be incorporated into any assessment of the value of a "typical" Carolina estate from this era. It is not surprising to find such holdings in three of six inventoried estates, for even a cursory glance at the index in *Warrants for*

Lands under the headings for Charles Town, James Town, Oyster Point, or Town Lots gives the unavoidable impression that a huge number of town lots were measured and laid out, involving perhaps half of the warrants issued to settlers in the colony. Moreover, by incorporating the value assigned to town lots into the total worth of these estates, it is possible to get at a kind of real property acquisition by the 1670-1680 servants and 1671 free immigrants to Carolina which before could not be measured precisely.

The total value, in sterling, of the six inventoried estates was a little over £1182. This averages to £197 each, which means, of course, that these six are fairly representative of the entire group of 22, whose average value was just over £150. The value of the farming land included in these six estates was exactly £325. Thus, the kind of land whose size can be measured and which, therefore, has served as the only means at our disposal for assessing the "success" of Carolina's early settlers, accounted for 27.5% of the total value of estates amassed by settlers who held such property.[46]

It is important to consider the sample employed here, for merely to say that the average estate was valued at £197 does not necessarily ensure that the six inventories detail the possessions of settlers who fairly represented Carolina's early population. John Williamson was a "marriner," and a wealthy man with five slaves valued at £83, and "silver and gold in cash and plate" valued at over £192, contributing to a total estate worth over £663.[47] At the other end of the social and economic spectrum was William Brett, planter, whose detailed estate inventory included 59 individual entries which were valued at a total of just under £27.[48] Joseph Dalton, "Esquire," was a prominent colonist. But his estate was worth less than £78.[49] Similarly, James Collins was a "Gentleman," with six slaves, but held property valued at less than £101.[50] John Hill's

[46] When these six settlers' town lots are excluded, the percentage of total estate value contributed by farming land rises to 32%.

[47] *Records of the Secretary 1675-95* (MSV), p. 301.

[48] *Ibid.*, p. 67.

[49] *Ibid.*, p. 125.

[50] *Ibid.*, p. 137.

occupation is not known. His estate was appraised at a little over £88.[51] And Margaret Sympson, widow of a carpenter, held an estate valued at £222 which included "1 Negro man by name Dick" worth £20, and "1 Negro boy named Sampson a Cripple" worth £1 10s.[52] Thus the six represent a fair cross-section of Carolina society, with perhaps a bias in favor of men with titles of distinction, which, it is clear, did not always relate directly to great wealth.

If farming land represented 27.5% of the total values of these estates, and if we assume that such property comprised a similar proportion of the estates accumulated by other early Carolinians, we can deduce the value of a "typical" estate for those property acquirers who arrived in Carolina as servants before 1680 and as free settlers in 1671. The 83 servants who secured real property averaged 369 acres each. This land would have been worth (at the rate of one shilling per acre at which the proprietors sold land during the second decade of settlement) £18.45. Assuming that value represented 27.5% of a typical former servant's estate, the total property acquired by that servant in Carolina would have been worth £67. The "typical" 1671 free immigrant, acquiring 532 acres in the colony, would have amassed an estate whose value was a little under £97. When we employ the numbers derived from considering the middle 80% of each group, the total estate values compute to £36 for former servants, and £61 for free immigrants. The chart on page 182 compares these numbers with those derived for settlers in Maryland.

It would, of course, be unwise to give too much credence to the estate values postulated for Carolinians through deductive reasoning as opposed to close examination of hard data. But it does seem clear that early Carolinians, especially servant immigrants, did enter an environment which provided them with widely accessible opportunities to acquire property, and that a really significant number took advantage of those opportunities. If the total estate value computed for the middle 80% of the 1670 to 1680 servant group seems depressingly low, it is important to recall that these settlers still possessed about 200 acres of land, which observers suggested was sufficient to maintain a family in relative security, if not in abundance. It is also clear that Carolinians fared about as well as did their fellow colonists to the north, perhaps even better in terms of property acquisition. If, therefore, one were to search for the origin of the typically American

---

[51] *Ibid.*, p. 111.

[52] *Ibid.*, p. 192.

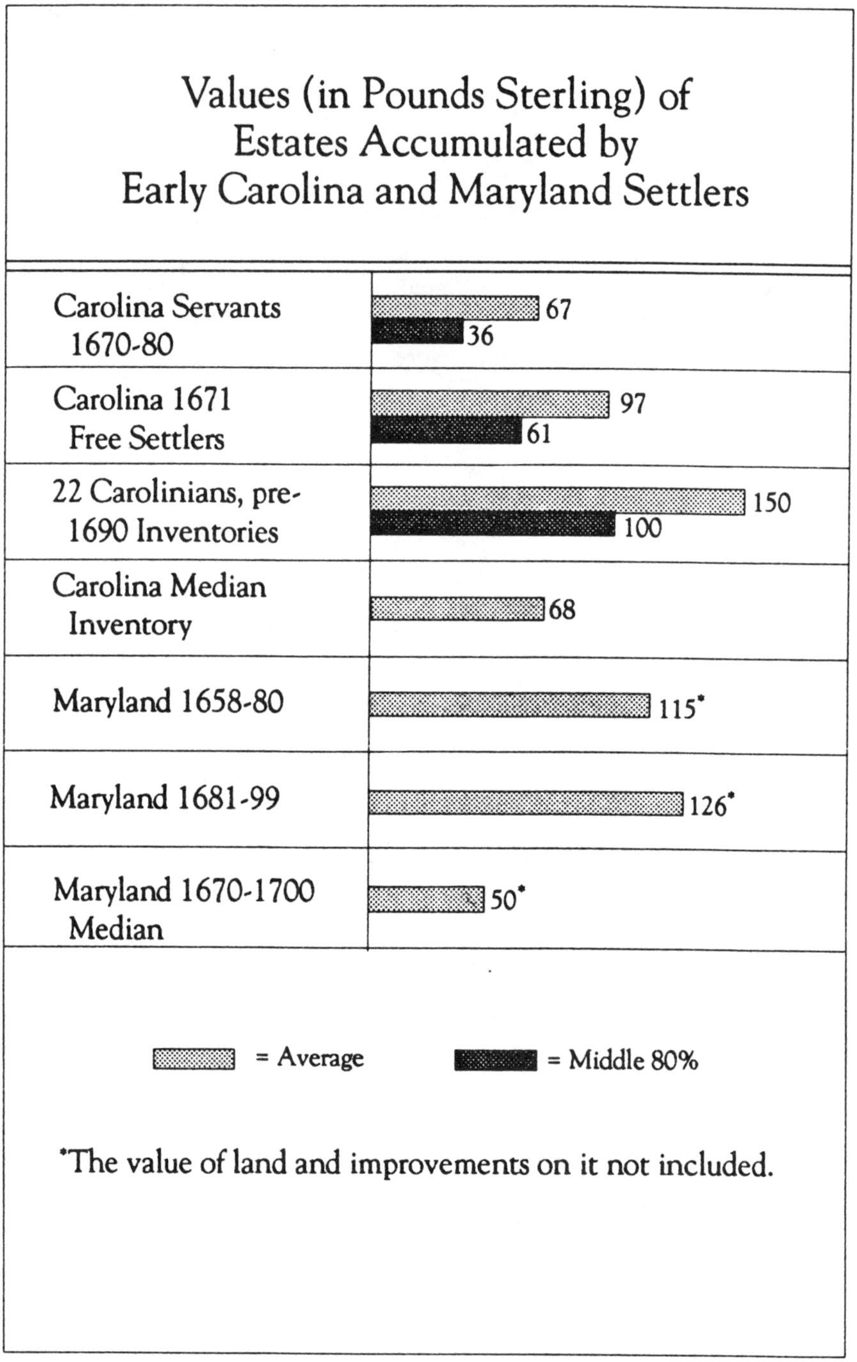

Values (in Pounds Sterling) of Estates Accumulated by Early Carolina and Maryland Settlers

image of large numbers of immigrants arriving with no property and low social rank, and, through effort and endurance ultimately achieving upward economic and social mobility of a sort linked to no other land, then the southern part of what would more than a century later become the United States might be the area and the time upon which to fix attention.

One last issue—the relationship between literacy and economic achievement—ought to be considered in a discussion of how mobility by former servants compares to that of free immigrants.[53] Over 62% of those who immigrated to Carolina between 1670 and 1680 as servants, and who later acquired land, were illiterate. And there was little difference in the total number of acres secured by illiterate as opposed to literate former servants during their careers in the colony. However, those whose literacy can be assessed—whether they were literate or not—did display markedly greater success in securing real property than those who failed to sign or mark any document in the public records.[54]

As we have seen, free immigrants to Carolina arriving in 1671 were far more likely than the colony's servant immigrants to have occasion to either sign or mark a document. And they were also, as a group, far more literate than the servants, with more than three of four displaying the ability to sign their names. But were free immigrants who could read and write more successful than their illiterate counterparts? Did literacy

---

[53] We have, as yet, no information from scholars working in Maryland about the ways literacy related to property accumulation in that colony.

[54] See pages 133-138, *supra*. Carole Shammas, "The Determinants of Personal Wealth in Seventeenth-Century England and America," *Journal of Economic History*, XXXVII (September, 1977), 675-89, looks at factors which seemed to influence economic advancement in three areas inhabited by Englishmen in the seventeenth century—Worcestershire, East London, and Virginia. She concludes that occupational status was a principal determinant of wealth in all three locations. So, she says, was age. Education (literacy) "had an effect of its own on wealth apart from the influence it shared with *Occupational Status*" (p. 682). She has devised a table in which she compares the mean wealth of various occupational groups on the basis of their literacy. Among "privileged orders" literate persons' estates averaged £503, while illiterates accumulated, on average, only £65.6. Literate craftsmen amassed estates valued at £91.2, while their illiterate counterparts' estates averaged only £48.5 in value. Laborers who could read and write secured property worth £35.7, while those who could not sign their names held only £24.8 in property when they died. And literate farmers displayed estates valued at £144.4 as opposed to estates worth £111.3 for illiterate farmers (page 687). Thus, while literacy had a positive effect on property accumulation by all the occupational groups, it had the least influence on the fortunes of laborers and farmers—the types of people likely to have begun their lives in Carolina as servants.

matter for those who entered the colony in freedom—did it affect their subsequent careers?

Of the 34 individuals whose literacy can be ascertained, 29 secured real property whose size can be measured. Of these, eight were illiterate, while 21 could sign their names. The literate free immigrants accumulated a total of 11,464 acres, or an average of 546 acres each. When the two most and two least "successful" literate free immigrants are ignored, the remaining 80% of the group held 5511 acres, or an average of 324 acres for each individual. The eight illiterate 1671 free immigrants secured 2630 acres, or an average of 329 acres each. If only the most typical six are considered, the average for the group plummets to 222 acres. Thus, literate free immigrants did, in fact, secure more land on average than did illiterate free immigrants.

The average size estate acquired by the free immigrants of 1671 whose literacy can be assessed was 486 acres. This number adjusts to 299 acres when the six most atypical estates are excluded from the calculation. Fourteen members of the free immigrant group acquired measurable land but failed to sign or mark a public document and, therefore, left no record of their literacy. These 14 colonists secured 7590 acres, or an average of 542 acres each. When we ignore the land acquired by the most and least successful individuals, the remaining 12 averaged 301 acres each. Thus, the careers of these free immigrants fail to confirm the notion that men and women who left a record of their literacy were, in general, more successful than those who failed to do so. It is clear, when looking at Carolina's early free immigrants, that participation in activities requiring a mark or signature did not necessarily signify that an individual was more successful than a fellow colonist who did not sign or mark a document during his or her life in the province.

Servants whose literacy can be determined—whether or not they actually were able to read and write—were, as a group, more successful than servants who never signed or marked a document that has survived. The careers of servants, then, tend to confirm the common assumption that merely having had the opportunity to display literacy signified that an individual possessed substance, and that such persons were more successful than men and women whose literacy is unknown.

Free immigrants who arrived in 1671, on the other hand, provide significant evidence to counter that view. For both the mean as well as the adjusted average acreage secured by members of the group whose literacy cannot be gauged were greater than the levels attained by those who did

Literacy and Wealth (in Acres) of Early Carolinians

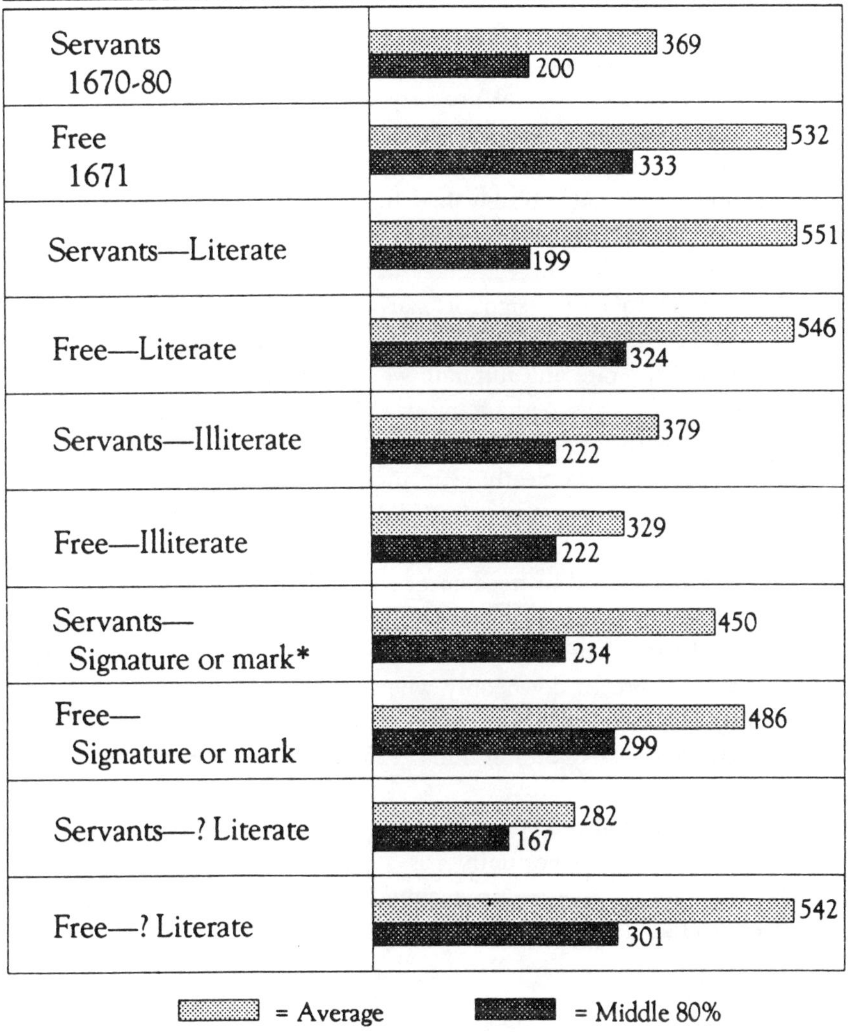

*Here I have been able to include Patrick Steward's 860 acre estate which was not used in the calculation of land accumulation by those who definitely were literate and those who definitely were illiterate because, while it is not possible to determine whether or not Steward could read and write, he *did* participate in activities that required a signature or mark.

sign or mark documents, and approached (but did not quite equal) the levels of property acquisition reached by those who clearly were literate. The table on page 185 displays these numbers in a more readily comprehensible format.

What is clear from all this is that in general, if a colonist definitely could read and write, he was likely to secure more property than a neighbor who was illiterate. Only in the case of the middle 80% of those who began as servants does literacy seem to have had a negligible effect on success as measured by real property acquisition. But, of course, that group probably was composed mostly of settlers who focused their existence on the use of land for planting crops or raising livestock. For them, an ability to read probably had little impact upon their economic fate. Yet this limited influence of education on economic success relates only to former servants whose literacy can be determined. Servants who, once free, failed to either sign or mark a document, accumulated less property than those who were literate, than those who were illiterate, or than those, both literate and illiterate whose ability to read and write can be determined. What is perhaps most striking about these numbers on literacy and property accumulation by various groups in early Carolina is that former servants who clearly were literate secured, on average, estates that were larger by a few acres than did free immigrants who were able to read and write; and that early Carolinians who clearly were illiterate, whether they had arrived in freedom or servitude, achieved similar (and in the case of the most typical 80% of each group, identical) levels of property acquisition. The similarity between the two groups *whose literacy can be determined* breaks down only when we examine the careers of the middle 80% who were clearly literate. In that group, Carolinians arriving as free settlers amassed estates fully 125 acres larger than those who came in servitude.

In sum, the numbers above make a strong case for portraying early Carolina as a land of opportunity—as a place where immigrants, *if they survived*, were able, over time, to acquire land whose size was sufficient to allow them to live decent lives.

CHAPTER EIGHT

Conclusion

This study has examined the lives of many of the men and women who established the English colony of Carolina during the last quarter of the seventeenth century. It has detailed the difficulties encountered by students seeking to comprehend life in the early colonial south caused by incomplete or confusing sources and by subjects for study who, because they were neither wealthy, nor eminent, nor powerful tended to appear in the colonial records infrequently. Nevertheless, close reading of the volumes of Carolina records which have survived can, it is now clear, yield sufficient data on a large enough group of "common" settlers that many questions historians ask about colonial American societies can be answered. Too often, given the limitations imposed by incomplete or inadequate records, the answers must be speculative or suggestive in nature. But among the speculations we can discern some hard evidence on the achievements of ordinary men and women who came to English South Carolina with neither wealth nor high status, but rather with hope for the future.

A number of themes run through this essay on life in early Carolina. Paramount is the notion that the opportunity for economic, and, to a lesser extent, social advancement was great—if a settler survived. Colonial officials clearly wanted to attract white colonists, and they seem to have perceived indentured servants as a valuable source of future permanent settlers. Thus, the interests of servants were protected, and opportunities for full participation in the Carolina economy and society were kept open for these immigrants once they achieved freedom. And masters, those Carolinians who paid for the importation of a labor force, seem to have delayed turning to black slaves until they found crops which would prove profitable, were certain that the environment would be suitable for slaves, and accumulated the capital to pay for them. In any case, it is clear that a very large proportion of early Carolina's population consisted of servants, or of men and women who had arrived in servitude. It is also clear that, because of the need to accomplish tasks which involved heavy labor, and because of the immaturity of the emerging society, male servants far outnumbered female servants.

These immigrants were not of the lowest orders of English or Barbadian society. They came to Carolina voluntarily. Many were literate. A vast majority of those who endured their period of servitude accumulated real property, and perhaps more important since all freed servants were entitled to receive land, added to their initial land acquisition over time. Upward mobility, in other words, was a reality for these men and women, and continued in the course of their lives in Carolina. Their achievements compared favorably with those of settlers who came to the colony in freedom. In fact, the levels of property accumulation beyond the amount of land with which they began their careers were similar both for those who came in freedom and those who came in servitude. And the property acquired by early Carolinians seems to have been equivalent to what settlers in other parts of English America were amassing.

If the proprietors who sought to rule Carolina from England experienced disappointments as the revenues they had anticipated failed to come from their colony, and their design for the society failed to develop according to their master plan, at least they succeeded where other Europeans had failed in establishing an enduring presence in America.

And the men and women who actually settled the colony, in spite of individual failures and personal catastrophes, as a group achieved real success. The notion of upward mobility as an attainable goal truly typified the society created by Englishmen in Carolina.

Afterword

A study such as this, which is the product of a long-term search for discrete pieces of information about individuals who were neither wealthy nor prominent when they came to America, and who, in most cases, achieved neither great riches nor eminence in the course of their lives in the New World, compels the student to see and to think about the European colonization of America on a tiny scale. Concentrating on individuals rather than on large events, and, moreover, on individuals who were not directly involved in important provincial, continental, or international matters can lead one to lose sight of the way the lives of such "common" men and women relate to the larger story of the European colonization of the Americas. The research discussed here has involved really only a few years in the lives of a small number of men and women who lived in a little community in the wilderness. The effect of this narrow focus is striking, for it means that the process of colonization is portrayed in intimate and personal terms. While surely that perspective is valuable, it is important to place such individual histories in a larger context—to look at how the lives of these people fit into a wider framework.

Seen in a global context, the story of European settlement in the New World involves the Europeanization of the Americas. Native peoples, customs, political and social systems were displaced or eliminated as men and women from Europe seized, settled, and ruled the New World, in the process imposing their own patterns of life upon it. However, in one sense the story related here leads to a quite different view of the European settlement of the Americas. For the preceding pages detail not the Europeanization of America; rather they chronicle the Americanization of Europeans—the way such notions as mobility, change in status, alteration of inherited roles, the future as not only different from but also better than the past came to be accepted as both normal and desirable aspects of life. These are American images, and they marked the experience of Europeans here from the very outset of settlement in places such as English Carolina. The servant immigrants whose accomplishments in Carolina provided much of the data for this study of status mobility and property accumulation, came to the colony specifically in order to experience *change* in their lives. They sought to transform themselves.

They did not, of course, wish to cease being English. They did not desire to give up their European intellectual or religious heritage. And such dramatic changes, needless to say, did not occur. In fact, recent scholarship has demonstrated that in many respects the eighteenth century in English America can best be described by employing such terms as Anglicization, and by noting how Americans came to think and to act more *English* over time. Nevertheless, the men and women whose lives have been examined here, did not come to Carolina in order to live according to a master plan devised in England. Rather, they came in order to alter the pattern of existence which marked their lives prior to their departure for Carolina.

And what they achieved had a remarkable effect on the future. For it shaped the way people both in America and in other lands visualized the New World, and specifically that part of it which would become the United States. If the Old World seemed to represent an environment in which tradition and inherited patterns of life counted, America, in the minds of many observers came to represent something quite different. "America" implied change and innovation. "America" meant opportunity.

Many of the Europeans who came to America at the outset of the era of colonization sought to create communities which would be so perfect that their example might change the way people lived everywhere in the world. Some wanted, in other words, to offer the world a message of hope and salvation, to provide by their example a beacon of promise for mankind. They aimed to do this by living in accordance with plans that had originated in Europe, which stressed rigid adherence to set standards of behavior, and which dictated how societies should be organized. The Carolina proprietors can be counted among such social and political planners. Their Fundamental Constitutions represent only one example of a master plan from Europe whose execution was meant to be carried out in the free open space of the New World.

And, in fact, America did come ultimately to serve as a "city on a hill" for the world to observe, a land which offered a message to mankind. Ironically, that message argued against giving heed to inherited or imported patterns of status, wealth or behavior. Instead, the message of

America to the men and women who so desperately strived to come from other lands was that change was not only *possible*, but that it was also *good*. In America, no matter where one had begun, upward mobility, both economically and socially, might well result if a person had ability and worked hard. In America, talent, not background, could determine one's future. That image and that message originated in the seventeenth century. And the 241 men and women who came to Carolina as indentured servants during the first decade of the colony's life contributed significantly to the creation of that image. Their story writ large over many years in many parts of America became the message of salvation America offered the world. If historically America has been a land open to immigrants who, once here, could exercise freedom to take advantage of opportunity, and in so doing move upward socially and economically, then that heritage extends back to the very earliest period of our history, when the first Englishmen came to live in places such as Carolina.

Bibliography

This bibliography includes original sources (both published and unpublished), secondary sources (books and articles), and unpublished university dissertations.

I. Original Documents

A. *South Carolina Department of Archives and History*

In the South Carolina Department of Archives in History, where I conducted most of my research, are stored virtually all of the original sources which have survived from the colonial period. For scholars interested in social history the most important documents are contained in the manuscript volumes referred to as "Wills, Inventories, and Miscellaneous Records." While the researcher will encounter all sorts of documents in these volumes, it is clear that two colonial offices, that of the Secretary of the Province and that of the Register of the Province, were the places where these materials originated. While the Secretary seems to have recorded all kinds of documents, the Register (now the Register of Mesne Conveyance in Charleston) exercised the responsibility of recording land transfers. There are no reliable indexes to these volumes. However, both the Civil Works Administration and the Works Project Administration supported programs which copied some of these volumes. The C.W.A. workers transcribed only wills. The W.P.A. workers, on the other hand, copied entire volumes. Needless to say, the dates on bound volumes of these transcribed records do not correspond either to each other or, more importantly, to the original manuscript records themselves. For the copies were made before the manuscript records were laminated, rebound, and re-dated. Below I cite the title of the original manuscript volume, the control number (shelf) for that volume in the S.C.D.A.H., and the C.W. A. or W. P. A. transcript of that volume if such a transcript was made.

Records of the Secretary of the Province and the Register of the Province of South Carolina, 1671-1675 (published in 1944)—control 1.

Records of the Register and of the Secretary of the Province, 1675-1696, 1703-1709—control 2.

Miscellaneous Records, 1682-1690—control 3. (This volume contains pages 339-44 and 369-78 of a volume originally called *Will Book, 1692-1693*, now titled *Records of the Secretary of the Province, 1692-1700*.)

Grant Book C 1694-1707 Register of the Province, 1722-1740, Secretary of the Province—control 4.

Records of the Register of the Province, 1696-1703 (originally titled A *Register of Deeds, Leases, Judgments, Mortgages, and all Manner of Conveyances of Land within the County of Berkly in the Province of Carolina.—Stephen Bull Esq*r*—Register:—Anno Dom: MDCXCVI*)—control 5.

Records of the Register of the Province, 1705-1709 (originally titled *Grants Mortgages Bills of Sales and other Records from 1704-1709*)—control 6.

Records of the Register of the Province F 1707-1711—control 7.

Records of the Register of the Province, 1709-1712—control 8.

Records of the Register & of the Secretary of the Province, 1711-1715 (originally titled *Indentures of Lease & Release Begun this 13th Day of December 1701 and Ends the 9th Febry 1714/15*)—control 9.

Records of the Register & of the Secretary of the Province, 1712-1713—control 10.

Warrants for Lands, 1672-1692 (published in 1910-and 1915)—control 11.

Records of the Secretary of the Province, 1675-1695 (originally titled*Court of Ordinary, 1672-1692, Grants 7, Green's Binding*)—control 12.

Commissions and Instructions of the Lords Proprietors, 1685-1715 (published in 1916)—control 13.

Abstracts of Grants and Commissions of Lords Proprietors, 1692-1718, 1733-1736, 1775-1820 (2 Vols.), Part One, pp. 1-275, Part Two, pp. 276-487—control 14 and 15.

Warrants for Lands, 1692-1711 (published in 1915)—control 16.

Record of the Secretary of the Province, 1694-1705 (originally titled*Will Book, 1692-1693)*—control 17—C.W.A. VOL. 1; W.P.A. Vol. 60, *1692-1693.*

Records of the Secretary of the Province, 1694-1705 (originally titled *Record, 1694-1705)*—control 18—C.W.A. Vol. 1; W.P.A. Vol. 61, *1694-1704.*

Records of the Secretary of the Province, 1700-1710—control 19—C.W.A. Vol. 1; W.P.A. Vol. 52, *1687-1710.*

Records of the Secretary of the Province Vol. D, 1704-1709 (originally titled *Grants Mortgages Bills of Sales &c. Records begun 1703 and Ends 1709*)—control 20.

Records of the Secretary of the Province, 1709-1725 (originally titled *A Book for Recording Powers of Attorney & Other Writtings &c.*)—control 21.

Records of the Secretary of the Province, 1709-1721—control 22—C.W.A. Vol. 1; W.P.A. *1716-1721.*

Miscellaneous Record Book N (a copy made in 1904 dated 1716-1721)—control 23.

Records of the Secretary of the Province, 1711-1719—control 24—C.W.A. Vol. 1; W.P.A. Vol. 62, *1711-1718.*

Records of the Secretary of the Province, 1711-1717—control 25.

I have examined an additional 20 volumes in this series of records, through *Miscellaneous Records EE, 1741-1743*—control 42 (there are two volumes on control 33 which are covered by three volumes in the C.W.A. and W.P.A. series of copies, and two volumes on control 36). However, these records yielded no data used in this work, and are therefore not included in the bibliography.

Other manuscript volumes in the S.C.D.A.H. which I have used extensively are cited below.

Last Resort. This is the final volume in the series of bound plats. It contains copies of records from a variety of sources. Its origin is unknown.

Proprietary Grants No. 1, Vol. 38.

Proprietary Grants No. 2, Vol. 39.

Index to Grants, Warrants, and Conveyances 1675-1776 by John S. Green. This manuscript index is not authoritative, and refers to volumes which have been rebound, and whose pages have been renumbered. Nevertheless, it has proved useful, serving as a starting place in the search for data on individuals in volumes which are not themselves indexed. Green's *Index* covers the volumes on control shelves 2, 4, 5, 7, 8, and 9 in the S.C.D.A.H.

Memorial Books, Vols. 1-5.

B. Other Original Documents

Cheves Langdon, ed. The Shaftsbury Papers and Other Records Relating to Carolina and the First Settlement on Ashley River Prior to the Year 1676. *South Carolina Historical Society*, Collections, *Vol.* V *(Richmond, 1897)*.

Chalmers, Lionel. An Account of the Weather and Diseases of South Carolina *(London, 1776)*.

Crafford, John. A New and Most Exact Account of the Fertiles and Famous Colony of Carolina (On the Continent of America) *(Dublin, 1683)*.

Cooper, Thomas, and McCord, *David J., eds.* The Statutes at Large of South Carolina, *10 vols. (Columbia, 1836-1841)*.

Gregorie, Anne King, ed. Records of the Court of Chancery of South Carolina 1671-1779 *(Washington, 1950)*.

Nairne, Thomas. A Letter from South Carolina *(London, 1718)*.

Public Record Office, London. CO *5/398. Colonial Office, America and West Indies, South Carolina. "An Abstract of the Records of All Grants Made in this Province from the First Establishment...to 1765." Microfilm at* S.C.D.A.H.

Records in the British Public Record Office Relating to South Carolina, *vols. 1-5, 1663-1710. Facsimile edition of handwritten transcripts in the* S.C.D.A.H. *(Columbia, 1928-1946)*.

Salley, Alexander S., ed. "Abstracts from the Records of the Court of Ordinary of the Province of South Carolina, 1692-1700." S.C.H.G.M., *Vols. 8-10, 1907-1909.*

———, *ed.* Commissions and Instructions from the Lords Proprietors of Carolina to Public Officials of South Carolina 1685-1715 *(Columbia, 1916).*

———, *ed.* Journal of the Grand Council of South Carolina, 1671-1680 *(Columbia, 1907).*

———, *ed.* Journal of the Grand Council of South Carolina, 1691-1692 *(Columbia, 1907).*

———, *ed.* Journals of the Commons House of Assembly, 1692-1735, *21 vols. (Columbia, 1907-1946).*

———, *ed.* Narratives of Early Carolina, 1650-1708 *(New York, 1967).*

———, *ed.* Warrants for Lands in South Carolina, 1672-1679 *(Columbia, 1910).*

———, *ed.* Warrants for Lands in South Carolina, 1680-1692 *(Columbia, 1915).*

———, *ed.* Warrants for Lands in South Carolina, 1692-1711 *(Columbia, 1915).*

Sainsbury, W. Noel, et al., eds. Calendar of State Papers, Colonial Series, America and the West Indies, 1669-1674, 1675-1676, 1677, 1680 *(vols. 8-10) (London, 1889).*

Thibou, Louis. "Letter," Sept. 20, 1683. South Caroliniana Library, Columbia.

II. Secondary Books

Andrews, Charles M. The Colonial Period of American History, *Vol. III (New Haven, 1964).*

Baird, Charles W. History of the Huguenot Emigration to America, *Vol. 2 (New York, 1885).*

Baldwin, Agnes Leland. First Settlers of South Carolina, 1670-1680 *(Columbia, 1969).*

Boorstin, Daniel J. The Americans: The National Experience *(New York, 1967).*

Brinsfield, John W. Religion and Politics in Colonial South Carolina *(Easley, SC, 1983).*

Bull, Henry DeSaussure. The Family of Stephen Bull of Kinghurst Hall, County Warwick, England, and Ashley Hall, South Carolina 1600-1960 *(Georgetown, 1961).*

Childs, St. Julien Ravenel. Malaria and Colonization in the Carolina Low Country, 1526-1696 *(Baltimore, 1940).*

Clowse, Converse D. Economic Beginnings in Colonial South Carolina, 1670-1730 *(Columbia, 1971).*

Craven, Wesley Frank. The Southern Colonies in the Seventeenth Century, 1607-1689 *(Baton Rouge, 1970).*

———. White, Red, and Black: The Seventeenth-Century Virginian *(New York, 1977).*

Duffy, John. Epidemics in Colonial America *(Baton Rouge, 1953).*

Dunn, Richard S. Sugar and Slaves: The Rise of the Planter Class in the English West Indies, 1624-1713 *(Chapel Hill, 1972).*

Edgar, Walter B., ed. *Biographical Directory of the South Carolina House of Representatives,Vol. 1, Session Lists 1692-1673* (Columbia, 1974).

Galenson, David W.*White Servitude in Colonial America: An Economic Analysis* (Cambridge, 1981).

Gray, Lewis C. *History of Agriculture in the Southern United States To 1680*, Vol. I (Gloucester, 1958).

Harlow, Vincent T. *A History of Barbados, 1625-1685* (Oxford, 1926).

Hartz, Louis B. *The Founding of New Societies: Studies in the History of the United States, Latin America, South Africa, Canada, and Australia* (New York, 1964).

Jordan, Winthrop D. *The White Man's Burden: Historical Origins of Racism in the United States* (New York, 1974).

———. *White Over Black: American Attitudes Toward the Negro, 1550-1812* (Chapel Hill, 1968).

Lockridge, Kenneth A. *Literacy in Colonial New England: An Enquiry into the Social Context of Literacy in the Early Modern West* (New York, 1974).

Massey, Jr., Frank J., and Dixon, Wilfrid J. *Introduction to Statistical Analysis*, 3rd ed. (New York, 1969).

Morgan, Edmund S. *American Slavery, American Freedom: The Ordeal of Colonial Virginia* (New York, 1975).

Rivers, William J. A *Sketch of the History of South Carolina to the Close of the Proprietary Government by the Revolution of 1719 with An Appendix Containing many Valuable Records hitherto unpublished* (Charleston,1856).

Salley, Alexander S. *The Origin of Carolina* (Columbia, 1926).

Sirmans, M. Eugene. *Colonial South Carolina: A Political History, 1663-1763* (Chapel Hill, 1966).

Smith, Abbot E. *Colonists in Bondage: White Servitude and Convict Labor in America 1607-1776* (New York, 1971).

Smith, Warren B. *White Servitude in Colonial South Carolina* (Columbia, 1961).

Waring, Joseph Ioor. A *History of Medicine in South Carolina, 1670-1825* (Columbia, 1964).

———. *The First Voyage and Settlement at Charles Town 1670-1680* (Columbia, 1970).

Weir, Robert M. *Colonial South Carolina: A History* (Millwood, NY, 1983).

Wood, Peter H. *Black Majority: Negroes in Colonial South Carolina from 1670 through the Stono Rebellion* (New York, 1975).

III. Articles

Bailyn, Bernard. "Politics and Social Structure in Virginia." In Paul Goodman, ed., *Essays in American Colonial History*. New York, 1967. Pp. 90-115.

Bolton, S.C. "South Carolina and the Reverend Doctor Francis LeJau: Southern Society and the Conscience of an Anglican Missionary."

Historical Magazine of the Protestant Episcopal Church, XL (March, 1971), 63-79.

Campbell, Mildred. "Social Origins of Some Early Americans." In James M. Smith, ed., *Seventeenth-Century America: Essays in Colonial History*. Chapel Hill, 1959. Pp. 63-89.

———. "Mildred Campbell Replies." *William and Mary Quarterly*, 3rd ser., XXXVI (April, 1979), 277-286.

———. "Mildred Campbell's Response." *William and Mary Quarterly*, 3rd ser., XXV (July,1978), 525-540.

Carr, Lois Green, and Menard, Russell R. "Immigration and Opportunity: The Freedman in Early Colonial Maryland." In Thad W. Tate and David L. Ammerman, eds., *The Chesapeake in the Seventeenth Century: Essays on Anglo-American Society* (Chapel Hill, 1979). Pp. 206–242.

Childs, St. Julien Ravenel. "The First Carolinians." *South Carolina Historical Magazine* 71 (April, 1970), 101-108.

Diamond, Sigmund. "An Experiment in 'Feudalism': French Canada in the Seventeenth Century." *William and Mary Quarterly*, 3rd ser., XVIII (January, 1961), 1-34.

Galenson, David W. "'Middling People' or 'Common Sort'?: The Social Origins of Some Early Americans Reexamined." *William and Mary Quarterly, 3rd ser., XXXV (July, 1978), 499-524.*

———. *"The Social Origins of Some Early Americans: Rejoinder."* William and Mary Quarterly, 3rd ser., XXXVI (April, 1979), 264-277.

Dunn, Richard S. "The English Sugar Islands and the Founding of South Carolina." *South Carolina Historical Magazine* 72 (April, 1971), 81-93.

Jervey, Theo. D. "The White Indentured Servants of South Carolina." *South Carolina Historical and Geneological Magazine XII (October, 1911), 163-171.*

Kupperman, Karen O. "Apathy and Death in Early Jamestown." *Journal of American History* 66 (June, 1979), 24-40.

Menard, Russell R., Harris, P.M.G., and Carr, Lois Green. "Opportunity and Inequality: The Distribution of Wealth on the Lower Western

Shore of Maryland,1638-1705."*Maryland Historical Magazine* 69 (Summer, 1974), 169-184.

Menard, Russell R. "From Servant to Freeholder: Status Mobility and Property Accumulation in Seventeenth-Century Maryland." *William and Mary Quarterly*, 3rd ser., XXX (January, 1973), 37-64.

Morgan, Edmund S. "The Labor Problem at Jamestown, 1607-1618." *American Historical Review* 76 (June, 1971), 595-611.

Rutman, Darrett B., and Anita H. "Of Agues and Fevers: Malaria in the Early Chesapeake."*William and Mary Quarterly*, 3rd ser., XXXIII (January, 1976), 31-60.

Shammas, Carole. "The Determinants of Personal Wealth in Seventeenth-Century England and America." *Journal of Economic History*, XXXVII (September, 1977), 675-689.

Walsh, Lorena S. "Servitude and Opportunity in Charles County Maryland, 1658-1705." In Aubrey C. Land, Lois Green Carr, and Edward C. Papenfuse, eds., *Law, Society, and Politics in Early Maryland* (Baltimore, 1977), 111–133.

Walsh, Lorena S., and Menard, Russell R. "Death in the Chesapeake: Two Life Tables for Men in Early Colonial Maryland." *Maryland Historical Magazine* 69 (Summer, 1974), 211-227.

Waterhouse, Richard. "England, the Caribbean, and the Settlement of Carolina." *American Studies* 9 (December, 1975), 259-281.

Weber, Mabel L. "Hyrne Family." *South Carolina Historical and Geneological Magazine*, XXII (October, 1921), 101-118.

IV. Dissertations

Ackerman, Robert K. "South Carolina Colonial Land Policies." Diss. University of South Carolina, 1960.

Duncan, John D. "Servitude and Slavery in Colonial South Carolina, 1670-1776." Diss. Emory University, 1971.

Kane, Hope Frances. "Colonial Promotion and Promotion Literature of Carolina, 1660-1700." Diss. Brown University, 1930.

Sirmans, M. Eugene. "Masters of Ashley Hall: A Study of the Bull Family in Colonial South Carolina, 1670-1737." Diss. Princeton University, 1959.

Waterhouse, Richard. "South Carolina's Colonial Elite: A Study in the Social Structure and Political Culture of a Southern Colony, 1670-1760." Diss. The Johns Hopkins University, 1973.

Wood, Peter H. "Black Majority: Negroes in Colonial South Carolina from 1670 Through the Stono Rebellion." Diss. Harvard University, 1972.